1200

UNIVERSITY OF

NEBRASKA

NATIONAL CHAMPIONS

UNIVERSITY OF
NEBRASKA
NATIONAL CHAMPIONS

Acknowledgments

Dear Husker fan,

It is with great pleasure and pride that we present the *University of Nebraska National Champions 1994* book. Our goal was to produce the most comprehensive book possible on Nebraska's championship season so that you, the loyal fan, could relive every moment of the Huskers' incredible journey for years to come. It's all here. ... The trials, victories and determination of a team with "Unfinished Business" are documented from fall practice to the Huskers' sensational Orange Bowl victory.

This book is the work of many dedicated people, to whom we are extremely grateful. First, we would like to thank head coach Tom Osborne and his staff. Without their tireless efforts on and off the field, none of this would have been possible.

We would also like to thank everyone who made this book a reality. Special thanks go to Bill Byrne, Chris Peterson, Chris Anderson, Chris Bahl, Jeff Abele and everyone else in the Nebraska athletic department. Their dedication to this project was immeasurable. Thanks also Mr. Bill Battle and Mr. Kit Walsh at the Collegiate Licensing Company for their assistance.

And, of course, special thanks go to our writer, Tom Vint. Tom was selected to author this publication because he faithfully followed the Huskers all season and on to the Orange Bowl. Tom knows everything there is to know about Nebraska football. His expertise within the following pages speaks for itself.

But what is a story without pictures? We are especially thankful for the work of Joe Mixan, John Williamson and Dennis Hubbard, which vividly tells the tale of Nebraska's season. Thanks also to contributing photographers Rick Anderson, Gary Clarke, Jeff Jacobsen, Bob Berry, Billy Ward, Richard C. Lewis, Lisa Hall, Tim Benko, Tom Finn and Bob Rosato for providing us with so many good photographs. Each spent a good deal of time selecting their best work for this publication.

Special thanks also to the editors of *Husker Illustrated*, including Bob Bennett and Chris Greer, for their help with this publication.

One of the most popular features of our championship books are the reprints of the media's coverage of the national championship. Extra-special thanks to *Sports Illustrated* for allowing us to reprint the covers of their magazines which featured Nebraska. Thanks also to the *Daily Nebraskan*, the student paper, and the *Omaha World-Herald* for permitting us to reprint their front pages. Finally, thanks to PSP, Inc. for granting us permission to reprint the cover of the Orange Bowl program.

Last, but certainly not least, we thank the players. Watching the team throughout the season has been a pleasure, and we are honored to produce this book for and about you.

Please enjoy.

 The University of Nebraska National Champions 1994 book is officially licensed by the University of Nebraska through the Collegiate Licensing Co.

University of Nebraska National Champions 1994 Staff: Publisher, Ivan Mothershead; Associate Publisher, Charlie Keiger; Production Manager, Amy Vail; Editors: Jeff Huneycutt and Ward Woodbury; Art Director, Brett Shippy; Layout and Design: Paul Bond and Michael McBride; Administrative Staff: Wendy Baum, Henry Boardman, Mark Cantey, Mary Cartee, Mary Costner, Carla Green, Shelley McDaniel and Lewis Patton.

ISBN 0-943860-10-5

Table of Contents

Foreword

On the night of January 1, 1995, the University of Nebraska Cornhuskers finished the "Unfinished Business" that had haunted Coach Tom Osborne, his staff, players and their multitude of fans since the night of January 1, 1994.

Both business opportunities occurred in the confines of the venerable Orange Bowl Stadium in Miami, Florida. Nebraska lost the National Championship to Florida State in 1994 when the Seminoles managed an 18-16 victory in the final seconds of a game that Husker players and coaches, the fans and the national media felt rightfully should have belonged to Nebraska.

Rather than tossing in the towel and wallowing in self-pity and bitter disappointment, the family that really lives under the banner "Nebraska Huskers" made a commitment to finishing the business that didn't quite get accomplished when the 1994 football season rolled around. And the "family" made it happen in grand style, all pulling together to win a Kickoff Classic, 11 regular-season games and a fourth consecutive Big Eight Conference championship before getting down to completing the unfinished business.

The family was complex, but a truer family never existed. There was Tom Osborne as the patriarch, leading, driving, believing, improvising and always preparing. Traditional trademarks of his 22-year career that have taken him to the top of his profession and kept him there for years, to be sure, but in 1994 there seemed to be a quiet confidence and "Dad-gum the Torpedoes, Full Speed Ahead" attitude.

There were assistant coaches, long a part of Osborne's veteran staff, who spent hours and hours meeting, teaching and encouraging players. There were players with experience leading through example and youngsters rising to challenges, all focused on finishing the business at hand. There were trainers, doctors, student-trainers, nutritionists and psychologists who faced difficult times and performed in magnificent style. There were people in Sports Information, the Ticket Office, the Academic Department, the Business Office, the Facilities Department, the Grounds Department, the External Operations Department, the Video Department, the Athletic Performance Department — all pulling together in any way possible to assist in culmination of the 1994 dream.

Athletic Director Bill Byrne, members of the Senior Staff and many others met continually and joined with all the other family members in providing whatever support possible to the players and coaches as they battled toward their lofty goal.

There were more family members helping, too — the fans and people of Nebraska, without whose support through 104 years there would be no Husker Spirit to ignite the propulsion toward fulfilling the unfinished business goal.

Well, it all came together on that New Year's Night in Miami's Orange Bowl. All those months of hard work, all those days of agonizing about serious injuries to Tommie Frazier, Brook Berringer and Mike Minter, all the apprehension about once again playing Miami on Miami's home field, all the hoopla about No. 1 Nebraska and No. 2 Penn State were put aside for a historic evening of college football.

Tom Osborne, the master coach, and 87 players who would not be denied, represented the Husker family and college football in style and manner not soon forgotten by anyone who witnessed the Huskers spot Miami 10 points and then proceed to dismantle the Hurricanes for a 24-17 victory and the long-awaited National Championship.

True, it was only football. But in retrospect, 1994 was not only about winning games. It was also about the importance of challenging the human spirit in a positive manner, the necessity for perseverance when adversity strikes, faith in one's self and one's associates, caring about other people, unity, and plain, old-fashioned hard work.

That's the real story of the 1994 Nebraska Cornhuskers and Tom Osborne's first National Championship and Coach of the Year Award. And that's what this beautiful book is all about — a salute to the Great Husker Family that finished some unfinished business.

Sincerely,
Don Bryant
Associate Athletic Director
Sports Information Director, 1963-93
University of Nebraska

Tom Osborne

When Bob Devaney announced his resignation in 1972 and handed the head coaching duties to a lanky, redheaded assistant, moans could be heard across the state.

Tom Osborne was Nebraska's receivers coach; he had no head coaching experience. The Hastings College all-star athlete, who had played a couple of years in the NFL as a wide receiver, joined the Devaney staff as a graduate assistant in 1962-63. He was promoted to part-time coach and teacher in 1964 before becoming a full-time receivers coach in 1967. Osborne was named assistant head coach when Devaney made the announcement that '72 would be his last season.

But Devaney still had a few years left, didn't he?

Yes, Devaney admitted later. He could have coached longer, but he might have lost the best coach in America if he'd done so. Tom Osborne was ready to be the head man somewhere, and Devaney wanted him at Nebraska.

Devaney knew what he had in Osborne and never interfered with what the young coach did on his own. Even early in Osborne's tenure, when he struggled to beat rival Oklahoma, Devaney (then the Athletic Director) stood by him without waver.

More than two decades later, if you asked Devaney about Osborne, one would hear words that speak volumes about the pride he felt while watching his young assistant become what Devaney thought he could be. Nobody could have done it better. The retired athletic director probably would end such a conversation with one of those sly smiles that told you he had known it all along.

Yes, Tom Osborne had made Devaney proud well before Jan. 1, 1995, when Osborne finally joined his former mentor as coach of a national champion.

Osborne did it with calm, class and confidence. He's always done it that way. "I'm still the same coach I've always been. I'm not any smarter," Osborne said in dozens of post-championship interviews.

In 22 seasons as Nebraska's head coach, Osborne has gone about the business of preparing football teams to be the best they can be, his players to be good people and his assistants to be examples of hard work and dedication. The formula has worked beyond anyone's wildest dreams.

In his 22 seasons, Osborne's teams have NEVER failed to win at least nine games. They have won 10 or more games 12 times, won or shared 11 Big Eight Conference championships (seven outright) and gone to a bowl game every year.

Those teams have included 33 first-team Academic All-Americans, of whom nine won the honor twice. With six previous scholar-athletes, Nebraska leads the nation with 48 academic first-teamers. Seven of his players have earned the NCAA's highest honor for student athletes: a Top Six or Top Eight Award.

Husker players also have earned 23 NCAA postgraduate scholarships and 15 National Football Foundation and Hall of Fame Scholar-Athlete Awards. This year, a Husker — Rob Zatechka — was named the sport's top scholar-athlete.

Nebraska players under Osborne have won the Heisman Trophy (once), Butkus Award (once), Lombardi Trophy (twice) and Outland Trophy (five times). Forty-one players have earned All-America status, of whom five earned two-time selection.

Osborne was named 1983 Coach-of-the-Year by the Fellowship of Christian Athletes, a Christian organization in which he remains active, and was a finalist for virtually every coach of the year award given in 1994. He also was honored as winner by his fellow coaches.

As head coach at Nebraska, he entered the Orange Bowl with a 218-47-3 record; he has never lost more than three games in any one season.

Osborne didn't just take a successful program from Devaney — he grabbed it and ran.

Former Missouri coach Bob Stull, one of the many past and present Big Eight coaches who have never beaten Osborne, said that what the Nebraska coach has done is "impossible." A person simply can't win at least nine games every year at the NCAA Division I-A level. Not every year. But Osborne has.

"There's probably four or five (teams) in the country that there's not a lot of difference between, and Nebraska is one of the top ones. They always are ... sometimes a little bit better than others," former Oklahoma State coach Pat Jones said prior to his team's 1994 loss to Nebraska. He never beat Osborne, either.

Tom Osborne has filled his office with reminders of the three things he treasures most: his family, football and fishing. Osborne now has the national championship trophy to add to the three Kickoff Classic trophies behind him.

UCLA coach Terry Donahue, who did beat Osborne once, admitted that he hasn't seen a bad Nebraska team in all the years he has faced them, whether it was with the Bruins or earlier when he was an assistant at Kansas.

"It's a traditional, vintage, national championship-caliber team," he said just before the Bruins lost to NU in the Huskers' fourth game of 1994.

Osborne established Big Eight records for most wins as a head coach (219) and most games coached (269). His Nebraska teams have continued the school's on-going NCAA records for consecutive nine-win seasons (26), years with a bowl bid (26), winning seasons (33) and New Year's Day bowl appearances (14).

The Hastings, Neb., native and former state high school and college athlete-of-the-year headed to the Orange Bowl with the best winning percentage among active coaches with 10 or more years of experience (.820). He was the first coach in NCAA Division I-A history to win 200 games in 21 seasons, and his teams have been ranked in *The Associated Press* poll for 223 consecutive weeks.

The only dark cloud hanging over Osborne as he headed into the 1994 season was his lack of a national championship. And that seemed to bother other people more than it did Osborne, whose standard has always been to do your best and let the rest take care of itself.

He had been close to winning the prize several times. His 1982 team finished with a 12-1 record; its only blemish was a controversial loss at Penn State. But it finished third in the final poll.

The 1983 team demolished Penn State in the Kickoff Classic and went 12-0. The team headed to the Orange Bowl with a No. 1 ranking, which it had held all season. The media pressure was severe. Newspaper, magazine and television reporters from across the country swarmed Lincoln daily for interviews from mid-season on.

Osborne admitted then that his perfect world would be to coach football, go fishing and never have to deal with all the outside (media) distractions. Working with young people is what pleases him most.

The 1983 Orange Bowl appearance that seemed certain to end in a win and the national championship instead ended in a crushing upset loss to an upstart Hurricane team (31-30). The two-point conversion pass that would have won the game for Nebraska was tipped away in the closing minutes.

Osborne was asked many times why he hadn't

kicked for the extra point and the tie, which probably would have given him the national title. He has always answered that you play the game to win. He never considered anything else.

Nebraska ended the season second in the final polls.

The 1993 team was 11-0 when it lost to eventual national champion Florida State, 18-16, in the Orange Bowl. This time, a Nebraska field goal went wide in the final seconds. The Huskers finished third in the final polls.

Osborne had weathered storms like that before. He had taken a lot of heat, even from Nebraska faithful, when his early teams lost to Oklahoma five times before they finally beat his friendly rival, Barry Switzer, 17-14 in 1978.

As fate would have it, the Orange Bowl Committee invited Oklahoma to be Nebraska's opponent in the bowl that year, and Switzer turned the tables in a 31-24 win.

Switzer would beat Osborne the next two years before Nebraska won three in a row. Osborne now has a four-game winning streak against the Sooners.

The stinging loss to Florida State in the 1994 Orange Bowl was yet another addition to a seven-game losing streak in bowl games for Osborne. Never mind that none of the opponents in those games had been ranked lower than fifth and that six of them were No. 1, 2 or 3. Never mind that the games, with the exception of two meetings with Florida State in the Fiesta Bowl, were in the opponents' backyards, or, in the case of Miami, on their home field.

Osborne admitted it probably wasn't fair to his teams to play opponents in those types of settings, but those were the best games he could get, and he always wanted the best games.

He related the bowl losses to the Miamis and Florida States in terms that paralleled those early sufferings at the hands of Oklahoma.

"We didn't do very well in those early years against Oklahoma, but we got better." And when it came to playing with the 'Canes and Seminoles, the Huskers again got better.

Through it all, Osborne held his head high. His teams played as well as they could, and that's how he measured success.

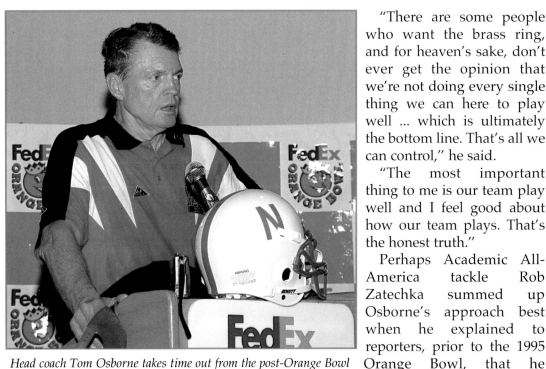

Head coach Tom Osborne takes time out from the post-Orange Bowl celebration to field questions from the media. His Huskers prevailed over Miami in Miami's backyard, 24-17.

"There are some people who want the brass ring, and for heaven's sake, don't ever get the opinion that we're not doing every single thing we can here to play well ... which is ultimately the bottom line. That's all we can control," he said.

"The most important thing to me is our team play well and I feel good about how our team plays. That's the honest truth."

Perhaps Academic All-America tackle Rob Zatechka summed up Osborne's approach best when he explained to reporters, prior to the 1995 Orange Bowl, that he believed the thrill for his coach was the chase, not necessarily the prize. He wanted to be in position to win it all, then have his teams play the best they could, even if they came up short.

"Last year we played well enough to win a national championship," Osborne said of the Florida State game. "That was very satisfying to me. To many people, it was a great frustration because we didn't have the trophy sitting here in Lincoln, but we did everything we could to win that championship.

"We played at that level. We did it in 1983, probably did it pretty close in 1982, and I take those things with me. There's nothing anybody can do to take that away. The trophy itself is nice, but that's not what we're playing for. We're playing to play as well as we can play."

Osborne's players have, over the years, learned his philosophy. The man with the doctorate degree in educational philosophy has coached his young men to worry about the things they can control, not the things they can't.

The national polls were among those things Osborne learned he couldn't control, and he refused to lobby voters even when it appeared that some other coaches would.

"I will not lobby," he said after beating Colorado and climbing to No. 1 in the polls in 1994. "I will not prostrate myself to the polls. All we want to do is play well. If people think we deserve to be No. 1, great. If not, then we've done all we can."

During Osborne's near-miss years of the early '80s, his friend at Penn State, Joe Paterno, told the Nebraska coach that he would win a national championship when he least expected it. It was prophesy.

Osborne and his staff worked around team-crippling injuries to quarterbacks Tommie Frazier and Brook Berringer and safety Mike Minter to mold a winning machine. Six games into the season, not many people would have given Nebraska a chance.

Unfortunately for Paterno, Osborne's championship victory occurred in a season in which Penn State also had an unbeaten team. Osborne said he knew how his friend would feel about that, and he'd call and talk later.

Many coaches across the nation applauded Osborne's ultimate victory, saying good guys don't always finish last.

There was a telling smile on Osborne's face when his players hoisted him on their shoulders after winning the Orange Bowl and the national championship. For a moment, the pressure of not disappointing the thousands of fans back home had been lifted. He wanted the win for his players and fans. His players wanted to win for him.

It was an unbelievable season for Osborne. Four Big Eight coaches had resigned during the fall, some under pressure, one just wanting to spend more time with his family.

Osborne considered that last rationale at one of his late-season press conferences. Asked if he would do it all over again, he revealed a good deal about himself when he said he probably wouldn't. He missed raising his three children with his wife, Nancy. And that was something he couldn't get back.

And maybe he could have done more hunting and fishing, which rate among his cherished pursuits behind religion, family and football.

Working with the young people, however, was special. He wouldn't have wanted to miss that.

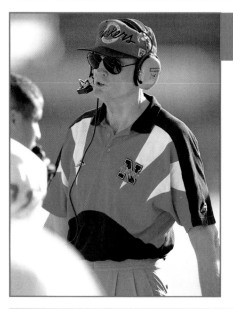

1994 Awards for Coach Osborne

- All-Big Eight Coach-of-the-Year (*Associated Press & Big Eight Coaches*)
- National Coach-of-the-Year (*Football Quarterly*)
- Alonzo Stagg Coach-of-the-Year
- AFCA Coach-of-the-Year
- Chevrolet Division 1A Coach-of-the-Year
- Giant Steps Award
- Coach-of-the-Year (*TD Club of Columbus*)
- Downtown Athletic Club of Glenwood, Iowa, Coach-of-the-Year
- Bear Bryant National Coach-of-the-Year Finalist
- National Coach-of-the-Year Finalist (*Football News*)

THE OSBORNE RECORD

Year	Won	Lost	Tied	Pct.	Pts.	Opp.	Bowl
1973	9	2	1	.792	306	163	Cotton
1974	9	3	0	.750	373	132	Sugar
1975*	10	2	0	.833	367	137	Fiesta
1976	9	3	1	.731	416	181	Bluebonnet
1977	9	3	0	.750	315	200	Liberty
1978*	9	3	0	.750	444	216	Orange
1979	10	2	0	.833	380	131	Cotton
1980	10	2	0	.833	470	110	Sun
1981**	9	3	0	.750	364	125	Orange
1982**	12	1	0	.923	514	167	Orange
1983**	12	1	0	.923	654	217	Orange
1984*	10	2	0	.833	387	115	Sugar
1985	9	3	0	.750	421	163	Fiesta
1986	10	2	0	.833	446	165	Sugar
1987	10	2	0	.833	451	164	Fiesta
1988**	11	2	0	.846	477	205	Orange
1989	10	2	0	.833	509	215	Fiesta
1990	9	3	0	.750	434	192	Citrus
1991*	9	1	1	.864	454	230	Orange
1992**	9	3	0	.750	441	199	Orange
1993**	11	1	0	.917	437	194	Orange
1994**	13	0	0	1.000	479	162	Orange
Totals	**219**	**47**	**3**	**.820**	**9,539**	**3,783**	**22 Consecutive Bowls**
(Bowl Games	9	13	0	.409	433	487)	

*Big Eight co-champions. **Big Eight champions.*

OSBORNE IN THE BOWLS

Most Bowl Games — All Time
1. Paul "Bear" Bryant   29
2. Joe Paterno*   25
3. *Tom Osborne**   22
4. Vince Dooley   20
5. Three tied with   18

Most Bowl Victories by Active Coaches
1. Joe Paterno   16
2. Bobby Bowden   14
3. Lou Holtz   10
4. Johnny Majors   9
    Tom Osborne   9
5. Terry Donahue   8

All-Time "Big-Four" Bowl Appearances
1. Paul "Bear" Bryant   20
2. *Tom Osborne**   14
3. Darrell Royal   12
    Bo Schembechler   12
5. Joe Paterno*   11

Most Years with One College Going to a Bowl
Bowls/Consecutive
1. Paul "Bear" Bryant   24/24
2. Joe Paterno*   25/15
3. *Tom Osborne**   22/22
4. Vince Dooley   20/9
5. John Vaught   18/14
    LaVell Edwards*   18/16

* Active Coaches.
"Big-Four" refers to the traditional New Year's Day bowls: Cotton, Orange, Rose and Sugar.

Assistant Head Coach/Running Backs Coach

Frank Solich

Winning has followed Frank Solich wherever he has gone. In the mid-1960s, the Cleveland native came to Nebraska from Holy Name High School to play fullback under coach Bob Devaney.

Despite weighing less than 160 pounds, Solich earned All-Big Eight honors as co-captain of the 1965 Huskers. In that same year, he set a single-game school rushing record during a game against Air Force; the 204 yards he gained was a record that held up for a decade.

He also set an Orange Bowl record in 1966 for most return yards with 166. That record still stands.

Solich, who also lettered in baseball at NU, graduated and returned to Omaha Holy Name to become its head coach (1966-68). He then coached Lincoln Southeast to state powerhouse status in 1968-79 and won state championships in 1976 and '77. In 1983, he left Southeast to become Nebraska's freshman and assistant varsity coach in charge of running backs.

As a freshman coach, Solich led his teams to three undefeated seasons. Overall, he compiled a 19-1 record in his four seasons as freshman coach.

Since he became the running backs coach, Nebraska has finished no lower than third in rushing nationally and has won the NCAA rushing title seven times, including 1994. He has had 12 all-conference backs — at least one in 11 of the 12 seasons he has been the position coach. He coached four academic all-conference players and two first-team All-Americans. Eight of his players have gone on to play professionally.

At the conclusion of Solich's first year as running back coach, Mike Rozier was awarded the Heisman Trophy.

The stable of running backs with which he worked in 1994 may be the most gifted group he has ever had. Sophomore Lawrence Phillips made a name for himself with 1,722 yards rushing to set a school sophomore record and earn second-team All-America honors. Backups Damon Benning, another sophomore, and junior Clinton Childs also were considered standouts who could start for most teams across the country.

Rozier was also among the many East Coast recruiting prizes Solich brought to Nebraska. Others include outside linebacker Mike Croel and current Huskers Christian and Jason Peter and Doug Colman.

Solich is considered a future head coach prize and was named Osborne's assistant head coach in 1991. Athlon Magazine named Solich its Assistant Coach-of-the-Year prior to the 1993 season, and the former Husker fullback was inducted into the Nebraska Football Hall of Fame in 1992.

Defensive Coordinator/Interior Line Coach

Charlie McBride

Charlie McBride's 18th season as an assistant to coach Tom Osborne may have been his most successful coaching year. McBride built a dominating defense that he compared to the Georgia "Junkyard Dogs," who led the Bulldogs to the national championship in 1980.

The Colorado graduate and former assistant at Colorado, Arizona State and Wisconsin had to do some shuffling early in the fall of his 13th year as defensive coordinator, however. Safety Mike Minter suffered a season-ending knee injury in the second game of the season, and his youthful backups needed time to adjust.

But by the start of the Big Eight season, the new mix had started to click, and Nebraska's Blackshirts became one of the best defenses in school history and one of the best in the nation.

Nebraska ranked in the Top 10 in rushing defense, allowing, on average, only 79.3 yards per game, 12.1 points per game and only 258.8 total yards per game. The combination of a strong pass rush and a solid secondary also held opponents to a combined pass-efficiency rating of 96.7. NU ranked second in the nation in scoring defense, fourth in rushing and total yards and 10th in pass efficiency.

1994 marked only the third time since 1946 that Nebraska had ranked in the Top 10 in each of the four major defensive categories.

Osborne rated this defense as possibly the best, even though the 1984 team and prior Devaney national championship teams were also very talented.

But there was no doubt this Husker defensive unit was the fastest, as a whole. The '94 season was only the second year the 4-3 alignment — which Miami and Florida State had used so successfully against the Huskers — was utilized at Nebraska. Nebraska scrapped the 5-2 it had used for nearly three decades in 1993 and instead showcased the talents of All-American and Butkus Award winner Trev Alberts in its new 4-3 base scheme.

This time, linebacker Ed Stewart was the All-American and Butkus finalist who led the defensive charge for McBride and his Blackshirts.

McBride, coach of the interior line as well as defensive coordinator, took both of his jobs seriously. His front charges, Terry Connealy and Christian Peter, made the simple task of running difficult for any and all opponents. Connealy was McBride's 15th All-Big Eight player and ninth all-league academic first-teamer. Connealy also earned first-team Academic All-America honors, the fourth such player to do so under McBride. The coach has also had four first-team All-America linemen and nine players who have gone on to pro careers.

Ron Brown

Regarded as one of the nation's most gifted young coaches, Ron Brown is in his eighth season as Nebraska receivers coach. In recent years, Brown has been considered for several coaching positions, including the head coaching job at Brown University, his alma mater. After the 1994 Orange Bowl meeting between Nebraska and FSU, Florida State coach Bobby Bowden offered Brown a position on the Seminoles' coaching staff.

But Brown declined both offers to stay at Nebraska, where he has built a reputation as an excellent coach. He is also known as a model for young minorities both on the job and within his off-duty Christian ministry. Active in the Fellowship of Christian Athletes, Brown also has established youth programs on Nebraska Indian reservations and has hosted a regularly-aired show on a Christian radio station in the state.

Despite the fact that he coaches receivers at a school noted for running the football, 15 of Brown's former Nebraska players have gone on to play in the pros. Most notable is tight end Johnny Mitchell, who was a first-round draft pick by the New York Jets in 1992. Another prize was Tyrone Hughes, a 1994 NFL Pro Bowl selection for the New Orleans Saints.

In the eight years he has been in Lincoln, an average of slightly more than two Husker receivers annually have been drafted or have signed free-agent contracts with the NFL.

Current wide receiver Reggie Baul summarized the situation well when he said that he elected to walk on at Nebraska rather than accept scholarship offers from a number of other schools known for their passing games because he wanted to raise his game to the next level. And if he could play at Nebraska, he would have to learn to block, run patterns and play an overall game of football, not just catch passes.

Baul became a big-play addition to the Huskers of 1994.

Downfield blocking by Nebraska's receivers was a key ingredient in the Huskers' success while running the football; Brown always has emphasized the importance of blocking to his players. He also had them ready to catch the ball when it was thrown, a readiness which may never have been more evident than when Brook Berringer took over at quarterback in 1994. The Huskers threw the ball with confidence and scored 16 times through the air, preventing teams from overplaying the Nebraska running game.

George Darlington

Although Nebraska's coaching staff is one of the most stable in the nation, only one assistant has been with Osborne throughout his 22-year head coaching tenure: George Darlington. Of those 22 seasons, Darlington has been the secondary coach for the past nine.

Because more and more colleges have begun to utilize elaborate passing games, Darlington has been forced to build a better crew of man-to-man coverage defenders. Considering the many swift, tall and gifted receivers in the college ranks, his task presented a sizable challenge. But Darlington seems to have met it.

In the course of coaching Nebraska's defensive ends for 13 seasons, Darlington has had eight All-Big Eight selections on the defense. He has coached nine All-Big Eight defensive ends, including four first-team All-Americans.

One of his four Academic All-Americans was in the secondary. That player, Mark Blazek, was named Toyota Leader of the Year in 1988.

Nine of Darlington's defensive backs have gone on to pro careers, and two more were NFL draft picks in 1993.

Darlington's past two seasons as secondary coach have been among his most challenging. Nebraska went to a 4-3 defense, and man-to-man pass coverage became more of a norm. Plus, the Huskers had some great passing teams on the schedule.

But a group of speedy recruits helped to ease the transition. Players such as 1994 cornerbacks Barron Miles and Tyrone Williams earned all-league honors for their play. Miles, a third-team AP All-American, had four blocked kicks, broke up 13 passes and had five interceptions.

Nebraska has led the Big Eight in pass efficiency defense three of the last seven years and ranked 10th in the nation in that category this year despite playing pass-happy teams from Wyoming, Kansas State, Colorado and Miami.

Heading into the '95 Orange Bowl, Husker defenders had recorded 17 interceptions and had held their opponents to a 47.3 completion percentage.

A Rutgers University graduate ('61), Darlington coached several high school teams in the East before joining San Jose State as an assistant coach in 1969. He came to Nebraska in 1973 and has been there ever since.

Turner Gill

Turner Gill is still considered the prototype option quarterback with regard to the skills — mental and physical —that are necessary to operate the type of offense Tom Osborne has made standard at Nebraska.

Gill's play in 1982 and 1983 made Nebraska a national championship contender. And although he narrowly missed the championship in both of those seasons, the offense he led became one of the most productive in NCAA history.

Gill was a three-time All-Big Eight quarterback; he compiled a 28-2 record as a starter. His second year, while playing with Heisman Trophy winner Mike Rozier and All-Americans Irving Fryar at receiver and Dean Steinkuhler at guard, Gill earned second-team All-America honors behind BYU's Steve Young, now a star for the San Francisco 49ers.

In his career as a player, Gill completed 231 of 428 passes (54 percent) for 3,317 yards and 34 touchdowns. He also rushed for 1,317 yards and 18 touchdowns.

Athletic skill led Gill to the Canadian Football League. When, after two seasons, injuries forced him to stop playing football, he played three seasons in the Cleveland and Detroit minor league baseball programs.

When Gill quit baseball, he enrolled in North Texas State to earn a bachelor's degree in behavior analysis and also serve as a volunteer assistant. He spent the 1991 season at Southern Methodist as a receivers coach. He then returned to Nebraska in August 1992 to become quarterbacks coach for Tom Osborne.

Gill may have been the perfect mentor for Florida recruit Tommie Frazier, who, in 1992, became the first true freshman ever to start for Nebraska at quarterback. Frazier earned Big Eight Newcomer-of-the-Year honors in 1992 and was second-team all-conference in 1993.

When Frazier was sidelined by injuries in 1994, Gill helped the youngster win the mental battle of recovery by recalling his own experiences with a leg injury in the 1980s. Meanwhile, Gill had Brook Berringer more than ready to fill Frazier's shoes. Berringer was 7-0 in his starts and earned second-team All-Big Eight honors as the league's most proficient passer.

Tony Samuel

Former Husker defensive end Tony Samuel learned his trade under NU assistant George Darlington from 1975-77. He was a part-time assistant at NU from 1978-81 and also made assistant coaching stops at Western Michigan and Stanford.

Samuel returned to Nebraska in 1986 to become coach of outside linebackers, and in 1994, he completed his ninth very successful year.

Since Bob Devaney began building a national power in the 1960s, Nebraska has regularly produced some of the Big Eight's (and the nation's) top defensive ends — Nebraska now labels them outside linebackers. Samuel has done his part; he's coached seven All-Big Eight players, two Butkus Award finalists (Trev Alberts in 1993 and Broderick Thomas in 1988), one Butkus winner (Alberts) and three first-team All-Americans (Thomas in '87 and '88, Travis Hill in 1992 and Alberts in 1993).

Three of Samuel's Huskers have earned academic all-conference honors, and one, Alberts, earned Academic All-America first-team status and was named one of the NCAA's Top Six Award winners.

Thomas, Mike Croel (1990) and Alberts also were first-round NFL draft picks.

Since the college game has become more pass-oriented, pass rushes have been critical to a successful defense. Samuel's outside linebackers have changed with the times. Alberts set a school record for quarterback sacks in 1993 with 15.

The 1993 team had 44 sacks for 294 yards in losses. Heading to the Orange Bowl, the 1994 team, with seniors Dwayne Harris and Donta Jones leading the pack, had 43 sacks for 263 yards in losses. During the Orange Bowl, they recorded five more sacks for 24 yards in losses and helped shut down the Miami offense in the final quarter. Harris had three of those sacks, which gave him a team-leading eight for the season.

Samuel may have lost Harris and Jones to graduation, but he has coached sophomore Jared Tomich and freshman Grant Wistrom, and they are ready to take their places. Both had seasons which indicated that they may be the next pair of Husker outside linebacking stars.

Inside Linebackers Coach

Kevin Steele

Kevin Steele, the newest member of the Nebraska defensive coaching staff, had another banner year in 1994, his sixth as inside linebackers coach.

One of the main reasons for that success was senior Ed Stewart, a Butkus Award finalist and first-team All-American. Stewart, who also had earned some first-team All-America honors as a junior, was the field general for the defense and again had a nose for the football during his senior season.

The Big Eight's Defensive Player-of-the-Year led the Huskers in tackles with 96. Stewart, in a defense that made the most of the fastest group of linebackers in Nebraska history, also had 18 quarterback hurries.

Steele has admitted that Stewart made his job easy. The senior needed only to discuss strategies with his coach before he put them to work on the field. Steele said Stewart was so good that opposing offenses would change their game plans to keep the ball out of that particular Husker's territory.

Steele's first star at the position was two-time All-Big Eight linebacker Pat Tyrance (1989-90). Tyrance also earned first-team Academic All-America honors, was one of Steele's four academic all-conference players and was named an NCAA Big Six Award and Woody Hayes Award winner.

Steele came to Nebraska after stops at Tennessee (his alma mater), New Mexico State, Oklahoma State and again at Tennessee. The 1981 Tennessee graduate also helped the Volunteers as the recruiting coordinator. He later brought those skills to Nebraska.

Steele dove into the fertile Florida recruiting territory and convinced current Huskers Tommie Frazier and Tyrone Williams to come north to Nebraska.

However, shortly after the Orange Bowl victory, Steele made a difficult decision: He has resigned from the Nebraska staff to join the NFL expansion Carolina Panthers' coaching staff.

Offensive Line Coach

Milt Tenopir

Of all the offensive lines Nebraska coach Milt Tenopir has overseen in his 21 seasons, he would rate his 1994 line as the best, from one end to the other, he has ever had.

Even that acclaim would not be such a big deal if it weren't for the fact that the Huskers have, over the past three decades, established a reputation for having one of the best offensive lines in the nation each year. Tenopir can take much of the credit for their success.

Under this Harvard, Neb., native's guidance, Nebraska has won five Outland trophies. In 1994, the nation's top interior line prize was awarded to Zach Wiegert. Guard Will Shields won that same award in 1992.

Wiegert, also a first-team All-American, teamed with guard Brenden Stai to form what many considered to be the best guard-tackle combination on one side of the ball in Nebraska's history. Considering that guard Dean Steinkuhler, an Outland and Lombardi winner, teamed with All-Big Eight tackle Scott Raridon in 1983, that is quite an accomplishment. Stai made several All-American first teams and was a member of *The Associated Press* second-team.

Over the years, Tenopir has developed a system that plugs the graduation holes with young players who generally have had at least two years of backup seasoning and have practiced against all-conference Husker defenders while readying themselves to play.

In the past two decades, 16 Nebraska offensive linemen have earned All-America honors, 38 have been All-Big Eight, 10 have been academic All-Americans and 26 have been academic All-Big Eight.

In 1994, Tenopir not only had the pleasure of coaching Wiegert and Stai but had the good fortune to coach the nation's top academic football player, tackle Rob Zatechka.

If the ability to run the football depends on what happens at the line, it is clear that Tenopir has done his job well. Nebraska has finished no lower than third in the nation in rushing since 1978 and has won nine national rushing titles since then, including three of the last four.

Tenopir graduated from Sterling College (Kansas) in 1961 and compiled a 76-34-1 high school coaching record in Kansas, Colorado and Nebraska before joining the Nebraska staff in 1974.

Offensive Line/Kickers Coach

Dan Young

Kicking and assistant offensive line coach Dan Young could credit one of his own with much of the success the Huskers enjoyed in critical games during 1994. Kicking was a major factor in Nebraska's wins over Kansas State, Colorado, Oklahoma and Miami.

First-year punter/place-kicker Darin Erstad became the find of the year after he asked for a spring tryout. Erstad already was a member of one Husker team; he was a standout player on coach John Sanders' baseball team.

Erstad jumped in to fill the shoes of graduated punter/place-kicker Byron Bennett and became one of the nation's top punters in terms of net yards. Erstad averaged 42.6 yards per punt and sent 20 inside the opponents' 20-yard line. In 50 attempts, none of his punts were blocked. He also recorded a punt of 73 yards, his longest of the season.

Erstad and short-distance specialist Tom Sieler also kicked 7 of 14 field goals through the uprights and scored 50 points on post-touchdown kicks.

According to Tom Osborne, the kicking game led to key field position advantages that helped Nebraska win its four toughest games: K-State, Colorado, Oklahoma and Miami. In all four, Erstad's punts pinned opponents deep in their own territory, which made it difficult for them to work their way upfield against the Husker defense.

In 1985, Young also began assisting Tenopir as an offensive line coach. He helped build one of the most consistent and talented offensive lines to come out of college football in the past decade.

A Primrose, Neb., native, Young graduated from Kearney State College and had successful high school coaching stops at Barneston, St. Paul and Omaha Westside before he joined the Nebraska staff as freshman coach in 1983. In three seasons, he had a 14-1 record as freshman coach. He then stepped up to the varsity staff and helped make the Husker special teams one of the key ingredients in Nebraska's consistent success.

Associate A.D. Football Operations

Steve Pederson

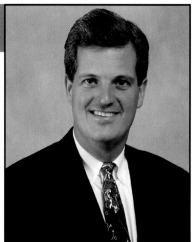

Steve Pederson returned to Nebraska in April 1994 to become the associate athletic director for football operations.

The North Platte, Neb., native graduated from Nebraska in 1980. He worked two years in the sports information office as an assistant before joining the football staff as the recruiting coordinator in 1982. Steve held that post until 1986, when he left to enter private business for a year.

Pederson went back to football in 1988 as the recruiting coordinator at Ohio State and was named assistant athletic director for recruiting and football operations at Tennessee in 1991.

He returned to Nebraska three years later — after helping the Volunteers collect three of the nation's top recruiting classes, including a 1994 group that was ranked No. 1 by many of the experts.

With Pederson on board, Nebraska already had secured oral commitments from what is considered a prized group of recruits before the Orange Bowl was played Jan. 1. And several other very good players who could not be added to the scholarship list indicated that they would walk on at Nebraska for a chance to play for the Huskers in years to come.

Graduate Assistant-Secondary

Clayton Carlin

First-year graduate assistant Clayton Carlin was a great catch for the Huskers, and his expertise was particularly useful when it came time to plan the defense for Miami quarterback Frank Costa prior to the Orange Bowl. Costa had played high school ball for then-coach Carlin at St. Joseph's High School in Philadelphia, Pa.

Carlin came to Nebraska after acting as secondary coach at Delaware Valley College in Doylestown, Pa., for two years.

Graduate Assistant-Receivers

Mike Grant

1994 marked the first year former Nebraska quarterback Mike Grant, a three-year Husker letterman, acted as a graduate assistant for his former coach. Grant assisted Ron Brown with Nebraska's receivers.

The Tampa, Fla., native graduated from Nebraska in December 1992 with a degree in communications studies and is working on a master's degree in mass communications. In 1993, he worked in the recruiting office as an assistant to former recruiting coordinator Dave Gillespie.

Assistant A.D./Director of Athletic Performance

Boyd Epley

Nebraska's assistant athletic director and Director of Athletic Performance, Boyd Epley, is the man who can be credited with building the Husker strength program to the standard for which other colleges aim. Today, 27 of Epley's former assistants are head strength coaches at the college and professional levels.

The former Nebraska track competitor turned his attention to strength training when his college days came to an end.

He was the Big Eight's first strength coach. Over the years, his abilities have made the Huskers bigger, stronger and faster — results which have earned him praise from across the country.

Head Trainer

George Sullivan

Nebraska's longtime head football trainer, George Sullivan, announced his retirement after 42 years on the job for the Huskers. But he stayed long enough to help coach Tom Osborne claim his first national championship and conceded that it was worth the wait.

"Sully" won the inaugural Tim Kerin Award for Excellence in Athletic Training in 1994. The award is regarded as "the Heisman Trophy for athletic training."

And while the coaches may have done one of the best jobs of their careers as they tried to keep a winning football team together in 1994, Sullivan may have given his best effort ever for those who were sidelined; he was in charge of patching up the injured and helping them return to playing shape.

He has commented that the blood clots that sidelined quarterback Tommie Frazier (from after the fourth game of the season until the Orange Bowl) were something he had never seen in such an athlete. But Sully helped Frazier return in time to become the Most Valuable Player in the Orange Bowl.

Throughout his career, the likable, easy-going Sullivan has been awarded nearly every honor an athletic trainer can receive. During his tenure, his staff has grown to three therapist-trainers, a physician's assistant-trainer, three other certified trainers, five graduate certified trainers and 17 student trainers, all of whom care for more than 600 Husker student-athletes.

THE 1994 NATIONAL CHAMPIONS

UNIVERSITY OF NEBRASKA HUSKERS

The Quarterback Shuffle

The only two scholarship quarterbacks on the Husker roster, Frazier (left) and Berringer (right), have contrasting styles, but both performed well at the controls of the Nebraska offensive juggernaut.

Coach Tom Osborne didn't have time to worry about controversy during the 1994 season. Oh, sure, there was the flap over who should be ranked No. 1 in the polls — first with Florida, then with Penn State. But those disturbances were nothing compared to the ever-present question of who would be healthy enough to quarterback his team.

Osborne's fall had started in fine shape. Junior Tommie Frazier was back for his third starting season. He was one of the best option quarterbacks in the nation and in Nebraska history. No problems there.

Brook Berringer, another junior, was a solid backup. He was rated a better passer than a runner but could handle the option fine in a pinch. Everything fine there, too.

But then everything started to unravel. Sophomore walk-on Matt Turman was bumped up to third in the QB line when Ben Rutz decided to transfer rather than wait for playing time. Jon Elder, Nebraska's lone 1994 scholarship quarterback recruit, had already left, early in fall camp.

That left walk-on freshman Monte Christo from Kearney fourth on the quarterback depth chart. It wasn't the most desirable situation, but Nebraska's coaches figured all would be OK if things held together. They didn't.

Frazier went down after the fourth game of the season with recurring blood clots in his right leg. So Berringer stepped in and grew better every week as he guided one of the nation's most potent offenses. He did so despite a partially collapsed lung, which he had suffered in his first career start.

Turman gave Berringer time to heal when he stepped in against Oklahoma State and Kansas State. Berringer then returned to complete the unbeaten regular season. He gave Nebraska a passing game that hadn't been seen on campus for more than a decade and earned himself second-team All-Big Eight honors as the top-proficiency quarterback in the conference.

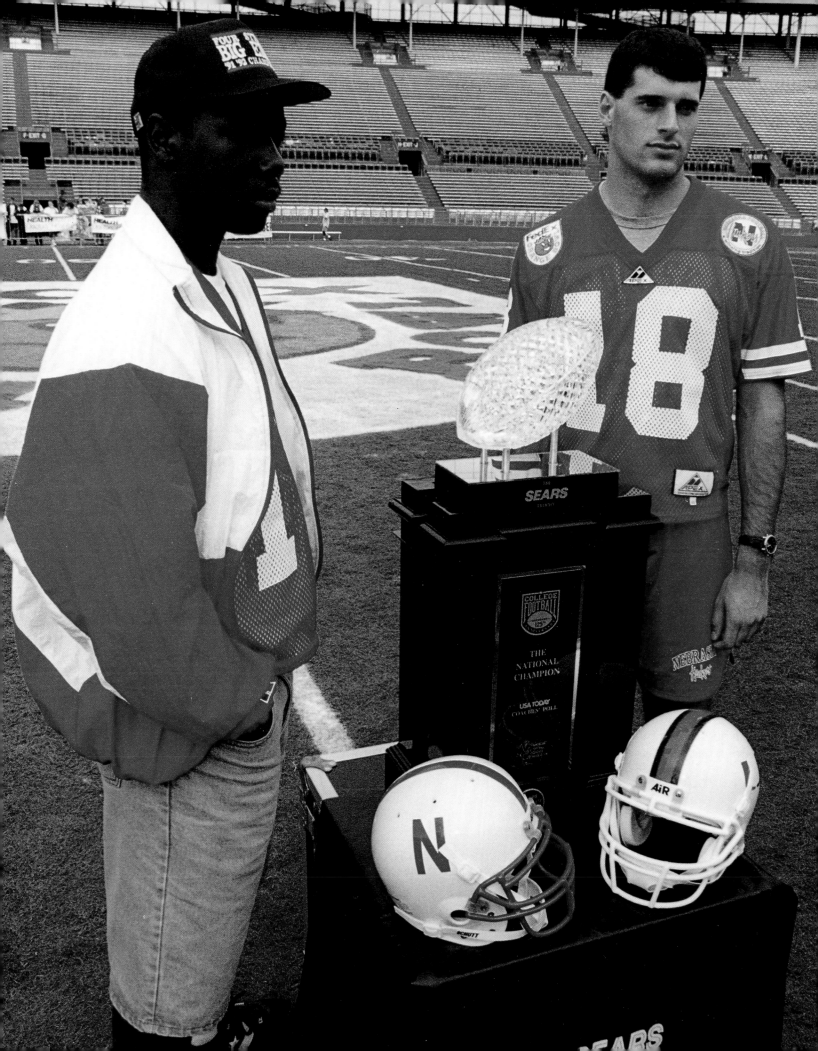

In the Orange Bowl, Frazier teamed with Cory Schlesinger (40) on fullback traps for both the tying and winning touchdowns in a fourth-quarter comeback.

Berringer played with confidence and an obvious knowledge of the system. He never seemed to panic, even when Wyoming, Iowa State and Oklahoma had probably given him reason to do so. Preparation, he often said, was always the key. He knew he was prepared to handle every situation for Nebraska, so there was no reason to panic.

By the season finale against Oklahoma, in which Berringer had, once again, led the Huskers to victory, it was hard to imagine that he was not the seasoned two-year starter that Frazier was.

Logic dictated that Berringer should start when No. 1 Nebraska met No. 3 Miami in the Orange Bowl. He was 7-0 as a starter, had a streak of good play and had the confidence to attack the Miami defense.

He was a youngster who had hit better than 62 percent of his passes and thrown for 1,295 yards and 10 touchdowns. Although he didn't have the passes-per-game to qualify for the national charts, his NCAA pass rating of 149.5 was one of the best in the nation.

He was also more than just a passer. Even though a lung injury prevented him from running in three games, he averaged nearly 4 yards per carry. Clearly, Brook could run the option effectively. He was good enough to keep defenses honest on the option and make them pay if they weren't.

Yes, logically, a healthy Berringer should start for Nebraska in the Orange Bowl.

But then the one factor which had been dismissed as impossible became probable: Frazier would be cleared to play again before the end of the season.

Osborne was faced with a dilemma. Who to start?

The question was whether to go with the season's original starter, Frazier, a Heisman candidate and master of the option, or go with Berringer, the passing game QB and a confident 7-0 player on a roll?

Both players wanted to start but refused to get into a war of words. An argument would divide the team, and they would have none of that. The game was too important.

In public, each player said all the right things. Whatever the coaches decided would be OK. They both would play and play well. There was no animosity or division on the team. Either of them was good enough to win.

Oklahoma State coach Pat Jones had said as much prior to the fifth game of the season. He had said that the only difference between Berringer and Frazier was that Frazier was faster.

The Orange Bowl media, however, had no qualms about picking sides. They threw their own rationales into the mix and drew attention away from the Nebraska defensive and offensive lines, which were among the best in school history. The BIG DEAL of the week was — who would be NU's quarterback?

Even the Miami players had a say in the debate. Most of the Hurricanes said it didn't matter to them who started — either one would be buried before the end of the Orange Bowl. One said it wouldn't have mattered even if Superman was to quarterback Nebraska.

Unfortunately, Superman wasn't one of Osborne's options.

Finally, just days before the game, Osborne announced that Frazier would start and Berringer would play sometime in the first half. Frazier, Osborne reasoned, had had the best pre-bowl scrimmage and had demonstrated he was ready to play at his previous level.

Scrimmage grades always have been important in deciding Nebraska's starting rotations. Casual observers have sometimes questioned their real worth, but Osborne has proven that the system works. The players Osborne has who aren't working hard in practice seldom get better and rarely get playing time.

Osborne's pick, in the end, was the logical choice. Frazier, after all, had been the starter before he was injured. The coach traditionally has given injured players their former spots in the lineup when they were healthy enough to return. Failure to do so for this youngster in particular, who had been racing toward a serious Heisman Trophy challenge at the time of his injury, just wouldn't make sense.

Also, if Berringer started but couldn't move the ball with the option and the pass, Miami could load up to stop Frazier's running game when he was brought in. Reversing that order would keep Miami more off balance. Besides, the order also would give Frazier a chance to rest his legs and observe the game; he could plan strategy for a later return, if needed.

Frazier had the Huskers moving early, but he couldn't get them into the end zone. His inability to get the score was not due to rustiness, however. In fact, as the coach had expected, Frazier looked as though he had never missed a game. The coach said that Frazier had been running the option offense for two months in practice and hadn't shown any sign of losing anything.

Frazier had gotten the ground game moving for Nebraska, but he tried to surprise the Hurricanes with a long pass. It was intercepted near the goal line.

Enter Berringer. The lanky quarterback drove NU to its first score with a 19-yard pass to tight end Mark Gilman in the second quarter. His touch pass, lofted over the Miami defense, made it 10-7 at the half.

Although Brook Berringer saw significant playing time in only eight games in 1994 (not including the Orange Bowl), he still managed to throw 10 touchdown passes — second only to Chad May in the Big Eight — in Nebraska's run-oriented system. He also ran the Big Red ground attack so effectively that it led the nation in rushing (340.0 ypg).

Berringer started the third quarter. He had the team moving on one drive (with three pass completions to Abdul Muhammad), but as the fourth quarter approached, a turnover and a few team errors kept Berringer from getting another score.

That prompted Osborne to make another change. Osborne discussed the game situation with quarterback coach Turner Gill on the headsets, and they both agreed it would be a good idea to get the option game up and running at full speed.

With Frazier out for the rest of the regular season and Berringer sidelined for the second half after he reinjured his lung, sophomore walk-on Matt Turman came on to lead the Huskers to 23 second-half points and the win over Oklahoma State.

"I just felt it was time for Tommie. It was a gut feeling," Osborne said. He brought the fresh legs of his option wizard back into the game, and Frazier guided the team to the game-tying and game-winning touchdowns in the fourth quarter.

Osborne later commented that, before the game, people were questioning his intelligence. Afterwards, they were calling him a genius. For weeks to come, he would joke with banquet audiences about how smart he had become after 22 years of coaching.

"I was prepared to go the rest of the way with Brook, but Tommie had fresh legs," Osborne said.

"We thought Brook played pretty well," Osborne said. "Then we had a couple of mistakes. ... There wasn't any great deliberation. We just thought (Frazier) might give us a little changeup at that point. It all worked out. Both guys played about half the game. And they deserved to play half the game for what they had done in the past."

Frazier said he never doubted he would come back in.

He won the game's Most Valuable Player honor for the second-straight year. But he also credited his teammate, Berringer, with keeping the game close.

Berringer ended the game with 8-of-15 passing for 81 yards. He ran seven times for minus 4 yards rushing. Frazier ran seven times for 31 yards and hit 3 of 5 passes for 25 yards. Both threw an interception. Berringer had the touchdown pass.

"It was an emotional roller coaster," Berringer said several times after the game. "I think we did the best we could to stay focused and get through this deal. I think we both contributed to the whole thing."

After the game, quarterback coach Turner Gill was bombarded with questions about who would call the signals for Nebraska in 1995. Gill said, considering the play of the two leaders, the race was wide open. But he continued to say that after what Nebraska had gone through in 1994, it was nice to be faced with that type of controversy.

(Right) Brook Berringer had never started for Nebraska until Frazier went down with blood clots during the fourth game of the season. Nonetheless, Berringer performed admirably; he threw for 1,295 yards for the season and was named second-team All-Big Eight.

(Below) The only true freshman ever to start at quarterback for Nebraska, Tommie Frazier, was one of the leading preseason candidates for the Heisman Trophy. Despite injuries which sidelined him for most of the regular season, Frazier ended the year on a high note by winning the Orange Bowl MVP award.

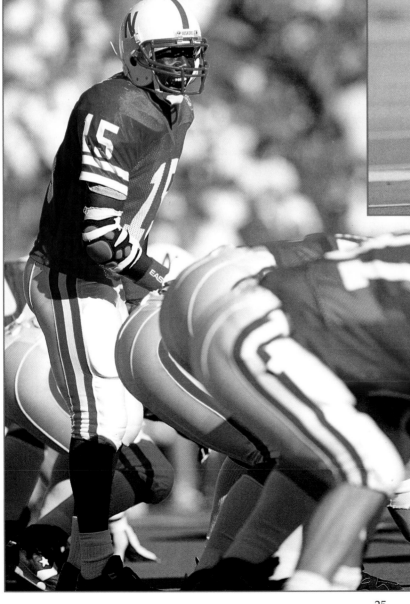

Husker All-Americans

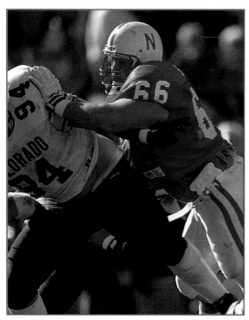

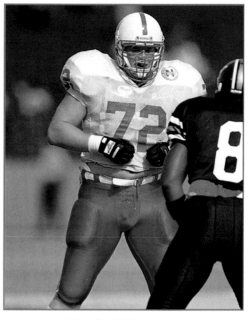

Brenden Stai
Senior Offensive Guard

First-Team All-American
Walter Camp
Football Writers
UPI

Second-Team All-American
Associated Press
College Sports
The Sporting News

First-Team All-Big Eight
Associated Press
Big Eight Coaches

Ed Stewart
Senior Linebacker

First-Team All-American
AFCA Coaches
Walter Camp
Football Writers
Associated Press
UPI
College Sports

Second-Team All-American
Football News
Sporting News

Butkus Award Finalist

Defensive Player-of-the-Year Finalist
Football Writers

Defensive Player-of-the-Year Semifinalist
Football News

All-Big Eight Defensive Player-of-the-Year
Associated Press
Big Eight Coaches

First-Team All-Big Eight
Associated Press
Big Eight Coaches

Big Eight Defensive Player-of-the-Week vs.
Oklahoma State

Zach Wiegert
Senior Offensive Tackle

First-Team All American
AFCA Coaches
Football News
Walter Camp
Football Writers
Associated Press
UPI
College Sports
Sporting News

Outland Trophy Winner

Lombardi Finalist

Offensive Lineman-of-the-Year
TD Club of Columbus

UPI Lineman-of-the-Year

First-Team All-Big Eight
Associated Press
Big Eight Coaches

ABC/Chevrolet
Player-of-the-Game vs. UCLA

Awards and Honors

BROOK BERRINGER
Junior Quarterback
Second-Team All-Big Eight (*Associated Press*)
Honorable-Mention All-Big Eight (*Big Eight Coaches*)
Big Eight Offensive Player-of-the-Week (CU)
ABC/Chevrolet Player-of-the-Game (OU)

CLINT BROWN
Senior Linebacker
CFA/Hitachi Promise of Tomorrow Scholarship

TERRY CONNEALY
Senior Defensive Tackle
Second-Team All-Big Eight (*Associated Press & Big Eight Coaches*)
Kickoff Classic Participants NACDA Scholarship
Second-Team All-American (*The Sporting News*)
Third-Team All-American (*College Sports*)
CFA/Hitachi Scholar-Athlete
GTE Academic All-American
Phillips 66 Academic All-Big Eight

TROY DUMAS
Senior Linebacker
Butkus Watch List
First-Team All-Big Eight (*Associated Press*)
Honorable-Mention All-Big Eight (*Big Eight Coaches*)

DARIN ERSTAD
Sophomore Punter/Place-Kicker
Honorable-Mention All-Big Eight (*Associated Press*)
Phillips 66 Academic All-Big Eight

TOMMIE FRAZIER
Junior Quarterback
Orange Bowl MVP
Kickoff Classic William J. Flynn MVP
ABC/Chevrolet Player-of-the-Game (WVU)

AARON GRAHAM
Junior Center
First-Team All-Big Eight (*Big Eight Coaches*)
Honorable-Mention All-Big Eight (*Associated Press*)
Phillips 66 Academic All-Big Eight
GTE Second-Team Academic All-American

DWAYNE HARRIS
Senior Outside Linebacker
Honorable-Mention All-Big Eight (*Associated Press*)
Second-Team All-Big Eight (*Big Eight Coaches*)

DONTA JONES
Senior Outside Linebacker
Honorable-Mention All-American (*UPI*)
First-Team All-Big Eight (*Associated Press & Big Eight Coaches*)
CFA Good Works Team
ABC/Chevrolet Player-of-the-Game (CU)

BARRON MILES
Senior Cornerback
First-Team All-Big Eight (*Associated Press & Big Eight Coaches*)
Third-Team All-American (*Associated Press*)
Honorable-Mention All-American (*Football News*)
Athlon Defensive Player-of-the-Week (Kansas State)
Big Eight Defensive Player-of-the-Week (Kansas State)
ABC/Chevrolet Player-of-the-Game (Kansas State)
New Jersey Sportswriters Defensive-Back-of-the-Year

KAREEM MOSS
Senior Rover
Second-Team All-Big Eight (*Associated Press & Big Eight Coaches*)

CHRISTIAN PETER
Junior Defensive Tackle
Honorable-Mention All-Big Eight (*Associated Press*)
Second-Team All-Big Eight (*Big Eight Coaches*)

LAWRENCE PHILLIPS
Sophomore I-Back
Second-Team All-American (*Associated Press, Football News, UPI & College Sports*)
First-Team All-Big Eight (*Associated Press & Big Eight Coaches*)
Offensive Player-of-the-Year Finalist (*Football News*)
Athlon Offensive Player-of-the-Week (UCLA, Oklahoma State)
Big Eight Offensive Player-of-the-Week (Texas Tech)
ESPN Player-of-the-Game (Texas Tech)

CORY SCHLESINGER
Senior Fullback
Phillips 66 Academic All-Big Eight
Honorable-Mention All-Big Eight (*Big Eight Coaches*)

MATT SHAW
Senior Tight End
GTE Academic All-American
Phillips 66 Academic All-Big Eight

RYAN TERWILLIGER
Sophomore Linebacker
GTE Academic All-District

TYRONE WILLIAMS
Junior Cornerback
Honorable-Mention All-Big Eight (*Associated Press*)
First-Team All-Big Eight (*Big Eight Coaches*)

ROB ZATECHKA
Senior Offensive Tackle
Second-Team All-Big Eight (*Associated Press & Big Eight Coaches*)
NCAA Today's Top Eight Scholar-Athlete
Rhodes Fellowship Candidate
National Honda Scholar-Athlete
GTE Football Academic All-American-of-the-Year
NFF/HOF Fellowship
CFA/Hitachi Scholar-Athlete
GTE Academic All-American
Phillips 66 Academic All-Big Eight
Vincent DePaul Draddy Trophy
Woody Hays National Scholar-Athlete

#88

ERIC ALFORD

The 6-foot-2, 225-pound senior tight end entered the 1994 season with a new position and a lot of encouraging words. Alford, who had served as a wingback in 1993 after transferring from Garden City (Kan.) Community College, was converted to tight end because the coaches felt his combination of size and speed would be a blessing at that position.

Coach Tom Osborne said Alford had a great deal of big-play potential because of his quickness, which was equal to that of former Husker tight end and first-round NFL draft pick Johnny Mitchell.

Alford proved the coach correct.

The sure-handed receiver split time with Mark Gilman and Matt Shaw but still managed 14 receptions on the season. He scored four times on those pass catches, including a big 30-yard TD via Brook Berringer in the win over Colorado. His career-best game was against the highly ranked Buffaloes; he hauled in five of Berringer's tosses for 78 yards.

Alford led the team in touchdown receptions with his four TDs and averaged 19.4 yards per catch. His longest TD was the result of a 64-yard pass from Berringer against Pacific.

Five of his catches during the year went for 25 yards or more, but he also was a clutch possession receiver. He hauled in one two-point conversion pass from quarterback Matt Turman against Oklahoma State and, in the fourth quarter of the Orange Bowl against Miami, caught a bullet of a throw on a crossing pattern from Tommie Frazier for the game-tying two-point conversion.

His talents and versatility were among the talents Husker recruiters were impressed with when they grabbed Alford from the junior college ranks. Nebraska doesn't often recruit from the juco ranks, but when the recruiters find a nugget, they pounce on it. Alford earned honorable-mention All-America honors at Garden City while playing split end, tight end, running back, defensive back and a return specialist.

In Alford's first season at Nebraska, he had three pass catches for 27 yards as a wingback and returned one punt for 13 yards.

SENIOR TIGHT END
6-2, 225; HIGH POINT, N.C.

REGGIE BAUL

Reggie Baul, a walk-on wide receiver from Bellevue, Neb., earned his way into a starting spot among Nebraska's "itty-bitty" receiver corps with seven pass catches and an average of 16.6 yards per reception in 1993.

Baul had turned down several scholarship offers from other schools noted for passing to come to Nebraska. He said he knew that to play at the next level, he had to become a more complete player than he was as a high school standout at Papillion-LaVista. That meant learning how to block.

Baul joined a good group of down-field blockers in the receiving corps and helped Nebraska backs win another national rushing title by helping block for many big gainers with the run.

When star option quarterback Tommie Frazier was sidelined by recurring blood clots, passing quarterback Brook Berringer took over, and the NU receivers benefited from the increased number of balls in the air.

Baul, with 4.47-second speed in the 40-yard dash, became another of the Husker big-play threats. He caught three touchdown passes on the season, including one from 51 yards out against Kansas. In that game, he had three catches for a team-high 106 yards.

For the season, Baul had 17 catches for 300 yards, a 17.7-yard average. His reception total tied him for third on the team.

Baul also caught one pass for 7 yards against Miami in the 1995 Orange Bowl. He had a 34-yard TD catch against Florida State in the 1994 Orange Bowl.

In addition to his pass-catching and run-blocking duties, Baul joined Kareem Moss on punt returns. Baul had 11 returns on the season for 119 yards.

JUNIOR SPLIT END
5-8, 170; BELLEVUE, NEB.

DAMON BENNING

During fall camp, sophomore Damon Benning battled junior Clinton Childs for the backup spot at I-back behind sophomore Lawrence Phillips. In the end, both played all 12 games and the Orange Bowl, which gave the Huskers a trio of very talented running backs.

But Benning provided the Huskers with some additional firepower as a kickoff returner; he averaged 25.7 yards on 12 returns for 1994. One 58-yard return sparked the Husker offense in the second game of the season on the road against Texas Tech.

He had two kickoff returns totaling 61 yards against UCLA (including a 37-yarder) and added a 32-yard runback against Wyoming the following week. Against Iowa State, he returned two for 51 yards, including a 26-yarder, and against Oklahoma in the regular-season finale, Benning recorded his fifth return of 25 yards or more (a 25-yarder).

Against Miami in the Orange Bowl, Benning averaged 17.6 yards on five returns and added three carries from the I-back spot for 18 yards.

The Omaha Northwest all-state high school player averaged 5.5 yards per rush in 1994 and scored five times in action behind Phillips. He was the fourth-leading rusher on the team with a year-end total of 367 yards.

He also caught five passes for 68 yards (13.6-yard average) in 1994, including a 37-yarder against Kansas.

In addition to his offensive skills, Benning was key to the Nebraska kicking game. He was among the first men downfield to cover Nebraska's punts, and he helped the Huskers finish second in the nation in net punting. NU allowed opponents only 2.9 yards per return.

Benning had four tackles on the season. He also was credited with the recovery of a fourth-quarter fumble in the game against Wyoming; his recovery set up Nebraska's winning touchdown.

SOPHOMORE I-BACK
5-11, 205; OMAHA, NEB.

BROOK BERRINGER

In 1994, the junior backup from Goodland, Kan., proved to everyone what he had known all along — he could play and play well for Nebraska if given the chance.

After he was called upon to fill in for the injured Tommie Frazier, Berringer scored three touchdowns against Wyoming, his first career start.

After the Wyoming game, during which he suffered a partially collapsed lung, Berringer played only the first half in the Big Eight opener against Oklahoma State. But during that half, he hit 10 of 15 passes for 75 yards.

He didn't start the following week at Kansas State, but in the second half, he came in to lead the Huskers to a 17-6 win.

Against Missouri, Berringer again was ordered to limit his running (to protect his injured lung), so the youngster threw for 152 yards and three touchdowns in a 42-7 win.

Then came No. 2-3-ranked Colorado in a nationally televised Big Eight championship showdown. Some questioned whether Berringer was good enough to help Nebraska overcome such a powerful team. He was. He got 142 yards on 12-of-17 passing. Berringer had Nebraska ahead 24-0 before Colorado could even get on the scoreboard.

The following week against Kansas, Berringer had the seventh-best passing day by a Nebraska quarterback; he threw for 267 yards and two touchdowns on a 13-of-18 day.

Berringer continued to impress with a 193-yard passing day (as well as 61 rushing yards) in a hard-fought win over Iowa State and had 166 passing and 48 rushing in an equally scrappy win over Oklahoma in the regular-season finale.

The Big Eight's top-efficiency passer earned second-team All-Big Eight honors for his play. He had 1,574 yards in total offense and a hand in 16 touchdowns. He completed 63 percent of his passes (94 of 151) with 10 touchdowns and five interceptions. He also rushed for 279 yards on 71 carries and scored six touchdowns.

In the Orange Bowl, Berringer came in during the second quarter and led Nebraska to its first touchdown against the Hurricanes with a 19-yard pass to tight end Mark Gilman.

Berringer hit 8 of 15 passes for 81 yards and was credited by Osborne and Frazier for doing his part to put Nebraska in position to take the win and, subsequently, the national championship.

JUNIOR QUARTERBACK
6-4, 210; GOODLAND, KAN.

#26 CLINTON CHILDS

Position coach Frank Solich was delighted with the trio of talents he had at I-back in 1994. The most senior member of that triumvirate was junior Clinton Childs, a big, hard-running former all-stater from Omaha's North High School.

Childs, along with sophomore Damon Benning, provided crucial backup for sophomore starter Lawrence Phillips, giving him opportunities to rest during the season.

Childs finished the fall as the third-leading rusher on the team with 62 carries for 395 yards and five touchdowns.

"Clinton really is one of three backs that certainly did an excellent job throughout the course of the season," Solich said. "He also contributed heavily on our special teams. In order to get in position to win a national championship, you need a great offense, great defense and great special teams."

Childs had nine kickoff returns in 1994 and averaged 21.1 yards per runback. His longest return was a 34-yarder in the game against Colorado, but his best overall game was against Wyoming, when he had three returns of 27, 29 and 21 yards. He also threw blocks for fellow return man Benning and made three tackles when he was given the chance to make a hit on the kick coverage teams.

The 6-foot, 215-pounder had the best per-carry average of the three I-backs with 6.4 yards per chance. He had a run of 30 yards — the longest of his season — against Texas Tech. He had 50 yards or more in four games, including a career-best 78 against UCLA.

He also caught five passes and posted an average of 11.6 yards per catch on the season.

"We thought we had a really talented trio of backs there," Solich said. "It's difficult, with guys of that quality, to get enough playing time for all three of them. But they remained team-oriented all season.

"Clinton is a very strong, physical type of running back who can get the extra yards after contact. He has the size and speed you like in a running back and was a valuable part of our national championship season."

JUNIOR I-BACK
6-0, 215; OMAHA, NEB.

DOUG COLMAN

One of the young talents to emerge on Nebraska's defense was 6-foot-3, 240-pound junior Doug Colman. The Ocean City High School standout from Ventnor, N.J., started the first eight games of 1994 then made room for teammate Phil Ellis, with whom he shared playing time.

Colman still finished as the seventh-leading tackler on the team with 51 tackles in his first year of extensive play. He had 11 stops in 11 games of backup duty his sophomore season.

Among 1994's 51 tackles were three tackles for 16 yards in losses, two quarterback sacks and four quarterback hurries. He also caused one fumble and recovered another. In addition, Doug broke up one pass while playing "Mike," or middle, linebacker for the Huskers.

Colman turned in perhaps his best effort of the season in front of a group of his homestate fans when he helped Nebraska shut out No. 24 West Virginia in the Kickoff Classic. The game is played in East Rutherford, N.J., and Colman said it was an emotional event because he was playing for his family and friends.

He led the team with a career-high eight tackles, had a 10-yard quarterback sack and caused, then recovered, a fumble that led to a Husker touchdown in the deciding 21-point second quarter.

Colman, who has good speed despite his size, also had eight tackles against Wyoming and seven against Missouri and Colorado. But he sprained an ankle against Iowa State and played little in the season finale at Oklahoma.

He returned in time for the Orange Bowl, however, and added five tackles, including one for a 2-yard loss, in one of the better Husker defensive efforts in recent years.

JUNIOR LINEBACKER
6-3, 240; VENTNOR, N.J.

#99

One of the senior co-captains and leaders of the defense, Terry Connealy has been the picture of consistency for three seasons at Nebraska. He has been credited with 47, 45 and 42 tackles in the three seasons during which he has played extensively at defensive tackle for the Huskers.

A two-time GTE first-team Academic All-American and three-time Big Eight academic first-teamer, Connealy teamed with tackle Christian Peter in 1994 to create a monumental problem for Nebraska opponents. They dominated the middle of the line and helped Nebraska's Blackshirts finish as the fourth-best rushing defense in the nation, allowing just 79.3 yards per game.

In 1994, Connealy, already ninth on the team in total tackles, improved his ability to make stops in the backfield. He was second on the team in tackles for losses with 7.5 for 38 negative yards for opponents. He had 6.5 sacks for 37 yards in losses. He had two sacks against No. 2-3 Colorado, and he also led the team with 13 tackles against stubborn Iowa State.

The 6-foot-5, 275-pounder also was credited with causing one fumble and 13 quarterback hurries.

The big agri-business major from tiny Hyannis, Neb., helped lead the defensive charge in the Orange Bowl against Miami quarterback Frank Costa. He was in on six tackles and had one sack for an 8-yard loss in the critical fourth quarter of the Orange Bowl, when Nebraska's defense shut down the Hurricane offense for the 24-17 national championship win.

The pressure that he and his teammates put on Costa in that fourth quarter was one of the factors that enabled Nebraska to pull out its first national championship for coach Tom Osborne.

Connealy was yet another home-grown success story; he made the jump from playing eight-man football in high school to playing a significant role on a national powerhouse Husker team.

In addition to his academic honors, he earned second-team All-Big Eight honors for his play in 1994.

SENIOR DEFENSIVE TACKLE
6-5, 275; HYANNIS, NEB.

TROY DUMAS

After shuffling through a number of positions in his previous three seasons at Nebraska, Cheyenne, Wyo., native Troy Dumas found a home in 1994. The 6-foot-4, 220-pound senior started every game as the "Sam," or strongside, linebacker in Nebraska's 4-3 defensive scheme.

Although he has occupied the positions of free safety, strong safety and linebacker in previous years, Dumas found that the Sam 'backer spot was his comfort zone. Dumas was a gifted athlete recruited out of East High School in Cheyenne in 1991, and Husker coaches expected him to be a future star. He made the grade in 1994.

The first-team All-Big Eight pick was among the players placed on the Butkus Award watch list for best linebackers in the nation. In 1994, thanks to his outstanding speed and good size, he finished third on the team in tackles with 69. His '94 total was higher than the previous three years' totals combined.

Four of the tackles were for losses. He had one quarterback sack, caused one fumble, blocked one kick, intercepted a pass and had seven quarterback hurries.

He rose to the occasion in big games with double-figure tackle totals against UCLA, Colorado and Oklahoma.

His interception, against Kansas State's Chad May, snapped an extended string of consecutive passes without an interception for the Wildcats' gifted thrower.

He also blocked an extra-point kick against K-State, which left the Wildcats behind 7-6 at halftime and gave Nebraska the edge it needed to carry that game to a 17-6 win.

Dumas and wingback Abdul Muhammad were the only two seniors who did not redshirt and who played in all four Orange Bowls in their careers. Dumas helped polish off the Huskers' 24-17 Orange Bowl win over third-ranked Miami with three tackles and a five-yard quarterback sack.

SENIOR LINEBACKER
6-4, 220; CHEYENNE, WYO.

#41 PHIL ELLIS

Phil Ellis, a 6-foot-2, 225-pound junior from Grand Island, was surprised when coaches told him he would get the start, his first, against second- and third-ranked Colorado.

He and junior Doug Colman had been sharing playing time at "Mike," or middle, linebacker in the first eight games of the season, but Colman had been the starter in each of the previous games.

Ellis thought that his slight speed advantage over Colman may have earned him his first start, especially considering Colorado's many offensive weapons and Nebraska's need for more pass coverage by the linebackers. But both juniors played interchangeably and played well for the Huskers in 1994.

He is blessed with excellent speed and has earned a reputation as a hard-hitter for the "Blackshirts." That's the way the coaches like it at Nebraska, especially in light of the importance of speed in their 4-3 defensive scheme.

Ellis started the final five games and gained extensive playing time in the regular-season finale against Oklahoma after Colman suffered an ankle injury against Iowa State.

Ellis ended 1994 with 58 tackles, the fifth-best record on the team. He had 24 solo stops, 7.5 tackles in the backfield for a total of 21 yards in losses, was credited with sharing a sack and had two quarterback hurries.

The two-year letterman had 32 of his tackles in the final five games of the regular season; he stepped up his play as he gained on-field experience. He had a career-high eight stops against Oklahoma, then matched Butkus Award finalist Ed Stewart with six stops and a pass breakup in the Orange Bowl win over Miami.

Ellis was named to the academic All-Big Eight honor roll his sophomore season in 1993.

JUNIOR LINEBACKER
6-2, 225; GRAND ISLAND, NEB.

DARIN ERSTAD

Darin Erstad took a lot of ribbing early in 1994 about being the best baseball player to play football at Nebraska. But no one could really challenge that. Erstad was an All-Big Eight outfielder for the Huskers, the MVP in the summer Cape Cod League for top amateur players and was projected to be a first-round pick in the 1995 professional baseball draft.

But when Nebraska football coaches saw what he could do with a football, the former North Dakota first-team all-stater in hockey, track, baseball and football was a wanted man. As a senior in high school, Erstad averaged 42 yards per punt, kicked a school-record 50-yard field goal and generally had a good time changing sports.

But he admitted that he was getting bored with playing just one sport at NU, so when Nebraska's punter/place-kicker Byron Bennett graduated at the end of the 1993 season, Erstad asked for a tryout.

He won the job and proved to be one of the best finds of the season for the No. 1 Huskers.

His lofty, long-distance punts helped Nebraska finish second in the nation in net punting. He averaged 42.6 yards per punt and allowed only 24 of 50 to be returned — for a total of 69 yards. He was adept at sticking opponents deep in their own territory; he would hang a punt high so coverage teams could keep it from getting into the end zone or kick it out of bounds before it reached touchback territory.

Coach Tom Osborne and kicking coach Dan Young said Erstad was key in Nebraska's victories over Kansas State, Colorado, Iowa State, Oklahoma and Miami. Once Erstad put the ball deep into the opponent's territory, they found it most difficult to go long-distance against Nebraska's heavy-hitting defense.

Erstad's driving kickoffs also regularly forced teams to start at or inside their own 20-yard line. And his talents extended to long-distance field goals. While sharing that duty with senior Tom Sieler, he made 2 of 6 from 40 yards or beyond and was perfect on all 10 of his extra-point tries.

SOPHOMORE PUNTER/PLACE-KICKER
6-2, 195; JAMESTOWN, N.D.

TOMMIE FRAZIER

The first true freshman ever to start at quarterback for Nebraska continued to make progress in '94 as the trigger man for the Huskers' potent option offense.

The junior from Bradenton, Fla., has displayed unusual confidence for an offensive player in the Osborne era. Coach Tom Osborne, who helps coach his own quarterbacks, has said that Frazier had the poise of a senior even in his first year ('92) and had picked up the offense better than anyone he could remember. After his first Orange Bowl game in 1993, Frazier predicted that Nebraska would be back to play for the championship in the 1994 Orange Bowl. And NU did just that, returning to the Orange Bowl with an 11-0 record to face off against Florida State.

After that game, any doubters of Frazier's big-play potential had to admit he could play. In the minds of many, he outplayed Heisman Trophy winner Charlie Ward even though Nebraska eventually lost the game, 18-16. Frazier was named the game's MVP.

Entering the fall of 1994, Frazier was listed among the Heisman, Davey O'Brien and All-America preseason candidates. He climbed from candidate to contender in the Heisman race after he opened the fall with three impressive wins (West Virginia, Texas Tech and UCLA).

Then, shortly after the game against Pacific, Frazier was diagnosed with blood clots in his right leg. Although the first clot was dissolved, another one formed within two weeks. Frazier's season and career were in question.

The NCAA denied a medical hardship exemption that would have given Frazier another year of eligibility. The two series he had played in the Pacific game had given him too many games. So the youngster decided that his goal was to return in 1994.

After months of medicines and surgery designed to cure the blood clots, Frazier was cleared to play, if necessary, in the season finale against Oklahoma. He was on the sidelines but did not enter the game.

He also was cleared for contact for the Orange Bowl. He won starting honors for the bowl game in a pre-bowl scrimmage, but he was unable to get any points on the board in the first quarter of the game.

In the fourth quarter, however, Frazier returned to the game to drive the Huskers to the tying and game-winning touchdowns for a 24-17 victory over Miami.

JUNIOR QUARTERBACK
6-4, 210; BRADENTON, FLA.

MARK GILMAN

Mark Gilman, a junior from Kalispell, Mont., had never been happier to be a receiver than he was in 1994. Why? When Nebraska's time-honored offense was scrapped out of necessity, Gilman saw more of the pigskin. A lot more. During the Colorado game, both he and fellow tight end Eric Alford had wondered if they were on the right team. Alford later admitted to checking his jersey to make sure the number being called in Nebraska's pass plays matched the one on his uniform.

Nebraska is not noted for passing the ball, and tight ends are used in games more for their blocking skills than their good hands. But when quarterback Tommie Frazier was injured and Brook Berringer took over the controls after the fourth game of the season, the passing game became a key part of the Husker offense. And the tight end position was one of Berringer's favorite targets.

Berringer's preferences were never more apparent than in the game against No. 2-3 Colorado. Gilman and Alford combined for nine of the team's 12 receptions and 124 of the squad's 142 yards in a huge Big Eight and national game. Nebraska's 24-7 victory vaulted the Huskers to No. 1 in the national rankings.

Gilman, who had caught only one pass in 1993, had already pulled in 17 as he headed to the Orange Bowl in Miami on Jan. 1. He had averaged 11.5 yards per catch, with a long of 48 yards against Iowa State, and scored a touchdown.

In the Orange Bowl, Gilman pulled down a 19-yard toss from Berringer and scrambled into the end zone for Nebraska's first score in what would eventually be a 24-17 championship win.

Gilman showed that, in addition to good blocking skills, he had great hands in 1994. He finished the season in a third-place tie with wide receiver Reggie Baul for most receptions on the team. He had a career-high four catches against Wyoming, and he had four more against Colorado. His lone touchdown catch came against Missouri.

Gilman played in all 12 games in 1994 and even started a few in the three-tight end rotation with Matt Shaw and Eric Alford.

Gilman was no slouch in the classroom, either: He earned a Phillips 66 Academic All-Big Eight honorable mention behind Academic All-American teammate Matt Shaw.

JUNIOR TIGHT END
6-3, 240; KALISPELL, MONT.

#54

AARON GRAHAM

It was a good year for this big Texas center. In the second game of the year, he had a chance to return to his home state and play in the same stadium in which he played youth football. Although he came to Nebraska from Denton, Texas, Graham played youth ball in Lubbock, the home of Texas Tech University. He also played a few of his youth super bowls in the very stadium in which Nebraska would drop Texas Tech, 42-16.

The 6-foot-4, 280-pound junior, in his second year at center, was the only underclassman on the powerful and gifted Nebraska offensive line. Graham moved into the top spot at center in the last four games of the 1993 regular season after serving as the No. 1 long-snapper in 1992.

Husker line coaches admitted that Graham had faced a challenge in the fall when he was forced to work with three different quarterbacks by the sixth game of the season. But despite working with all those signal callers, he had only one bad exchange all season.

One of his strengths has been his quickness in getting the ball to the punter and to the kick holders. The average snapper gets the ball to the punter in .72 seconds. Graham has consistently snapped in the .6 and .7 range. On PATs and field goals, his time is between .4 and .5 seconds. Coach Dan Young says Graham may be the best snapper the Huskers have ever had.

A two-time Academic All-Big Eight pick, Graham earned second-team All-America honors on the GTE academic team this season. He was named to the All-Big Eight first team by the coaches and was an honorable-mention pick on The Associated Press squad.

Graham also had his share of "pancake" blocks, in which a lineman flattens his opponent. He was credited with 12 such blocks in the Colorado game against the Buffaloes' gifted defensive front. From his center spot, he recorded 79 pancakes for the season and averaged 6.6 per game.

JUNIOR CENTER/LONG SNAPPER
6-4, 280; DENTON, TEXAS

DWAYNE HARRIS

Dwayne Harris, with his long arms and fingers, might aptly be nick-named "The Reach." Harris was the two-time letterman who faced the challenge of filling the shoes of gradu-ated Butkus Award winner Trev Alberts.

Harris introduced himself to the Husker faithful in 1993 in the game against Oklahoma. Harris stepped in when Alberts suffered an injury after just nine plays and was forced to depart for the day. Harris recorded a career-high seven tackles, including three sacks of OU's All-Big Eight quarterback Cale Gundy. Harris also had four quarterback hurries, one of which resulted in a Nebraska inter-ception which set up the Huskers' first score of the game.

The 6-foot-2, 225-pounder was anx-ious to build on that experience and his season totals of 22 tackles, eight sacks, two pass breakups and 14 quar-terback hurries. He had gained plenty of experience while sharing playing time with Donta Jones, Alberts and Bruce Moore, and 1994 was his year to step up.

Harris did just that. He used his 4.76-second time in the 40-yard dash, as well as his long reach, to claim five more sacks for 38 yards in losses. He totaled 43 tackles, 10 for losses, and caused a fumble on his way to earning second-team All-Big Eight honors.

His outside charge, 34-inch vertical leap and ever-present hands also earned him credit for 19 quarterback hurries, one of which led to another interception. Plus, he broke up four passes on his own.

While his play during the season was good, his Orange Bowl perfor-mance may have been his best. He was credited with six tackles on the day, but three of them were quarter-back sacks worth 11 yards in losses for Miami. He and his rush teammates were in Hurricane quarterback Frank Costa's face the entire second half, which proved to be a major factor in Nebraska's 24-17 win.

SENIOR OUTSIDE LINEBACKER
6-2, 225; BESSEMER, ALA.

BRENDAN HOLBEIN

Some veteran high school observers questioned the wisdom of Cozad High School star Brendan Holbein's college choice: Holbein turned down a scholarship offer from Iowa State to walk on at Nebraska.

Holbein had just rushed for 2,740 yards and 38 touchdowns to record the most impressive high school season in state history. The speedster averaged more than 10 yards per carry while leading his team to the Class B state title. The Touchdown Club of Atlanta awarded him the Bobby Dodd Award for the top running back in Nebraska.

But at Nebraska, the likes of Calvin Jones, Derek Brown, Damon Benning and Clinton Childs were unlikely to give Holbein, a 5-foot-9, 180-pounder, a chance to play as a running back.

So, Holbein redshirted his freshman year in 1992 and worked on his game as a wingback and wide receiver.

In 1993, Holbein played in four regular-season games and caught one pass for 18 yards. He also established himself as a hard-hitting downfield blocker, an important skill for Nebraska receivers in an option-oriented offense.

Holbein, whose quickness was documented by a 10-yard time of 1.56 seconds, was expected to join Brett Popplewell in '94 to provide quality backup for Reggie Baul at wide receiver. But Holbein played in all 12 games and improved to the level of starter for five games: UCLA, Pacific, Oklahoma State, Kansas and Iowa State.

He caught nine passes in 1994 and got into the end zone twice. His first career score was the result of a 9-yard toss from Tommie Frazier in the game against UCLA, and he scored on a 30-yard play from Brook Berringer against Missouri.

Holbein also played a good support role in the Orange Bowl win over Miami; he caught one pass for 7 yards and continued his season-long tradition of knocking defenders down beyond the line of scrimmage.

SOPHOMORE SPLIT END
5-9, 180; COZAD, NEB.

CLESTER JOHNSON

In 1994, former Bellevue West all-state quarterback Clester Johnson alternated with starter Abdul Muhammad at wingback for Nebraska.

Johnson started a pair of games (West Virginia and UCLA) and played in all 12. In the process, he caught four passes for 93 yards. He demonstrated his big-play potential with an average of 23.3 yards per catch and a season-long catch of 64 yards in a big-play day against Kansas. He also caught a 15-yard pass for a touchdown against Pacific.

Johnson gave the Huskers quality depth at the wingback spot since he had played, and played well, in 11 games in 1993. During his sophomore season, Johnson caught eight passes and scored once.

He also made his presence known in the 1994 Orange Bowl loss to Florida State; he caught three passes for 30 yards and tipped a pass that resulted in a 34-yard touchdown for teammate Reggie Baul.

The 5-foot-11, 210-pounder also was an excellent downfield blocker. He helped Nebraska's running game spring any number of big gainers in its NCAA-leading rushing season.

When Nebraska ran into quarterback problems (Tommie Frazier was lost to blood clots during the game against Pacific, and a lung injury sidelined backup Brook Berringer the following week), coaches considered Johnson as a possible backup.

The former prep star had thrown for 3,757 yards and rushed for 712 yards and 35 touchdowns in his career at Bellevue West. Although he took some practice snaps at quarterback prior to the Kansas State and Missouri games — as a precautionary measure — he never took a snap in a game.

JUNIOR WINGBACK
5-11, 210; BELLEVUE, NEB.

#84

DONTA JONES

After Butkus Award winner Trev Alberts graduated following the 1993 season, Donta Jones, his starting partner in the other outside linebacker position, planned to be the next standout linebacker in a long line of exceptional Nebraska products.

Jones, who played both end spots in 1993, made the right side his home in 1994. The right side was Alberts' old spot and was a good match for the athletically gifted Jones as well.

The senior from La Plata, Md., was an example of hard work on and off the football field for his teammates. He was named the team's Co-Lifter-of-the-Year in 1993 and Lifter-of-the-Year in 1994 for his accomplishments in the weight room. He set school position records for the pro-agility run and strength index as measured by strength coach Boyd Epley.

The three-year letterman and two-year starter recorded 52 tackles in 1994. Ten of those sacks were for losses totaling 52 yards and five were quarterback sacks for 31 yards in losses.

Jones also caused one fumble, broke up two passes and was credited with 22 quarterback hurries for the season.

Jones had one of his best days in the biggest game of the regular season. He had seven tackles, two pass break-ups and one sack against No. 2-3 Colorado, a performance for which he was named the ABC-Chevrolet Nebraska Player-of-the-Game.

Against Kansas State, he had seven more tackles, one of which was yet another solo sack. His season earned him a spot on the first-team All-Big Eight squad, CFA Good Works Team membership and honorable-mention on the UPI All-America squad.

And while his numbers against Miami in the Orange Bowl might not show it (only five tackles, no sacks or tackles for losses), Jones was right there with several of his Blackshirt teammates when they decided to meet at the quarterback late in the game. Their pressure helped snuff Miami's offensive drive for a tie and win the game, 24-17.

SENIOR OUTSIDE LINEBACKER
6-2, 220; LA PLATA, MD.

BARRON MILES

SENIOR CORNERBACK
5-8, 165; ROSELLE, N.J.

If there was one player whose size was deceptive with regard to the importance of his contribution to Nebraska's success in 1994, it would be 5-foot-8, 165-pound cornerback Barron Miles.

Perhaps one of the best athletes on an athletically gifted team, Miles became the big-play man on a big-play Blackshirt defense. He regularly drew the big-name receiver assignment in man-to-man pass coverage and seldom came out on the short end.

Miles finished 1994 with 40 tackles, four blocked kicks and five interceptions. He also caused one fumble and broke up 13 passes. Those numbers earned him third-team All-America status and a first-team spot on the All-Big Eight teams for a second year. That two-time All-Big Eight selection was the first for a Nebraska defensive back since Bruce Pickens garnered the honor in 1989-90.

The New Jersey Sports Writers Association named the Roselle, N.J., native its College Defensive Back-of-the-Year.

Miles' tackle total ranked 10th on the team's list. He blocked one punt against UCLA and two against Pacific on his way to a career-record total of seven blocked kicks. The other block (his school-record fourth of the year) came against Oklahoma in the season finale; he put his hands on a 33-yard field goal attempt at a critical point in the game.

He broke up a single-game record six passes against pass-happy Kansas State and finished with the season (13) and career (19) records for break-ups.

Coach Tom Osborne and defensive secondary coach George Darlington clearly thought much of Miles' athletic abilities: He was the team's backup punter in road games, was considered for a move from cornerback to safety when injuries thinned that position and even took snaps at quarterback when injuries at that position created a near-panic situation.

He had two interceptions that led to scores against Wyoming (one of Nebraska's closest games of the season) and came on to make a team-leading twelve tackles and three pass breakups against Miami in the 24-17 victory in the Orange Bowl. He even had one tackle for a 4-yard loss in that game.

Nebraska ended the season ranked in the Top 10 nationally in pass defense efficiency, and Miles was considered a major contributor to NU's success.

KAREEM MOSS

In his final year as a Husker, senior rover Kareem Moss seemed to be all over the field. The 5-foot-10, 190-pounder from Spartanburg, S.C., made the best of his first year as a starter and stepped up to become a key player in a secondary that had struggled when safety Mike Minter was lost to injury in the second game of the season.

Moss went on to record 66 tackles, the fourth-best total on a team that coach Tom Osborne said settled down to become one of the best defenses ever at Nebraska. Moss tied team leader Ed Stewart with 41 solo tackles during the season.

Moss had three tackles for 13 yards in losses, two sacks, four pass breakups and two interceptions, and he twice hurried the opposing quarterback.

After the secondary adjusted to Minter's absence, the play of Moss and his secondary teammates elevated to the levels needed to meet the challenges from nationally ranked Kansas State and Colorado. Both the Wildcats and the Buffaloes threw the ball well, but Nebraska's Blackshirts held them in check.

Despite the losses of NFL draft picks Toby Wright and John Reece, Nebraska's secondary became a solid presence on a good football team.

Moss was also the No. 1 punt returner for the Huskers; he brought back 31 punts for 234 yards, an average of 7.6 yards per return. And he set a Kickoff Classic record in the season opener with four returns for 81 yards, a 20.3-yard average.

Moss had double-digit tackle days against UCLA and Kansas, and a career-best six solo stops against Colorado.

One of his two interceptions occurred during the second offensive play for Oklahoma in the regular-season finale. In the end, Nebraska's defense stepped up to clinch a fourth-straight Big Eight championship.

Moss, who was one of very few junior college players to be recruited by Nebraska (Garden City, Kan., CC), had four tackles and a late-game interception in the Huskers' 24-17 national championship win over Miami in the Orange Bowl.

SENIOR ROVER
5-10, 190; SPARTANBURG, S.C.

ABDUL MUHAMMAD

The senior leader of the "itty-bitty" receivers for Nebraska, Abdul Muhammad, came very close to missing the 1994 championship season. He was hurting and didn't want to play his senior season in pain.

But it seems Muhammad regularly turns in his best seasons for Nebraska while in pain. In 1993, he returned from a summer visit to his Compton, Calif., home with a bullet in his backside, the result of a drive-by shooting in the neighborhood in which he was raised.

The 5-foot-9, 160-pounder finished 1993 with a team-leading 25 receptions for 383 yards and three touchdowns. He averaged 15.3 yards per catch and headed to the Orange Bowl with his unbeaten teammates to play Florida State for the national championship.

In that game, Muhammad took a crushing hit that left him with cracked ribs and a lacerated liver. He spent several weeks in the hospital and experienced continued soreness throughout the summer. Abdul considered redshirting in '94 because he wanted to play his senior season in good health.

But in two-a-day practice he took his first hits and decided he could play after all. And at season's end, he couldn't have been happier with his decision.

Muhammad was a key ingredient in Nebraska's passing attack. The sticky-handed speedster, who runs the 40-yard dash in 4.46 seconds, was NU's big-play receiver — eight of his catches went for 25 yards or more.

In 1994, he again led all NU receivers with 23 catches and 360 yards, an average of 15.7 yards per catch. And when the Huskers needed a big play, likely as not, Muhammad was the target.

He had a season-best five catches for 98 yards against Oklahoma, including a 44-yarder from Berringer in the third quarter that set up the game's only touchdown.

In the Orange Bowl, Berringer and Tommie Frazier found Muhammad four times for 60 yards.

But his biggest play may have been a downfield block in the fourth quarter of the Orange Bowl. His block gave full-back Cory Schlesinger free passage to the end zone for Nebraska's game-winning touchdown.

CHRISTIAN PETER

Junior Christian Peter's 6-foot-2, 285-pound frame was deceptive: Opposing offenses could have sworn the Locust, N.J., native was a lot bigger than that.

Peter took advantage of his first year as a starter and made a huge impact on Nebraska's defense. When Peter sided with senior tackle Terry Connealy, the two interior linemen made it almost impossible for opponents to run up the middle on Nebraska's Blackshirts.

By the end of the year, Nebraska ranked in the Top 10 nationally in all four major defensive categories. The rushing average allowed was only 79.3 yards per game, good for fourth nationally.

Peter, as well as outside linebacker Dwayne Harris, had a chance to see what their 1994 seasons would be like in the final regular-season game of 1993. Connealy and Danny Noonan both left the Oklahoma game with injuries, and Peter responded with four tackles, including three solo stops. On one play, he bulled through the Sooner line and tackled the Sooner ballcarrier in the backfield for a 4-yard loss deep in OU territory.

Peter also had a chance to play in the Orange Bowl against Florida State; he claimed two tackles.

Christian admitted that the playing time only made him hungry for more. In 1994, he demonstrated why the coaches had been anxious for him to turn the corner: He made use of his quickness and superior strength (460-pound bench press) to record 71 tackles. Fourteen of his stops were behind the line for 45 yards in losses. He had seven quarterback sacks and 20 quarterback hurries, and he broke up two passes.

In 1995, Christian is expected to be a key figure in another outstanding Nebraska defense. Line coach and defensive coordinator Charlie McBride said the defensive line may even become a family affair: Christian's younger brother Jason, as a freshman backup to Connealy will contend to win the other tackle spot next fall.

JUNIOR DEFENSIVE TACKLE
6-2, 285; LOCUST, N.J.

LAWRENCE PHILLIPS

This sophomore from West Covina, Calif., carved out his niche almost immediately upon his arrival in Lincoln. Not many freshmen running backs play for the Huskers, but Phillips earned and excelled in the coveted spot.

He played in every game in 1993 except the opener and finished as the team's third-leading rusher with 508 yards and five touchdowns.

Against UCLA during his freshman year, he came off the bench to rush for 137 yards on 28 carries in a one-point Husker win. He also came off the bench to sparkle in the Orange Bowl after starter Calvin Jones was injured in the second quarter. Phillips ended with 64 yards on 13 carries and scored against Florida State in an 18-16 loss.

When Jones decided to forego his senior season, Phillips was promoted to the No. 1 spot, and he filled it well. He opened the season with a 126-yard effort against No. 24 West Virginia in the Kickoff Classic. He had 175 yards and two touchdowns in the next game against Texas Tech.

The yardage only continued to pile up when Nebraska lost quarterbacks Tommie Frazier and Brook Berringer to injuries — Phillips was asked to carry the offensive load.

Lawrence had 168 yards on 27 carries against Wyoming and scored three touchdowns. The following week, he had the 12th-best rushing day ever by a Husker back with 221 yards on 33 carries on his way to scoring three more touchdowns against Oklahoma State.

He battled Kansas State for 117 yards on 31 carries the following week and provided a 24-carry, 103-yard effort to help beat national power Colorado. He added two more games of more than 150 yards each against Kansas and Iowa State before Oklahoma's defense snapped his 100-yard rushing streak at 11 games.

By season's end, Phillips was the all-time sophomore rushing leader for Nebraska with 1,722 yards. It was the second-best rushing season in Husker history behind only the Heisman Trophy-winning season of Mike Rozier (2,148 yards in 1983).

Phillips earned second-team All-America honors, was eighth in the Heisman Trophy voting, was named by Football News as an Offensive Player-of the-Year finalist and was a first-team All-Big Eight pick by the coaches and Associated Press.

Phillips also scored 16 touchdowns and had 172 more yards on 22 receptions.

Coach Tom Osborne said that the youngster has the potential to climb to Rozier's level. But with his 96-yard effort in the Orange Bowl (against a Miami defense that was ranked best in the nation going into the bowl game), Phillips caused many people to believe he might be very near that level already.

SOPHOMORE I-BACK
6-0, 200; WEST COVINA, CALIF.

#40 CORY SCHLESINGER

Cory Schlesinger was raised in the tiny town of Duncan, Neb., and played football in nearby Columbus, where he earned all-state honors and a scholarship to NU.

If he had one knock coming out of high school, it was a question of speed, even though he rushed for 1,514 yards and 23 touchdowns his senior year. At first, Husker recruiters were reluctant to offer him a scholarship, but they were convinced by those who knew Schlesinger's work habits and his heart to play. Cory got the scholarship, and he didn't disappoint.

Schlesinger's work ethic manifested itself in school position records and the strength and performance indexes formulated by Director of Athletic Performance Boyd Epley. Schlesinger was named Husker Co-Lifter-of-the Year by his teammates in 1993.

And on the field, that determination resulted in playing time and improvement. After playing backup to senior Lance Lewis in 1992, Schlesinger took over as the No. 1 fullback in 1993.

He finished that season as the team's fifth-leading rusher with 48 carries for 193 yards and one touchdown. He averaged 4 yards per carry, but coach Tom Osborne indicated that he wanted more big-play potential from the position.

In '94, Schlesinger gave him what he wanted. He nearly doubled his rushing total with 456 yards on 63 carries, good for an average of 7.2 yards per carry. He had a lost yardage total of 3 yards for the season and scored four touchdowns during the regular season.

But Schlesinger's biggest plays came during the Orange Bowl; his two fullback trap runs of 15 and 14 yards provided the tying and winning touchdowns in the 24-17 national championship victory over Miami.

Quarterback Tommie Frazier said that the Huskers liked to give the ball to Schlesinger in the fourth quarter because he always came through.

Schlesinger ended the Orange Bowl with six carries for 48 yards, an 8-yard average.

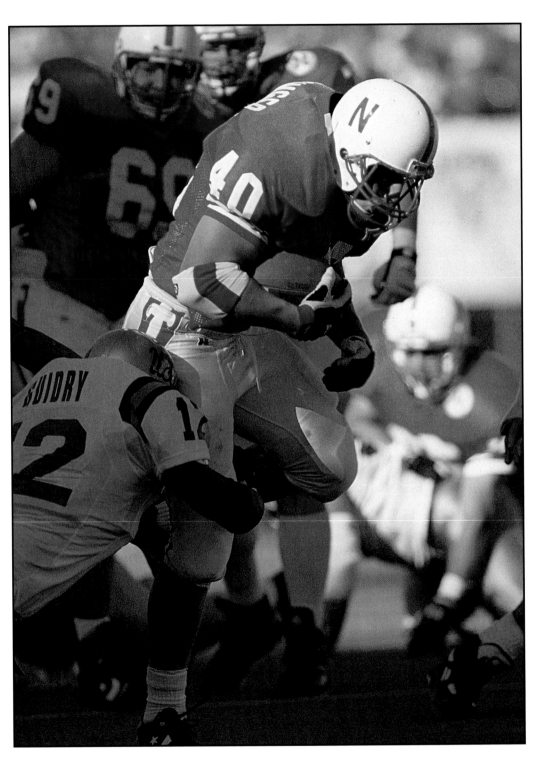

SENIOR FULLBACK
6-0, 230; DUNCAN, NEB.

MATT SHAW

#85

Matt Shaw is one of the most unusual success stories of Nebraska's 1994 season. The walk-on from Lincoln Northeast High proved again that there is more to a Husker receiver than pass-catching.

Shaw earned a starting role for the Huskers based on his prowess as a blocker. Although he never caught a pass during his college career, he proved that he more than deserved his spot on the line.

Shaw alternated with Mark Gilman and Eric Alford at tight end, a position which became critical to Nebraska's power rushing game when the Huskers began to struggle with the issue of their quarterbacks' health at midseason.

The 6-foot-3, 235-pounder played in every game during his final two seasons. And his performance in the classroom was just as impressive as his play on the turf. In 1994, Shaw earned GTE first-team Academic All-American honors and was named a Phillips 66 Academic All-Big Eight selection. He carried a 3.761 grade point average (out of a possible 4.0) in biological sciences.

Apparently, Shaw wasn't the only Husker to show a proclivity for both football and education: Shaw was one of Nebraska's three first-team Academic All-Americans in 1994; Terry Connealy and Rob Zatechka were also members of that elite squad.

The only games he failed to start in 1994 were against UCLA, Pacific and Oklahoma, and the only reason he did not start then was that Nebraska opened those three games in the spread formation.

Shaw was a key addition to an offensive line that was considered the best ever in Nebraska's football history. The Huskers won their 11th NCAA rushing title with a 340-yard average; they scored at a 36.3-point clip and amassed 477.8 yards in total offense per game.

SENIOR TIGHT END
6-3, 235; LINCOLN, NEB.

#12

TOM SIELER

When senior Byron Bennett used up his eligibility as Nebraska's place-kicker and punter in 1993, Nebraska coaches were confident that they had a quality kicker in the wings.

Senior Tom Sieler had shared some of the kickoff and extra-point duties with Bennett for two seasons. He kicked off much of 1993, displaying a strong leg, and often sailed kicks well into the end zone.

But in 1994, a surprise newcomer denied Sieler a chance to be THE man in the Husker kicking game. Baseball star Darin Erstad came on board and took over the punting duties, displaying a leg even stronger than that of Sieler.

Still, Sieler was a mainstay on short field goals, and his precision kicks earned him honors for the majority of point-after-TD kicks. And Nebraska's scoring proficiency provided Sieler with plenty of opportunities to showcase his talent.

The Las Vegas, Nev., native made the best of those chances, kicking 40 of 42 PATs through the uprights during the season.

Sieler also claimed short-yardage field goal duties and was 4 of 6 for the year. He hit both of his tries from inside the 30 and 2 of 4 from 30-to-39 yards out.

Sieler had the distinction of both kicking off and recording a tackle in the 1994 Orange Bowl game against Florida State.

He drew the PAT kicking assignment again when the Huskers returned to the Orange Bowl in 1995 to play Miami and hit both of his point-after-tries.

During his career, Sieler made 58 of 61 PATs and finished with a career total of 68 points.

SENIOR PLACE-KICKER
6-5, 205; LAS VEGAS, NEV.

BRENDEN STAI

SENIOR OFFENSIVE GUARD
6-5, 300; YORBA LINDA, CALIF.

Right guard Brenden Stai, returning from a disappointing 1993 season, had perhaps more to play for in 1994 than any other lineman. With four games remaining in the '93 regular season, he had broken a leg, and what was certain to have been an all-star year came to an abrupt end.

Without him in the lineup, Nebraska's powerful rushing game fell off by an average of 41 yards per game.

But Stai was exceptional in 1994, earning first-team All-America honors on the Walter Camp, Football Writers and UPI teams. He was a second-team pick by *The Associated Press*.

His first-team picks, coupled with those of tackle Zach Wiegert, marked only the fourth time since 1950 that two members of the same offensive line earned first-team All-America selections in the same year.

Writers and coaches made Stai a first-team All-Big Eight selection, but perhaps the greatest compliment came from his own coach.

Combined with right tackle Wiegert, Stai formed what coach Tom Osborne said was probably the best guard-tackle combination in Husker history. And that was saying a lot, considering the 1983 tandem of Outland- and Lombardi-winning All-America guard Dean Steinkuhler and All-Big Eight tackle Scott Rairdon.

Stai had 132 "pancake," or knockdown, blocks during the season, averaging 11 per game. He had 17 such blocks against Oklahoma and totaled 15 twice, including the huge game against Colorado.

Nebraska took advantage of Stai's 6-foot-5, 300-pound frame and team-leading strength in the Orange Bowl by switching sides with Joel Wilks. The move matched Stai against Miami's superb All-America tackle Warren Sapp. The strategy seemed to work: Sapp and his teammates on the defensive line faded in the fourth quarter from exhaustion.

And the switch didn't hurt Wilks, either, according to line coach Mile Tenopir. Tenopir said Wilks might have had his best game of the season against Miami.

#*32*

Senior "Will," or weakside, linebacker Ed Stewart saved his best for last. And what the senior from Chicago had done before wasn't too shabby.

Stewart shook off early-season concerns about a kidney ailment to turn in one of Nebraska's best defensive performances ever. He was one of three finalists for the Butkus Award for the nation's best linebacker. He was named Big Eight Defensive Player-of- the-Year by both *The Associated Press* and Big Eight coaches, was one of three finalists for the Football Writers Defensive Player-of-the-Year, was a semifinalist for Football News Defensive Player-of-the-Year and was a consensus first-team All-American.

Late in the season, when asked about all the honors which were being bestowed upon him, Stewart commented that they were all great, but they would mean a lot less if the Huskers didn't win a national championship.

But Stewart needn't have worried: He was the heart of a dominating defense that made that championship possible. His 96 tackles led the team for 1994. He had five games in which he recorded 10 or more stops, including 13 against Iowa State and 12 against Wyoming.

He also had 5.5 tackles for 23 yards in losses, including 3.5 quarterback sacks. He also had 18 quarterback hurries.

Linebacker coach Kevin Steele said Stewart was so good at what he did that opposing teams would run plays specifically designed to avoid Stewart's territory. And the Husker assistant went on to say that Stewart was the ideal player — he needed only to discuss strategies before he put them to use on the field.

The three-year letterman, named co-captain by his teammates, helped direct traffic and inspired his fellow players with the level of his play.

Stewart came up with five tackles in the 24-17 national championship win over Miami in the Orange Bowl, but his biggest contribution was the continual pressure he placed on Hurricane quarterback Frank Costa. Stewart's intensity helped wear down the Miami offense during the deciding fourth quarter.

SENIOR LINEBACKER
6-1, 220; CHICAGO, ILL.

ERIC STOKES

Eric Stokes, a gifted athlete recruited out of Lincoln East High School (in the Huskers' own backyard), was hailed as a Nebraska defensive secondary star in the making.

A running back and defender in high school, Stokes sat out 1992 as a redshirt. In 1993, he played in every game except one. But injuries slowed his progress and cut into his playing time in his rookie season. He was sidelined by a knee injury in the one game he missed in '93 and was also slowed by a hamstring pull, sore ribs and a sore hip.

He missed the entire spring after he underwent hip surgery, but he planned to return in the fall in good health. However, the hip still slowed him some when he returned to the squad.

Then, a season-ending knee injury to safety Mike Minter in the second game of the season created a gap in the secondary. Nebraska defensive coaches were forced to put junior Tony Veland and sophomore Stokes into action.

It took a few games for Veland, a converted quarterback, and Stokes, a former cornerback, to adjust to their new assignment in the defensive secondary. But once they turned the corner, their defensive play shone for Nebraska.

The Huskers finished the season ranked in the Top 10 in four major categories, including pass efficiency defense.

Stokes collected 36 tackles in his first season of substantial play. He also broke up two passes as he gained valuable experience in a relatively injury-free season.

The speedy Stokes plans to have a prominent role in continuing the Blackshirt tradition of success in 1995.

SOPHOMORE FREE SAFETY
5-11, 175; LINCOLN, NEB.

JARED TOMICH

Jared Tomich joined freshman Grant Wistrom at defensive end in 1994, and the two youngsters made a significant contribution to the Nebraska Blackshirt defense.

The 1994 edition of the Blackshirts, one of the fastest defenses in Nebraska history, earned praise from coach Tom Osborne as his best defense ever and possibly the best Nebraska has ever spawned in its long football history.

Tomich fit right into the modern mold of rush ends, or outside linebackers. Some compared the play of Tomich and Wistrom to that of a developing Trev Alberts. Alberts won the Butkus Award for the nation's best linebacker for Nebraska in 1993.

The 6-foot-2, 250-pound Tomich, who possesses explosive speed, was in on 23 tackles in 1994, four of which resulted in 15 yards in losses. He had one quarterback sack and 12 quarterback hurries. He also was credited with causing an interception in the Oklahoma State game. He had one tackle in the 1995 Orange Bowl win over Miami.

Statistically, one of his best games was the season opener against West Virginia in the Kickoff Classic; he made five tackles while in a four-player rotation with seniors Donta Jones and Dwayne Harris and freshman Wistrom.

"Jared contributed on all of our special teams, too," said position coach Tony Samuel. "We tried to rotate four guys at rush end so he played in every game. He made some big plays, including one on a fourth-and-one against UCLA when he came across the line and made a tackle for a loss. He has great potential. Wistrom and Tomich will definitely be the two leading candidates to start in 1995. They played under pressure and played well."

SOPHOMORE LINEBACKER
6-2, 250; ST. JOHN, IND.

MATT TURMAN

Sophomore walk-on Matt Turman took advantage of several unexpected occurrences to become a major player in Nebraska's 1994 championship season.

The 5-foot-11, 165-pounder from Wahoo was expected to begin the fall fairly far down the list of Nebraska quarterbacks, but he found himself No. 3 after Ben Rutz, Jon Elder and Monte Christo dropped from contention.

Rutz transferred, the Huskers' only '94 scholarship quarterback recruit, Jon Elder, also transferred and walk-on hopeful Monte Christo was injured.

But the losses weren't a great concern until Frazier was sidelined due to blood clots in his leg. Turman played significant minutes against Pacific, and that experience proved to be beneficial in the weeks ahead.

In the game against Wyoming, Berringer suffered a partially collapsed lung, and the following week, against Oklahoma State, he reinjured it in the first half. Turman was forced to play the entire second half against the Cowboys.

Turman, the son of Wahoo Neumann High coach Tim Turman, played like a veteran against OSU. Nebraska was in the lead 9-3 when he took over, but he led the Huskers to two quick scores in the third quarter. He added another score in the fourth to cement the 32-3 win.

Since Berringer's status was still questionable, Turman started against No. 11-16 Kansas State. Turman led the team to a 7-6 lead at the half. Berringer then came in to finish the job in a 17-6 win.

Turman himself gave the Husker coaches reason for concern the following week against Missouri. He had come into the game to give Berringer a chance to recuperate for the big Colorado game, now only a week away. But while running an option, Turman was hit after going out of bounds and suffered what was thought to be a shoulder separation. It later turned out to be just a sprain, so he was on the sidelines to support Berringer for the rest of the season.

In 11 games, Turman hit 6 of 12 passes for 81 yards and one touchdown. He also ran 19 times for 80 yards, an average of 4.2 yards per carry.

#9

In 1994, junior Tony Veland turned what could have been a disappointing Nebraska career into something special. Despite his ability to run the Husker option offense, Veland was plagued by injuries at the quarterback position. So, Veland tried to come back from serious knee surgery as a safety on defense.

Although slowed by continuing rehabilitation on his knee, Veland became Nebraska's starting safety after a knee injury ended sophomore starter Mike Minter's season.

Veland made the transition rapidly, even though he had missed all of spring ball due to his own knee injury, which he suffered in the second game of 1993. At the time of his injury, he was the No. 2 quarterback behind Frazier. Prior to that, in 1992, he had been listed as the No. 1 quarterback, but a broken collar bone ended his hopes two weeks before the season began.

The desire to play with less chance of injury brought him to the defensive side of the ball in 1994.

Veland started the final 10 games of the season at safety and ended with 26 tackles, one pass breakup and three interceptions.

The junior alternated with sophomore Eric Stokes in a rebuilt Husker secondary that regrouped after a disappointing showing against Wyoming to more than meet the challenges of the gifted passing attacks of Kansas State and Colorado.

Veland had one of his best games against Colorado, logging a career-high four tackles.

Prior to that game, the coaches had considered moving him back to quarterback — Frazier was sidelined for the regular season with recurring blood clots and backup Brook Berringer had suffered a partially collapsed lung.

Veland took some snaps in practice but was reluctant to return to quarterback unless it was absolutely necessary. The coaches elected to let him concentrate on his new defensive position, and he evolved into a solid player for the Blackshirts. He had six tackles in the Orange Bowl victory over Miami, the second-best total on the team, and helped NU capture the national championship.

JUNIOR FREE SAFETY
6-2, 200; OMAHA, NEB.

ZACH WIEGERT

SENIOR OFFENSIVE TACKLE
6-5, 300; FREMONT, NEB.

The image most Nebraskans have of Zach Wiegert's season is captured in a single play of the UCLA game: The big tackle pulled around the left side of the line and belted a defensive back so hard it knocked the outmatched defender backward 5 yards.

Wiegert loved such plays and made more than one defensive back pay for trying to defend Nebraska's option sweeps. One could almost hear the 6-foot-5, 300-pound Wiegert break into a sinister laugh when he turned the corner in front of a Husker running back.

And for his labors of love, Wiegert earned nearly every offensive line honor that was awarded in 1994. He won the Outland Trophy, the seventh such award presented to a Nebraska lineman; was a finalist for the Lombardi Award, which eventually went to Miami's gifted defensive tackle Warren Sapp; and was the TD Club of Columbus' Offensive-Lineman-of-the-Year.

He was on everybody's list as first-team All-American and was ninth in the voting for the Heisman Trophy, which is awarded to college football's best player.

The big tackle was named to the All-Big Eight team for the third time, won ABC's Player-of-the-Game award for Nebraska against UCLA and was a Big Eight Offensive Player-of-the-Week nominee for his play against Kansas. Coach Tom Osborne noted that Wiegert never missed a block in that Kansas game and commented that he couldn't recall any other offensive lineman accomplishing that feat for him. The coach also said that Wiegert didn't miss many blocks in any other game, either.

The three-year starter at tackle combined with right guard Brenden Stai to form what Osborne labeled probably the best right-side pair in Husker history.

Wiegert was one of the reasons Nebraska won another national rushing title (with a 340-yard average) and had one of the school's best passing seasons in recent years. He finished the entire season without one holding call, and the defenders he was assigned to block never sacked the quarterback. He had started 36 consecutive games for Nebraska heading into the Orange Bowl, and his position coaches said he had improved all the while.

Zach was credited with 113 "pancake," or knockdown, blocks — on at least one of the season's highlight game films, he had two on the same play.

JOEL WILKS

Joel Wilks, one of Nebraska's least-experienced offensive linemen entering the season, may have had the best season of the bunch.

The senior guard from Hastings, Neb., earned his first start when he was chosen to fill the guard position vacated by Rob Zatechka, who moved from left guard to tackle to replace the graduated Lance Lundberg.

The 1994 Nebraska line would clear enough holes to allow the Huskers to lead the nation in rushing with an average of 340 yards per game. And they earned that yardage despite playing several games with injured quarterbacks, a situation which dictated running the ball against defenses that knew what was coming.

Wilks played in six games at the end of the 1993 season after rebounding from an ankle sprain. He started one of those games and proved his value as a starter.

One of the smallest of the '94 linemen, the 6-foot-3 Wilks weighed in at 280 pounds. And while his longtime starting teammates drew headlines for their play in the fall, Wilks quietly recorded a team-leading 142 "pancake" blocks, named as such because the lineman upends and flattens his opponent.

Joel averaged 11.8 of those pancakes a game, including 17 against Oklahoma State, a game during which the Husker offense limited much of its plays to straight-ahead runs to protect injured quarterback Brook Berringer.

Another in a long line of successful walk-on players who earned spots on the offensive line, Wilks led the team in pancakes against West Virginia, Wyoming, Oklahoma State, Missouri and Kansas. He shared top honors with teammates against UCLA, Iowa State and Oklahoma.

If there was an unsung hero in this most notable of Nebraska offensive lines, Wilks would be the man. He, too, made headlines when he and Brenden Stai switched sides in the Orange Bowl so the heavier, stronger Stai would be matched against Miami's Lombardi Trophy winner Warren Sapp.

SENIOR OFFENSIVE GUARD
6-3, 280; HASTINGS, NEB.

TYRONE WILLIAMS

Junior cornerback Tyrone Williams, one of the speedy talents Nebraska was able to steal from the state of Florida, is one of the new breed of defensive backs coach George Darlington recruited for the 4-3 defense.

His new backs would need speed and the ability to cover people man to man, and Nebraska fans saw plenty of both after the Huskers swapped the 5-2 reaction defensive scheme for an aggressive, lightning-quick 4-3 in 1993.

Williams fit the model well with 4.45-second speed in the 40-yard dash and a 35-inch vertical leap. When Williams was combined with senior corner Barron Miles, the Huskers had what some considered one of the best cornerback pairs in the nation.

After sitting out the 1992 season, Williams bolted into the defensive picture in 1993. He filled in one of the many secondary spots left open by graduation and earned Big Eight Co-Defensive Newcomer-of-the-Year honors, as selected by the coaches.

He finished 1993 with 29 tackles, the 10th-best total on the team, broke up three passes and had one interception. One of his biggest games, however, was the Orange Bowl battle against Florida State, when he had nine tackles and three breakups.

Williams sat out the '94 season-opener, but he started the final 11 games of the regular season. He ended with 38 tackles, including 31 solo stops. Tyrone also had five pass breakups and three interceptions.

When the Husker defenders were asked to play man-to-man coverage for much of the Orange Bowl against Miami, one of the best big-play passing teams in the country, he had three tackles.

Miami did score twice on long passes in the first half, but the secondary and a vicious pass rush in the second half allowed Nebraska to win its first national championship for coach Tom Osborne.

Williams was considered a key ingredient in a Blackshirt defense that finished in the Top 10 in four major defensive categories, including pass efficiency defense.

Not many true freshmen earn a significant playing role at Nebraska, but in 1994, Grant Wistrom did.

The 6-foot-5, 230-pounder arrived at Nebraska fresh from Webb City, Mo., with a body developed beyond his years and a quick-study mentality that enabled him to learn the Husker system quickly.

"He wasn't like any other freshmen I've been associated with," outside linebacker coach Tony Samuel commented.

Wistrom quickly became an impact player on a Husker Blackshirt defense that was considered to be Tom Osborne's best ever. The youngster earned a spot within a four-player rotation at outside linebacker with seniors Donta Jones and Dwayne Harris and sophomore Jared Tomich.

Wistrom played in all 12 games during the regular season as well as in the Orange Bowl against Miami. He finished with 36 tackles, including 6.5 for 55 yards in losses and 4.5 sacks for 49 yards in losses. He also was credited with 11 quarterback hurries.

In the Orange Bowl victory over the Hurricanes, he made three tackles.

Wistrom's play caused even head coach Tom Osborne to sing his praises.

"He's playing at a level that is commensurate with a lot of our senior players," Osborne said late in the season. Osborne continued to say that few of the freshmen who had been able to contribute for Nebraska had had such an immediate impact.

"I've never seen anything like it," Osborne said. "He's really been a great asset to our team."

Samuel agrees, and he likes the idea of having a player of that caliber back for three more seasons.

"He also did a great job on special teams," Samuel said. "He was on about every special team we had. And he was a backup snapper and played extensively at rush end. He did a great job."

FRESHMAN LINEBACKER
6-5, 230; WEBB CITY, MO.

ROB ZATECHKA

Senior Rob Zatechka could be considered the brains of the 1994 offensive line or, at the very least, THE BRAIN.

The 6-foot-5, 315-pounder from Lincoln, Neb., finished his college career with a perfect 4.0 grade point average. He never received lower than an "A" in any class, which was nothing new. He did the same thing in high school at Lincoln East.

Zatechka won nearly every academic award given in 1994. He was named an NCAA Today's Top Eight winner as one of the nation's top student athletes. He was a two-time first-team GTE Academic All-America pick. He was a two-time CFA Hitachi Scholar-Athlete winner, a four-time Academic All-Big Eight pick, a Rhodes Fellowship candidate, the national Honda Scholar-Athlete-of-the -Year Award winner, a Woody Hayes Award winner and the Vincent DePaul Draddy $25,000 Scholarship winner.

(The Vincent DePaul award is the National Football Foundation and Hall of Fame prize for the national student athlete-of-the-year.)

In addition to his classroom honors, Zatechka, a three-year letterman, was named co-captain of the Huskers for the 1994 season. During the season, he played in all 13 games and earned second-team All-Big Eight honors.

Part of a powerful and quick offensive line that paved the way for the nation's top rushing attack, Zatechka had 79 "pancake" blocks or, in other words, blocks that flattened an opponent. The Huskers had an average of 6.6 pancakes per game, an exceptional number for a team that pulled tackles from either side of the line for sweeps around the end.

Coach Tom Osborne has commented that he had confidence that his team could run equally well either way. Much of that confidence could probably be traced to the talents of Zatechka and teammate Zach Wiegert, an All-American and Lombardi Trophy winner playing the opposite tackle position.

Seniors

36 Leonard Alexander
Linebacker
Detroit, Mich.

88 Eric Alford
Tight End
High Point, N.C.

45 Clint Brown
Linebacker
Arlington, Neb.

61 Brady Caskey
Offensive Tackle
Stanton, Neb.

99 Terry Connealy
Defensive Tackle
Hyannis, Neb.

17 Scott Davenport
I-Back
Rye Brook, N.Y.

4 Troy Dumas
Linebacker
Cheyenne, Wyo.

86 Dwayne Harris
Outside Linebacker
Bessemer, Ala.

92 Jerad Higman
Outside Linebacker
Akron, Iowa

51 Bill Humphrey
Center
Libertyville, Ill.

84 Donta Jones
Outside Linebacker
La Plata, Md.

49 John Martin
Outside Linebacker
Wahoo, Neb.

14 Barron Miles
Cornerback
Roselle, N.J.

29 Kareem Moss
Rover
Spartanburg, S.C.

27 Abdul Muhammad
Wingback
Compton, Calif.

57 Jason Pesterfield
Defensive Tackle
Pauls Valley, Okla.

40 Cory Schlesinger
Fullback
Duncan, Neb.

85 Matt Shaw
Tight End
Lincoln, Neb.

12 Tom Sieler
Place-Kicker
Las Vegas, Nev.

66 Brenden Stai
Offensive Guard
Yorba Linda, Calif.

32 Ed Stewart
Linebacker
Chicago, Ill.

72 Zach Wiegert
Offensive Tackle
Fremont, Neb.

76 Joel Wilks
Offensive Guard
Hastings, Neb.

56 Rob Zatechka
Offensive Tackle
Lincoln, Neb.

65 Bryan Pruitt
Offensive Guard
Midlothian, Ill.

82 Jacques Allen
Wingback
Kansas City, Mo.

7 Reggie Baul
Split End
Bellevue, Neb.

18 Brook Berringer
Quarterback
Goodland, Kan.

26 Clinton Childs
I-Back
Omaha, Neb.

46 Doug Colman
Linebacker
Ventnor, N.J.

41 Phil Ellis
Linebacker
Grand Island, Neb.

15 Tommie Frazier
Quarterback
Bradenton, Fla.

87 Mark Gilman
Tight End
Kalispell, Mont.

54 Aaron Graham
Center
Denton, Texas

58 Luther Hardin
Outside Linebacker
O'Fallon, Ill.

96 Jason Jenkins
Defensive Tackle
Hammonton, N.J.

33 Clester Johnson
Wingback
Bellevue, Neb.

30 Brian Knuckles
I-Back
Charlotte, N.C.

2 John Livingston
Split End
San Marcos, Calif.

22 Jeff Makovicka
Fullback
Brainard, Neb.

38 Chris Norris
Fullback
Papillion, Neb.

63 Brian Nunns
Offensive Tackle
Lincoln, Neb.

69 Steve Ott
Offensive Guard
Henderson, Neb.

52 Aaron Penland
Linebacker
Jacksonville, Fla.

55 Christian Peter
Defensive Tackle
Locust, N.J.

80 Brett Popplewell
Split End
Melbourne, Aust.

37 Darren Schmadeke
Cornerback
Albion, Neb.

31 Chad Stanley
Fullback
Lebanon, Kan.

9 Tony Veland
Free Safety
Omaha, Neb.

68 Steve Volin
Offensive Guard
Wahoo, Neb.

8 Tyrone Williams
Cornerback
Palmetto, Fla.

48 Dave Alderman
Rover
Omaha, Neb.

23 Larry Arnold
Linebacker
Copley, Ohio

7 Dennis Bailey
Free Safety
St. Louis, Mo.

21 Damon Benning
I-Back
Omaha, Neb.

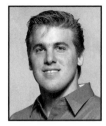

11 Chad Blahak
Cornerback
Lincoln, Neb.

20 Michael Booker
Cornerback
Oceanside, Calif.

9 Chad Brouse
Free Safety
Lincoln, Neb.

83 Aaron Davis
Split End
Lincoln, Neb.

75 Chris Dishman
Offensive Tackle
Cozad, Neb.

6 Darin Erstad
Punter/Place-Kicker
Jamestown, N.D.

44 Jon Hesse
Linebacker
Lincoln, Neb.

5 Brendan Holbein
Split End
Cozad, Neb.

78 Kory Mikos
Offensive Tackle
Seward, Neb.

83 Bryce Miller
Outside Linebacker
Elmwood, Neb.

10 Mike Minter
Free Safety
Lawton, Okla.

Ian Mitchell
Linebacker
Lincoln, Neb.

42 Ed Morrow
Outside Linebacker
Ferguson, Mo.

97 Jeff Ogard
Defensive Tackle
St. Paul, Neb.

1 Lawrence Phillips
I-Back
West Covina, Calif.

39 Mike Roberts
Rover
Omaha, Neb.

74 Scott Saltsman
Defensive Tackle
Wichita Falls, Texas

28 Brian Schuster
Fullback
Fullerton, Neb.

Mike Smith
Fullback
Dunning, Neb.

16 Eric Stokes
Free Safety
Lincoln, Neb.

91 Ryan Terwilliger
Linebacker
Grant, Neb.

93 Jared Tomich
Outside Linebacker
St. John, Ind.

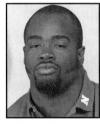

94 Larry Townsend
Defensive Tackle
San Jose, Calif.

77 Adam Treu
Offensive Tackle
Lincoln, Neb.

11 Matt Turman
Quarterback
Wahoo, Neb.

25 Jon Vedral
Wingback
Gregory, S.D.

53 Matt Vrzal
Center
Grand Island, Neb.

3 Riley Washington
Split End
Chula Vista, Calif.

28 Jamel Williams
Linebacker
Merrillville, Ind.

82 Shalis Winder
Outside Linebacker
Scottsbluff, Neb.

22 Trampis Wrice
Cornerback
Valdosta, Ga.

Freshmen

47 Matt Aden
Rover
Omaha, Neb.

70 Eric Anderson
Offensive Tackle
Lincoln, Neb.

81 Lance Brown
Wingback
Papillion, Neb.

87 Darren Brummond
Linebacker
Englewood, Colo.

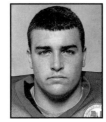
62 Ted Butler
Offensive Guard
Lincoln, Neb.

90 Tim Carpenter
Tight End
Columbus, Neb.

48 Kenny Cheatham
Receiver
Phoenix, Ariz.

9 Monte Christo
Quarterback
Kearney, Neb.

3 Tray Crayton
Defensive Back
Oceanside, Calif.

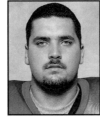
2 Leslie Dennis
Cornerback
Bradenton, Fla.

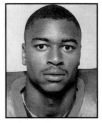
63 Constantine Dumitrescu
Offensive Lineman
Hayward, Calif.

7 Jay Foreman
Defensive Back
Eden Prairie, Minn.

81 Sean Gard
Outside Linebacker
Omaha, Neb.

53 Ben Gessford
Offensive Lineman
Lincoln, Neb.

81 Billy Haafke
Receiver
South Sioux City, Neb.

10 Ryan Held
Quarterback
Overland Park, Kan.

59 Josh Heskew
Center
Yukon, Okla.

59 Michael Hoffman
Defensive Tackle
Spencer, Neb.

40 Quint Hogrefe
Linebacker
Auburn, Neb.

62 Matt Hoskinson
Offensive Guard
Battle Creek, Neb.

38 Matt Hunting
Linebacker
Cozad, Neb.

5 Jai Jackson
Defensive Back
Lincoln, Neb.

84 Sheldon Jackson
Receiver
Diamond Bar, Calif.

34 Vershan Jackson
Fullback
Omaha, Neb.

19 Jesse Kosch
Punter
Columbus, Neb.

89 Jeff Lake
Split End
Columbus, Neb.

54 Charlie Leece
Linebacker
Grand Island, Neb.

79 Mike Lesser
Offensive Guard
Pierce, Neb.

13 Casey Macken
Linebacker
Cozad, Neb.

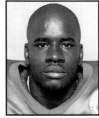
05 Octavious McFarlin
Defensive Back
Bastrop, Texas

Josh McGrane
Tight End
Lincoln, Neb.

38 Joel Makovicka
Fullback
Brainard, Neb.

39 Andy Miller
Receiver
Papillion, Neb.

6 Brian Morro
Punter/Place-Kicker
Middletown, N.J.

80 Erik Nelson
Defensive Line
Iowa City, Iowa

Freshmen

43 Sean Noster
Linebacker
San Antonio, Texas

95 Jason Peter
Defensive Tackle
Locust, N.J.

73 Fred Pollack
Offensive Tackle
Omaha, Neb.

34 David Reddick
Receiver
Camden, N.J.

13 Ted Retzlaff
Place-Kicker
Waverly, Neb.

82 Mike Rucker
Linebacker
St. Joseph, Mo.

35 Jeff Sakalosky
Linebacker
Omaha, Neb.

58 Anthony Schmode
Outside Linebacker
Battle Creek, Neb.

Adam Skoda
Linebacker
Lincoln, Neb.

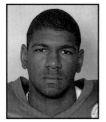

49 Larry Smith
Receiver
Lincoln, Neb.

67 Aaron Taylor
Offensive Guard
Wichita Falls, Texas

64 Ross Tessendorf
Outside Linebacker
Columbus, Neb.

83 Travis Toline
Linebacker
Wahoo, Neb.

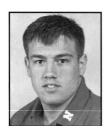

23 Todd Uhlir
I-Back
Battle Creek, Neb.

59 Mike Van Cleave
Offensive Guard
Huffman, Texas

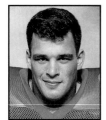

74 Brandt Wade
Outside Linebacker
Springfield, Neb.

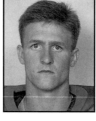

26 Eric Walther
Defensive Back
Junita, Neb.

23 Sean Wieting
Wingback
Tulatin, Ore.

68 Jason Wiltz
Defensive Line
New Orleans, La.

85 Grant Wistrom
Linebacker
Webb City, Mo.

64 Jon Zatechka
Offensive Tackle
Lincoln, Neb.

92 Joe Horst
Tight End
Wood River, Neb.

13 Trent Schlake
Quarterback
Gothenburg, Neb.

PICTURE NOT AVAILABLE:

Josh Cobb	Running Back	Wallace, Neb.
Chris Herron	Defensive Back	Scottsbluff, Neb.
Bill Lafleur	Punter/Place-Kicker	Norfolk, Neb.
Jason Luhr	Outside Linebacker	Osmond, Neb.
Dorrick Roy	Receiver	Inglewood, Calif.
Jeremy Shadrick	Outside Linebacker	Tulsa, Okla.
Jay Staehr	Quarterback	Kimball, Neb.
Andy Thompson	Defensive Back	Omaha, Neb.
Kyle Tully	Outside Linebacker	Jefferson, Wis.

The Husker Season Overview

This "revised" sign says it all. After a 13-0 season and a 24-17 Orange Bowl victory over Miami on its home turf, Nebraska's "business" was finally finished.

Nebraska football coach Tom Osborne has had some great football teams in his 22 years as head coach of the Huskers. He also was a member of the coaching staff that brought Lincoln back-to-back national championships (1970-'71); Osborne was the genius behind the offensive line under Bob Devaney.

But when the 1994 season came to a close, Osborne admitted that he had never had a team that was more driven than the one that walked off the Orange Bowl field with the winner's trophy as well as the inside track for the national championship.

"I've never been around a team so committed to one proposition — winning the national championship," Osborne said following the 24-17 Orange Bowl win over Miami. "The resolve from this team goes back to Jan. 1, 1994, when we lost the Orange Bowl. This team prevailed."

Nobody questioned the motivation of the Huskers after they narrowly missed a championship in an 18-16 loss to No. 1 Florida State in the 1994 Orange Bowl. Players hit the weight rooms in Lincoln shortly after returning from that bowl setback. They knew they were close but had more work to do.

And nobody questioned whether this team was good enough to get back to the Orange Bowl unbeaten, even as early as the beginning of fall practice in 1994. But in August, no one could have imagined the path Nebraska would take to get there.

Osborne and his staff may have done the best coaching job of their careers as they shuffled players and game plans to win them all.

The fall of 1994 began with No. 3 and 4 preseason rankings in the two major polls, plenty of attention and lots of national championship talk.

Seven starters returned on offense and six returned on defense from a team that had more than held its own against No. 1 Florida State before it finally fell in its lone loss of 1993.

Junior Tommie Frazier, perhaps the best option quarterback since Turner Gill (Nebraska, 1983), would be at the trigger of an offense that annually has been ranked among the nation's top three rushing leaders since the late-1970s.

Offensive linemen Rob Zatechka, Aaron Graham, Brenden Stai and Zach Wiegert, who together finished 1993 as one of the best lines in Nebraska history, also returned.

Tiny big-play man Abdul Muhammad returned from an Orange Bowl injury, and fullback Cory Schlesinger would be on hand to add quick-hitting rushing potential to his guard-like blocking.

The defense returned tackle Terry Connealy, outside linebacker Donta Jones, inside linebackers Troy Dumas and Ed Stewart, and cornerbacks Barron Miles and Tyrone Williams. All were guys with good speed who could fly around and give their opponents fits.

Then there was the supporting cast of lettermen, who frequently had nearly as much playing experience as the starters, on both sides of the ball.

The Huskers were favored to win a fourth-straight Big Eight championship and, after the Orange Bowl showing, were expected to make another run at the national championship as well.

The season opened with four impressive wins, which had people talking about Frazier in Heisman Trophy terms. He and a swarming defense had sparked a 31-0 win over 23rd- and 24th-ranked West Virginia in the Kickoff Classic to open the season.

Sophomore I-back Lawrence Phillips and Frazier teamed up for a pair of touchdowns each in a 42-16 win over unranked Texas Tech. Frazier passed for one and ran for another TD in Nebraska's (now ranked No. 1 and No. 2) 49-21 romp over No. 12-13 UCLA. Then, after directing two quick scores on the Huskers' first two possessions against Pacific, Frazier's season suddenly came to a halt. At first, it seemed a minor matter when he went

to the bench to rest a sore right calf.

But the day after the 70-21 shellacking of Pacific, Frazier was struggling to get out of a Lincoln hospital. Doctors had found blood clots in the right leg that had given the young quarterback trouble since after the UCLA game.

Frazier was ordered to the sidelines while on blood-thinners; he wouldn't see action again in the regular season.

So the reins of Nebraska's potent offense were handed to junior backup Brook Berringer, who had never started a college game.

Berringer's first call to duty came on Oct. 1 against Wyoming, and he played like a veteran.

However, for the first time all season, Nebraska's 4-3

(Top Right) Loyal Husker fans turned into rabid Husker fans once they sensed a national championship — and that didn't take long. At the conclusion of the Kickoff Classic (a 31-0 win over West Virginia), the crowd lofted oranges into the end zone in a not-so-subtle hint as to where they expected to be at the end of the season.

(Bottom Right) This was a familiar scene in '94. Although the opponents changed, the sight of Lawrence Phillips hurtling over and around defenders remained the same. Phillips logged 11 straight 100-yard rushing games during the season.

defense had trouble shutting down an opponent. It was reeling from the loss of sophomore safety Mike Minter, who was out for the season after suffering a knee injury in the second game against Texas Tech.

The Husker coaches shuffled people around in the secondary, trying to find the right mix. But Wyoming's freshman redshirt quarterback, Jeremy Dombek, was having a passing day he will long remember. He hit 17 of 35 passes for 264 yards in a 42-32 struggle with No. 1-2 Nebraska.

Fortunately for the Huskers, Berringer also shone. The fourth-year player, who had studied the Osborne option in Frazier's shadow, was supposed to be the best passer among NU quarterbacks. He had taken a back seat to Frazier in the running department, but that day, he ran for 74 yards and three touchdowns.

In the final two minutes of the first half, he hit 7 of 7 passes to get the Huskers in scoring range, and his first score was the result of a 5-yard option run. But Berringer took a savage hit from the side and back on the play, and he went to the lockers at halftime still trying to catch his breath.

He returned for the second half and ran 24 and 11 yards for two more scores, helping Nebraska hold off an inspired Wyoming team.

Later though, Berringer found himself in the hospital, literally passing Frazier in the emergency room halls. Frazier got one of his blood-thinning shots while Berringer was diagnosed and treated for a partially collapsed lung.

Early in the next week, Osborne wasn't sure who would quarterback his team in the Big Eight season-opener against Oklahoma State. Berringer was still questionable, and Frazier was an unlikely hope. That left third-team sophomore walk-on Matt Turman.

All of the other scholarship quarterbacks were gone. Ben Rutz had transferred out during the summer; he had not wanted to wait for playing time behind Frazier and Berringer. 1994 recruit Jon Elder had left at the start of fall camp.

Husker coaches had even recruited a student manager who had played quarterback in high school and converted a reserve split end to provide enough quarterbacks to run the scout teams in practice.

It was not the type of situation in which national championship-contending coaches wanted to find themselves.

Osborne even had former quarterback Tony Veland taking some snaps in practice. But Veland was the No. 1 safety, and pass-happy Kansas State and Oklahoma State were on the horizon.

Berringer was cleared to play against Oklahoma State but made it only to halftime. A prearranged X-ray determined that the lung had deflated again. Turman finished the game, and Phillips assumed the offensive load. The sophomore back had 33 carries for 221 yards and three touchdowns in the 32-3 game.

It was also during this game that the Blackshirts stepped forward to become one of the top defenses in the nation. Oklahoma State, with only one loss in four games, managed just 136 yards in total offense; only 24 yards were covered in the second half.

Linebacker Ed Stewart was leading the charge. He would become a finalist for the Butkus Award, which is given to the nation's top college linebacker.

Given the situation, Osborne had little choice but to be conservative. Turman started the following week on the road at unbeaten, 11th- and 16th-ranked Kansas State. The Wildcats were led by All-Big Eight quarterback Chad May, who had thrown for a conference-record 489 yards against Nebraska the year before.

The game plan was simple. Give the ball to Phillips and keep the ball away from May.

Even though Kansas State knew what was coming, the Huskers rushed for 210 yards. Phillips had 117 yards on 31 carries. But Nebraska led only 7-6 at the half.

Berringer came in to finish the game and drove NU to a touchdown and a field goal in the deciding fourth quarter. Nebraska would own a lot of fourth quarters before the season ended.

Again the defense dominated. K-State had minus 7-yards rushing, and May hit only 22 of 48 passes for 249 yards. May also was sacked six times. Nebraska (7-0) had clinched its 33rd consecutive winning season, an on-going NCAA record.

Concerned that Berringer needed more time to heal with the Colorado game only a week away, Osborne again played it close to the vest against Missouri on Oct. 22. The I-backs had 38 carries in this one. Phillips got the ball 22 times for 110 yards. Berringer, who was ordered not to run any options, also hit 9 of 13 passes for 152 yards and three touchdowns.

And, once more, the defense did its part well. Building on the philosophy that if the opponents can't score, they can't win, the Blackshirts allowed Missouri just 198 yards in total offense and one fourth-quarter touchdown.

Then came the game people across the nation wanted to watch. No. 2-3-ranked Colorado and No. 2-3 Nebraska would face off for the inside track for the Big Eight championship.

Both were unbeaten. Colorado was flying high with the help of one of the nation's most potent offenses, led by quarterback Kordell Stewart and Heisman Trophy contender Rashaan Salaam.

Berringer, finally, was given a clean bill of health for the option game. Combined with his pin-point accurate passing, his option game proved to be the undoing of Colorado's defense. He completed 12 of 17 passes for 142 yards, including a 30-yard TD to tight end Eric Alford.

That passing also opened up the running game. Phillips exceeded the 100-yard mark again with 103 yards on 24 carries. Fullback Cory Schlesinger scored on a 14-yard run, Tom Sieler kicked a 24-yard field goal and Clinton Childs ran in from 2 yards out to build Nebraska's lead to 24-0 in the third quarter. And the offensive line dominated a good Buffalo defensive front.

Colorado's previously high-flying offense was brought crashing back to earth by the Husker Blackshirts. Kordell Stewart was sacked four times and harassed to the point that he completed only 12 of 28 passes for 150 yards. Salaam, the nation's rushing leader, became the first back of the season to gain 100 yards on NU with 134 on 22 carries. Salaam's yardage did no damage, however, until he scored CU's only touchdown on a 7-yard run late in the third quarter.

During this game, Nebraska fully realized what a great catch it had in former baseball stand-out-turned-punter Darin Erstad. He had been among the national leaders in net punting, but his kicking in this game pinned Colorado deep in its own territory on several occasions. His kicking forced the Buffs to go long-distance against the Husker defense, a nearly impossible task.

A ninth win was in the bag, which continued Osborne's string of seasons during which he'd won nine games or more. He has accomplished that feat in every one of his 22 years as head coach. The '94 season also marked the 26th-straight year the school had attained that level — another on-going NCAA record.

The Colorado-Nebraska game also just happened to be the site of Nebraska's 200th-straight home sellout crowd. That, too, continued an NCAA mark.

Nebraska climbed to No. 1 in one national poll and narrowly trailed Penn State in the other. Osborne and his players were bombarded with questions from reporters about which team should be ranked higher. Osborne and Penn State coach and friend Joe Paterno refused to lobby for the top spot, but NU players claimed that, after the Colorado win, the honors should be theirs.

But three games remained in the regular season, and those games, in addition to bowl meetings, would

After clinching their fourth straight Big Eight championship with a win over Iowa State, the Huskers were more than ready to face the Hurricanes in the Orange Bowl.

decide a national title. Osborne said things would shake out.

Berringer continued to play like a veteran, attacking opposing defenses that stacked up to stop Nebraska's running game. Kansas' eight-man front gave him a chance to throw deep, and he came within 30 yards of Nebraska's single-game yardage passing record in the process.

Berringer hit 13 of 18 passes for 267 yards in the 45-17 victory over KU. The passing yardage was the most amassed by a Nebraska quarterback in 21 years and ranked seventh on the all-time school charts.

Phillips rushed for 153 yards on 21 carries and scored two touchdowns. He covered 118 of those yards in the third quarter, when the Jayhawks made some adjustments to counter Berringer's passing.

Then it was off to Ames, Iowa, site of the 1992 ambush (Iowa State had stunned a seventh-ranked Nebraska team with a 19-10 loss). The winless Cyclones (0-8-1) again would scare the powerful Huskers, but they let Berringer and company escape with a 28-12 win.

It was an emotional game for Iowa State. Coach Jim Walden, a former Husker assistant with Osborne under Devaney, had resigned earlier in the week. Then the Big Eight had announced that Walden couldn't coach ISU's final game of the season at Colorado. He had been critical of officiating, and the league office had suspended him a game. So, the Nebraska game would be Walden's final outing with this Cyclone squad.

An inspired Cyclone team, which featured several Nebraska natives in key roles, nearly took out all its frustrations on Nebraska, but Damon Benning and Phillips scored clinching touchdowns in the fourth quarter.

The following game was nearly a repeat of the Iowa State matchup, at least as far as emotions were concerned. Oklahoma coach Gary Gibbs also announced his resignation just prior to the game, giving the annual OU-NU scrap-to-the-finish new meaning.

Both defenses played "lights out" in this one, but Nebraska's defense, as well as its offense, was better. The Sooners managed just 47 total yards in the second half and totaled minus 5 yards in the fourth quarter.

At the end of the first half, the score was tied at 3-3. All Nebraska had to do was score —so they did. Tom Sieler kicked a 26-yard field goal in the third quarter after Berringer ran 28 yards on an option and threw to Muhammad for 24 more. Later, Muhammad and Berringer hooked up for another 44-yard pass play to set up a 1-yard touchdown run by Berringer, which completed the scoring in the game.

But despite clinching a fourth-straight Big Eight championship and another trip to Miami, the mood in the Husker locker room was less than celebratory. There was unfinished business awaiting the Huskers in the Orange Bowl. 10-1 Miami was poised for and confident about another shot at bumping off the Big Red.

Osborne had taken a 12-0 team to meet a Miami team in the Orange Bowl once before. That time, at the end of the 1983 season, Heisman Trophy winner Mike Rozier was the running back, All-American Turner Gill was the quarterback and All-Americans Irving Fryar and Dean Steinkuhler (the Outland and Lombardi winner) were at wide receiver and guard.

The Hurricanes won that one, 31-30, after Gill's two-point conversion pass was tipped away in the closing seconds.

This time, Osborne had guard Brenden Stai, a UPI First-Team All-American, tackle Zach Wiegert, the nation's best lineman and Outland Trophy winner, and Stewart, a finalist for the Butkus Award for best linebacker, as his first-team All-Americans. Wiegert finished 10th in the Heisman voting, two spots below I-back Lawrence Phillips, who was a second-team All-American after a 1,722-yard, 16-touchdown season.

Phillips' yardage was the most ever for a Nebraska sophomore and the second-most in school history, behind only Rozier's record 2,148 in 1983.

Also, Frazier had been cleared to play quarterback again. He had earned back his No. 1 spot in the team's final pre-bowl scrimmage. Berringer, the top-efficiency passer in the Big Eight and a second-team all-conference pick, also would play.

Awaiting the nation's rushing leaders was No. 3 Miami, the nation's top team defensively, which featured the nation's best defensive player, lineman Warren Sapp, the Lombardi Award winner.

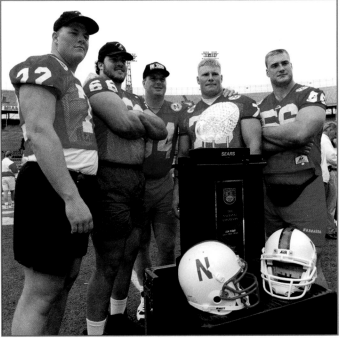

(From left) Zach Wiegert, Brenden Stai, Aaron Graham, Joel Wilks and Rob Zatechka – more commonly known as the Husker Pipeline – surround the fruits of their labor, The Sears Trophy, which annually is presented to the national football champion.

This meeting would be the fourth time the two schools had clashed in the Orange Bowl; Nebraska was 0-3.

"My desire is that No. 1 and No. 2 ought to get together ... but the Rose Bowl stands in the way," Osborne said later. "I wanted to play Penn State. The players wanted to play Miami in Miami because they saw that as their ultimate challenge. I would've rather gotten around it."

But this Nebraska team was different from any Miami had faced before, Osborne proclaimed repeatedly in the weeks prior to the game. This team could play offense nearly as well as the 1983 team, had the best offensive line in Husker history and had a defense.

Nebraska had learned its lessons while playing the Miamis and Florida States in bowl games over the past seven or eight years. Speed is a killer, and the 4-3 defense is an awfully good way to play with speed.

Frazier started the first quarter and had the Huskers moving on several drives but couldn't get the team into the end zone. Miami, on the other hand, put up 10 points with the aid of a 35-yard pass from Frank Costa to Trent Jones.

Berringer came in to play the second quarter and put Nebraska on the scoreboard with a 19-yard pass to tight end Mark Gilman.

Costa countered in the third quarter with another long TD pass. Then, the Husker defense shut the Hurricanes down in a big way. Miami had minus 35 yards in the fourth quarter, and Costa took a beating from the pass rush.

Meanwhile, Osborne played a hunch and brought Frazier back into the game. His fresh legs and quick feet left the 'Cane defenders gasping for air and set up a pair of fullback traps that allowed Cory Schlesinger to get into the end zone from 15 and 14 yards out for touchdowns that first tied the game and then allowed Nebraska to take the lead.

Osborne had his first national title after several near-misses. The Huskers had a 13-0 record. They had beaten a Florida team on its home turf. They made believers out of all those who had doubted they could ever win such a game.

Finally, Nebraska's business was finished.

Nebraska
West Virginia

31
0

Hands held in unity, the Huskers ran into the '94 season with a singular team goal: the national championship.

It was labeled the national championship game that should have been: Nebraska — ranked No. 3 and 4 in the college football polls — traveled to East Rutherford, N.J., to play against No. 23-24 West Virginia in the 12th-annual Kickoff Classic.

Both teams had finished the 1993 regular season 11-0, the only NCAA Division I-A teams to do so. But Nebraska had been locked in to play host in its third-straight Orange Bowl as the Big Eight champion, and the Orange Bowl Committee had extended its guest invitation to once-beaten Florida State. As for West Virginia, the Mountaineers went to the Sugar Bowl to meet Florida.

Both of the unbeaten teams lost.

Nebraska's loss was the driving force behind the theme for its 1994 season: "Unfinished Business." The Huskers' 18-16 near-miss against the powerful Seminoles, who won the national title when Nebraska missed a long field goal in the closing seconds of the Orange Bowl, served notice that Nebraska could play — and play well — against the southeastern teams.

Florida State, Miami and Georgia Tech had handed NU seven straight bowl losses in hostile territory.

The Kickoff Classic gave the Nebraska team of 1994 something to shoot for from the starting block. They had a chance to show the nation, in the country's first college football game, that this team could play. Quarterback Tommie Frazier also was set to establish himself as a contender for the Heisman Trophy.

(Right) In the Kickoff Classic, Phillips — here running over rather than around — raced to the first of his 11 straight 100-yard rushing games.

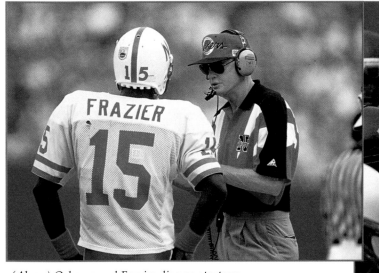

(Above) Osborne and Frazier discuss strategy.

(Right) Fullback Cory Schlesinger breaks free on a trap play — the first of many times he would do so in 1994.

A spring and summer of hard work was about to pay off on this hot August 28 afternoon in New Jersey, home to several of the Husker players. Tom Osborne said that part of the reason he'd accepted the bid for the Kickoff Classic was to reward the East Coast Huskers with a chance to play in front of many of their family members. (The West Coast Huskers, by the way, had had their chance the previous season with a game at UCLA.)

Nebraska displayed grit and determination early against an emotionally fired up Mountaineer squad that was trying to fill several key positions vacated by graduation. West Virginia entered the game with claims that it also had plenty to prove. After a humbling loss of its own — 41-7 in the Sugar Bowl against Florida — coach Don Nehlen's club was trying to earn back its respect and show it belonged with the nation's elite football programs.

Osborne was making his third appearance in the Classic. He made such appearances only when he had a veteran quarterback to guide his team. Osborne repeatedly pointed out that this is the kind of game that can make or break a team, send it off with renewed confidence or shatter hopes that could take several games to recover.

He had already witnessed that kind of devastation. His No. 1-ranked 1983 squad walloped a fourth-ranked Penn State team, 44-6, with senior Turner Gill at quarterback. Penn State, the defending national champion at the time, managed to recover well enough to end its season ranked 17th. Nebraska finished No. 2, suffering its only loss at the hands of Miami (31-30) in the Orange Bowl.

In 1988, Steve Taylor quarterbacked a second-ranked Husker team to a 23-14 win over No. 10 Texas A&M. Texas lost several key players to injury in that game and

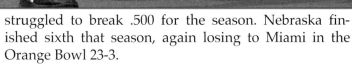

struggled to break .500 for the season. Nebraska finished sixth that season, again losing to Miami in the Orange Bowl 23-3.

Hopes were high in 1994 since the Huskers had Frazier, a two-year starter at quarterback, Lawrence Phillips returning at I-back and one of the best offensive lines in Husker history.

On the other side of the ball, linebacker Ed Stewart led a quick, swarming defense that had a whole season's experience running Nebraska's new, 4-3 scheme under its belt. The Miami-style defense suited the Huskers well, and the coaching staff could finally plug in enough speed to make it work.

Still, it took the Huskers a while to settle down against the Mountaineers offensively. Osborne and his staff had expected West Virginia's strongest feature to be its defense. Six starters had returned from a unit that, in 1993, had held four opponents to a touchdown or less.

Tom Sieler's 32-yard field goal for Nebraska was the only score of the first quarter as the Husker offense felt out the Mountaineers. Meanwhile, West Virginia's offense could do nothing against NU's Blackshirts.

Then Frazier took over with the option game. Nebraska rang up 21 points in the second period. Frazier got the season's first touchdown on a 25-yard option run.

Frazier then found split end Reggie Baul from 12 yards out less than 1:30 later. That followed a fumble caused and recovered by linebacker Doug Colman at the West Virginia 13. It was 17-0.

Few of the players on the field could have gotten a bigger emotional lift from playing big in this game than Colman. He was playing before his own personal fan club. The junior from Ventnor, N.J., said he had 106 friends and family members in the crowd of 58,233 at Giants Stadium.

Two possessions later, Frazier lent a hand in two of three big plays to get into the end zone again. The junior quarterback from Bradenton, Fla., hit Baul for a 23-yard gain on a short hitch pass that the speedy wide out turned into a big gainer. A roughing-the-kicker penalty allowed NU to keep possession shortly thereafter at the West Virginia 39.

Then Frazier capped the 74-yard drive with another option-keeper from 27 yards out. His quickness cutting the corner and his breakaway speed were too much for the hot and tired Mountaineers.

"I had a good game," Most Valuable Player Frazier said matter-of-factly after it was over. It was typical of the confidence, not cockiness, of the youngster.

His first game MVP of the season continued a trend: Gill and Taylor had both been named MVP in their own Kickoff Classics. And the questions of a Heisman Trophy challenge soon followed for the current Husker quarterback.

Frazier was not ready to hear that kind of talk, however. He had other things on his mind, such as team goals.

"If the Heisman comes, I'll be happy," Frazier said following the game, the first of many times he would make that assertion. "I'm not worried about the Heisman right now. All I'm worried about is winning week in and week out."

Frazier ended the scoring deluge with a 42-yard touchdown run midway through the fourth quarter. He finished with 12 carries for 130 yards and two touch-

A smothering Nebraska defense gave West Virginia little running room and allowed the Mountaineers to net only 8 yards for the game.

And after Nebraska's defensive performance (a shutout) against West Virginia, a league and possible national championship were what everyone expected.

Led by Colman's eight tackles, plus Stewart and lineman Christian Peter's (another New Jersey product) seven each, Nebraska's Blackshirts never let West Virginia's two young quarterbacks catch their breath. The Huskers had recorded their first shutout since blanking Oklahoma State 55-0 in 1992.

West Virginia's young quarterbacks got an education on defensive pressure courtesy of the Huskers. Donta Jones hurries Eric Boykin (left), then cashes in on a second chance at a tackle for a loss (below).

downs rushing for the day. He also was 8-for-16 passing for another 100 yards.

Phillips kicked in with 24 carries for 126 yards as the option offense rolled up 368 yards rushing on 60 carries.

But the offense wasn't perfect. Despite the rushing totals against what was considered a good defense, the Huskers had five turnovers: three lost fumbles and two interceptions.

"We're pleased with the outcome," said Osborne. "But sometimes people can get overly optimistic. We, at times, didn't play all that well. But we think we have a good team."

So did Nebraska's fans. They tossed oranges into the end zone, displaying their confidence with regard to where they expected the Huskers to spend their holiday season.

The Mountaineers had 8 yards rushing for the game on 38 carries. Part of that was Nebraska's eight quarterback sacks. Eric Boykin and Chad Johnston managed only six-of-19 passing for 81 yards, and they were picked off twice as they tried to force passes while running for their lives.

"We think we have a great defense," Osborne said. "And to be a great football team, you've got to have a great defense."

"We've talked since January that the key on defense is chemistry," linebacker coach Kevin Steele told reporters after the game. "You can have great athletes, but if you don't play together, you can be real average."

There was nothing average about Nebraska in its season-opener. And had it not been for the booming punts of West Virginia's Todd Sauerbrun, the score might have been worse. Sauerbrun averaged 60 yards on nine punts, including a 90-yarder in the first quarter that allowed Kareem Moss to return it 28 yards to the Husker 31.

Sauerbrun's punts did let Nebraska run up another 152 yards on nine returns for the game. The Mountaineer punter frequently outkicked his coverage, but had it not been for the distance on his kicks, Nebraska's improved field position might have resulted in a bigger margin of victory.

Nehlen had nothing but praise for the Huskers when all the hitting was done. He said they deserved their lofty ranking, and he admitted it would have been more fun to have played them at the end of the 1993 season.

Scoring Summary

	1st Quarter	2nd Quarter	3rd Quarter	4th Quarter	Final
Nebraska	3	21	0	7	31
West Virginia	0	0	0	0	0

NU - Tom Sieler 32-yard field goal, :34, Qtr. #1.
NU - Tommie Frazier 25-yard run (Sieler kick), 10:49, Qtr. #2.
NU - Reggie Baul 12-yard pass from Frazier (Sieler kick), 9:20, Qtr. #2.
NU - Frazier 27-yard run (Sieler kick), 1:20, Qtr. #2.
NU - Frazier 42-yard run (Sieler kick), 7:27, Qtr. #4.

Team Statistics

	NU	WVU
First downs	28	9
Rushing att.-yards	60-368	38-8
Passes	8-17-2	6-19-2
Passing yards	100	81
Total att.-yards	85-468	57-89
Returns-yards	9-152	4-10
Sacks by	8-48	0
Punts-average	3-48.3	9-60.1
Fumbles-lost	4-3	4-1
Penalties-yards	6-41	5-44
Time of poss.	33:52	26:08

Individual Leaders

Rushing:
NU: Tommie Frazier 12-130-3; Lawrence Phillips 24-126-0; Cory Schlesinger 8-31-0; Clinton Childs 4-30-0.
WVU: Robert Walker 12-46-0; Kantroy Barber 6-23-0.
Passing:
NU: Frazier 8-16-100-2.
WVU: Eric Boykin 4-13-62-1; Chad Johnston 2-6-19-1.
Receiving:
NU: Reggie Baul 3-46-1; Phillips 2-17-0.
WVU: Rashaan Vanterpool 3-50-0; Lovett Purnell 2-36-0.
Interceptions:
NU: Collins 1-8-0; Miles 1-7-0.
WVU: Kidd 1-0-0; Emanuel 1-0-0.
Tackles (UT-AT-TT):
NU: Doug Colman 4-4-8; Ed Stewart 4-3-7; Christian Peter 4-3-7; Jared Tomich 3-2-5.
WVU: Charles Emanuel 7-7-14; Bo Chatfield 4-6-10; Vann Washington 6-2-8; Aaron Beasley 4-4-8.
Sacks:
NU: Peter 2.5-5; Grant Wistrom 1.5-17; Colman 1-10; Tomich 1-7; Kareem Moss 1-7; Ryan Terwilliger 1-2.
WVU: None.

Nebraska
Texas Tech

42
16

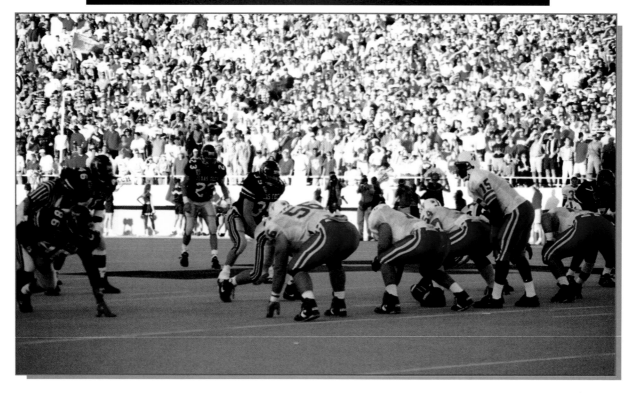

Frazier barks out an audible to adjust for Tech's defensive set en route to a 42-point day.

For the second game in a row, Nebraska (now ranked first in the nation) had a national television audience for which to perform. This time, the Huskers would face Texas Tech on a Thursday night ESPN telecast. The Huskers had enjoyed more than a week off since they had blanked West Virginia and climbed to the top spot in the coaches' football poll a week after the Kickoff Classic.

Coach Tom Osborne didn't care much for all the early poll attention. He hoped it wouldn't add too much pressure or detract from his team's focus on the task at hand — a good Texas Tech team.

"I think too much is made of the polls right now," he said for the first of many times.

Osborne indicated that while teams could benefit from the extra time between games, they could, on the other hand, also lose their sharpness. But the break had given the Huskers time to work on a few of the problem spots from the Kickoff Classic win over West Virginia, iron out a few rough areas and get mentally ready to take to the road for a second time.

This game was a homecoming for Nebraska junior center Aaron Graham, who was getting a chance to play in his old home stadium.

"Actually, I grew up in Lubbock," said Graham, whose family later moved to Denton, Texas. "It's kind of exciting because I played my youth football league in Lubbock. We got to play two of our Super Bowls in Jones Stadium. It'll be kind of neat going back there."

Graham and his offensive line teammates were among the best in the nation as a unit, as they were about to prove

(Right) Phillips made a habit of gaining yards after first contact.

84

to Texas Tech.

And again, it was showtime for Nebraska quarterback Tommie Frazier. This time, it didn't take him long to display his talents.

Frazier broke loose three minutes into the first quarter and outraced the Texas Tech defense. He put the Huskers on the board with a 58-yard score.

Nebraska didn't score again until the second quarter, when Frazier's 3-yard run capped a scoring drive.

NU's offense outgained Texas Tech 242 yards to 87 in the first half. The Blackshirts had again put on a clinic on how to play defense.

The only chink in the armor was a 49-yard Jon Davis field goal in the second quarter.

couldn't get by without scoring like we did in the second quarter. The defense can't play the whole game alone."

Nebraska also recalled its meeting with Texas Tech the season before in Lincoln. Tech scored first in the second half to take a 21-20 lead with 8:37 left in that third quarter.

That Tech team, featuring veteran quarterback Robert Hall and big running back Bam Morris, was staying with the Huskers then. But a Frazier touchdown pass sparked a 30-point second-half finish for Nebraska, which polished off a 50-27 win.

Despite their efforts, the Huskers did repeat some of that game's history. Nebraska's offense was again jarred

It took Nebraska a while to get its power game rolling against a good Tech defense.

Despite the lopsided yardage comparisons, Nebraska headed for the locker room at halftime leading only 14-3 and knowing they could do better. They did.

"The Tech defense really played the whole game real strong," Frazier said. "They'll have a great defense once they get everything together."

His prophesy proved true: The Tech defense led the Red Raiders to a share of the Southwest Conference title and a Cotton Bowl berth as the league champion.

But the Huskers weren't happy with the halftime score.

"I think we were tired," Frazier said. "I went into the locker room at halftime, and I said we'd explode. We

to its senses in the second half after Scott Aylor caught a 6-yard touchdown pass from Zebbie Letheridge. Tech had, once again, scored first after intermission.

Aylor's score, just 2:27 into the half, made the score 14-9. A run attempt for two points failed.

That's when Nebraska went to work.

Lawrence Phillips capped a drive with a 2-yard run 3:32 later. Phillips then sprinted 56 yards through the Tech defense for another score before the third quarter was completed.

Then, early in the fourth quarter, Frazier connected with tight end Eric Alford on a 35-yard touchdown toss for a 35-9 lead.

"I think any time you play the No. 1 team in the nation, you better be ready to play a full 60 minutes," said Tech coach Spike Dykes. "They've got some triple jeopardy. Everywhere you look, they have another tremendous player coming at you. I don't know if I've ever seen a team that is stronger or better prepared."

Texas Tech's Ben Kaufman recovered a fumble for a touchdown with 6:24 to go, but Clinton Childs countered for Nebraska with a 30-yard scoring run with 2:00 to play.

"First of all, Texas Tech played really well," Osborne said. "I'm proud of the way they played, especially with only five days of preparation. They had a good defense.

nosed football players.

"I don't think they have near the physical ability we have, but they have really played tough," Graham said. "They play past their capabilities. They play with a lot of enthusiasm."

Frazier said Nebraska's ranking had something to do with the opponent's effort, too.

"We expect a good effort from everyone we play," he said.

But this season, Tech's offensive unit didn't have the experience or talent that Hall and Morris brought to that 1993 team. This game against Nebraska was more of a struggle for the Red Raider offense.

"It felt really good playing against the No. 1 team in

Phillips slips a tackle on his way to two touchdowns and 175 yards rushing.

They played hard and did a good job."

"I like Spike Dykes, and he does a good job of coaching. And Dick Winder's offense is extremely tough to prepare for. I'm disappointed we missed a couple of field goals, and I made a couple of mistakes that can be corrected."

Graham and Frazier had expected a good effort from Tech even before they stepped onto the field.

"I think the thing about Tech is they're really a bunch of kids, the vast majority are kids," Graham said. But Graham continued to say that they were also talented, and with experience, those kids were going to be hard-

the nation," said Tech's Byron Hanspard. "It was a privilege to play against such wonderful people, and I thank the Lord for that privilege. We did real good being such a young offense, and the Lord really elevated us. They had a great defense, and they handled us real well."

Phillips led the rushing attack this time with 19 carries for 175 yards and two touchdowns. Frazier added 84 yards on 13 carries, and fullback Cory Schlesinger ran well off the trap play that would continue to work well all season; he totaled 84 yards rushing on just six carries.

(Above) Frazier watches as teammate Cory Schlesinger makes a hard run up the middle.

(Right) This time, Frazier does the dirty work himself – he slipped this tackle en route to gaining 82 yards on the ground.

Childs and NU's other I-back, Damon Benning, also pitched in 59 and 45 yards in backup duty. Benning contributed another 90 yards on three kickoff returns, including a career-long 58-yarder.

The Huskers rolled up 524 rushing yards against Tech and added 88 through the air. They cut their turnovers from five (in the Kickoff Classic) to one, which pleased Osborne greatly. Unfortunately, the rest of the game wasn't quite what he had expected.

"We did a job tonight, and that's about it," he said. "We played good but not inspired. I think they were more excited to play Nebraska than Nebraska was excited to play them."

Tech players weren't so sure.

"They've got a great team, and I think they've got a chance for a national championship," said Red Raider star linebacker Zach Thomas. "I think they have great talent, especially in the offensive line. Those guys can really move, and I think that's what makes them a great team.

"We played good at times, and then the next quarter, you don't know what happens. I think we lost our poise a little bit and didn't play like we can for 60 minutes."

Osborne also had second thoughts about those benefits reaped from the time off between games. He admitted that the 12-day layoff between games may have left his team flat.

"We need to throw better, and maybe the time off had something to do with that," he said. "We got sacked a couple of times, missed a couple of passes, dropped a couple of passes and then missed two field goals."

"People got awfully excited awfully fast after the

Kickoff Classic. We've got a long way to go and have a lot to prove."

In many ways, this was a repeat of the Kickoff Classic, in which West Virginia had tried to gets its offense established with new quarterbacks.

Tech used three young quarterbacks, of whom Letheridge caused the most problems. He led Tech rushers with 62 yards but hit only five of 14 passes for 46 yards under heavy pressure from the Nebraska defense.

Tech managed only 147 yards rushing on 42 tries and passed for 150 more. Its offense was outdistanced in the yardage game 612-297 overall.

Five of Nebraska's six touchdown drives covered 78 yards or more. The other covered 69. And the Husker Blackshirts denied Tech at every turn.

"They have great team speed, especially on defense," Tech's Alton Crain said.

Teammate Aylor agreed. "They are really fast on defense, and they run the ball a lot, which makes it tough. If they aren't No. 1, they are certainly up there."

But while Nebraska could rejoice about its win, it also would suffer from its loss. Free safety Mike Minter, the defensive secondary's quarterback, was lost for the season with a torn left ACL.

His replacement, converted quarterback Tony Veland, came in to intercept a pass. Veland, a junior coming back from a serious knee injury himself, displayed some of the gifts that made him Nebraska's top option quarterback at one time, returning that interception 35 yards.

Scoring Summary

	1st Quarter	2nd Quarter	3rd Quarter	4th Quarter	Final
Nebraska	7	7	14	14	42
Texas Tech	0	3	6	7	16

NU - Tommie Frazier 58-yard run (Tom Sieler kick), 12:59, Qtr. #1.
NU - Frazier 3-yard run (Sieler kick), 13:13, Qtr. #2.
TTU - Jon Davis 49-yard field goal, 10:43, Qtr. #2.
TTU - Scott Aylor 6-yard pass from Zebbie Lethridge (run failed), 12:33, Qtr. #3.
NU - Lawrence Phillips 2-yard run (Sieler kick), 9:01, Qtr. #3.
NU - Phillips 56-yard run (Sieler kick), 4:19, Qtr. #3.
NU - Eric Alford 35-yard pass from Frazier (Sieler kick), 10:56, Qtr. #4.
TTU - Ben Kaufman recovered fumble (Davis kick), 6:24, Qtr. #4.
NU - Clinton Childs 30-yard run (Sieler kick), 2:00, Qtr. #4.

Team Statistics

	NU	TTU
First downs	26	17
Rushing att.-yards	63-524	42-147
Passes	5-17-1	11-29-1
Passing yards	88	150
Total att.-yards	80-612	71-297
Returns-yards	4-40	3-11
Sacks by	3-16	0
Punts-average	3-47.0	8-41.4
Fumbles-lost	0-0	1-0
Penalties-yards	5-44	4-30
Time of poss.	33:50	26:10

Individual Leaders

Rushing:
NU: Lawrence Phillips 19-175-2; Tommie Frazier 13-84-2; Cory Schlesinger 6-84-0; Clinton Childs 10-59-1.
TTU: Zebbie Lethridge 6-62-0; Alton Crain 15-46-0; Byron Hanspard 12-27-0.
Passing:
NU: Frazier 5-15-88-0; Brook Berringer 0-2-0-1.
TTU: Tony Darden 3-10-64-0; Lethridge 5-14-46-1.
Receiving:
NU: Phillips 3-39-0; Eric Alford 1-35-1; Reggie Baul 1-14-0.
TTU: Field Scovell 4-74-0; Stacy Mitchell 3-24-0; Matt Dubuc 2-31-0.
Interceptions:
NU: Tony Veland 1-35-0.
TTU: Bart Thomas 1-4-0.
Tackles (UT-AT-TT):
NU: Kareem Moss 5-2-7; Ed Stewart 4-3-7; Donta Jones 2-4-6; Dwayne Harris 2-4-6.
TTU: Zach Thomas 7-7-14; Bart Thomas 7-3-10; Shawn Banks 4-6-10; Marcus Coleman 6-3-9.
Sacks:
NU: Ryan Terwilliger 1-6; Jason Pesterfield 1-5; Dwayne Harris 0.5-3; Christian Peter 0.5-3.
TTU: Damon Wickware 1-9.

Nebraska UCLA 49 21

SEPTEMBER 17, 1994 – AT MEMORIAL STADIUM

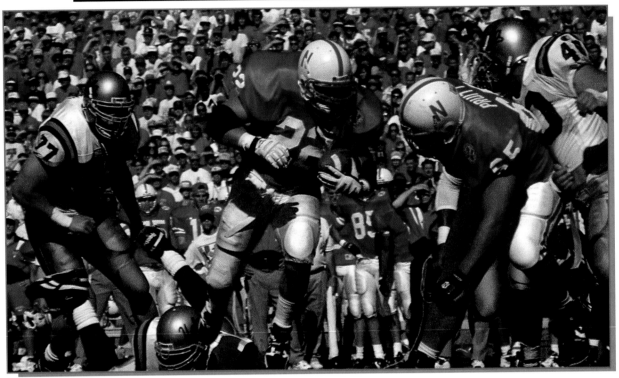

Fullback Jeff Makovicka (22) follows a Bryan Pruitt (65) block.
Many of Nebraska's backups played extensively against UCLA — Nebraska's first home game.

Home at last. In Nebraska's first home game of the season, UCLA — ranked No. 12 and 13 in the college football polls — came into Memorial Stadium with a 2-0 record to meet coach Tom Osborne's 2-0 Huskers, who were ranked No. 1 and 2 in the two major national polls.

It also was the third time Nebraska would play before a national television audience. The team's high national ranking was drawing a lot of attention.

It was a game Osborne viewed with anticipation, one he figured would tell him much about how good a football team he had. This Bruin squad was more capable of matching the Huskers man-for-man, physically as well as in the talent department, than either West Virginia or Texas Tech. UCLA owned a big win over Tennessee and had recently emerged from a struggle to beat lightly regarded SMU.

UCLA sounded hungry in pregame talk before this one. Not only had the SMU game left them anxious to prove they were better, but the Bruins indicated that the 14-13 loss to Nebraska in 1993 at Los Angeles had been tough to swallow. They wanted revenge.

"I think it probably helps us," UCLA coach Terry Donahue said of that close game with the Huskers. "I think any time you play a team as close as we played Nebraska last year, the players who participated in that game at least are going to feel confident, and they're going to feel, 'Hey, we're in the same league with these guys, and we can play with these guys.' But who knows. Every team is different."

(Right) Nebraska's Moss (29) and Dumas (4) swarm for anything with Bruin colors, and their focus pays off:
Each collected 10 tackles and knocked down a few passes in a big day against UCLA.

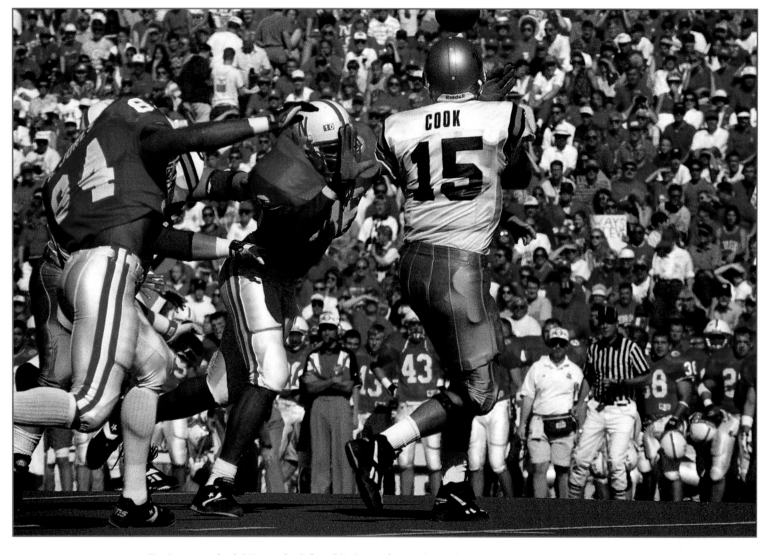

Bruin quarterback Wayne Cook found little comfort in the pocket against Nebraska's pass rush.

Nebraska apparently was. The Nebraska offensive line muscled its way through the UCLA defenders and created a mismatch that quarterback Tommie Frazier noticed when he went to the line.

"I saw fear in their eyes," Frazier said. "A couple of their linebackers looked at me like, 'What play are they going to run now? And is it going to be for a big gain?'"

Donahue had been in this predicament before. He admitted before the game that it seemed as though every time the Bruins' schedule featured Nebraska, the Huskers were ranked in the top three to five in the nation.

"It's a very, very impressive team," he said. "It apparently has no weaknesses. It's a team that appears extremely powerful in all phases of the game. They're very similar in that all those (former highly ranked Nebraska) teams always had a great athlete that was the driving force of that offensive unit. This year's case is obviously Frazier. He is an unbelievable player."

But Frazier, who ran for one touchdown and threw for two more, shared the spotlight in this one. Seven

Huskers scored as NU rolled up 484 yards rushing and another 71 through the air.

It was a big improvement from the 208-yard rushing day the Nebraska backs had at UCLA the year before, when the Huskers had to come from behind to win. The Bruins led 10-7 until Frazier hit tight end Gerald Armstrong for the winning touchdown with 6:56 remaining in the third quarter.

This time, tackle Zach Wiegert was so dominating that he was named the ABC Chevrolet Player-of-the-Game for Nebraska. The big senior lineman flattened anyone who got in his way.

And behind that line, Frazier was working on his game. He hooked up with tight end Eric Alford on a 23-yard pass to open the scoring about six minutes into the game. The extra point kick was blocked, but it didn't matter much.

Of Nebraska's first 65 rushing plays, 19 resulted in gains of 10 yards or more. The line simply blew the Bruins off the ball.

"We'd like to improve our passing game, but as long

as we can run it like this, we're going to," said Frazier, whose mastery of the option had Nebraska averaging 7.3 yards per rush through the first three games.

The Huskers marched back down the field for another first-quarter score. This time, I-back Lawrence Phillips caught a Frazier pitch one-handed to get into the end zone from 1 yard out.

Phillips, a sophomore from West Covina, Calif., topped the career-high 175 yards he had amassed the game before against Texas Tech with 178 yards against his home-state school. He had runs of 12 and 17 yards on the first Husker scoring drive and later added a 60-yarder to the UCLA 7 in the third quarter.

Down 12-0, UCLA put its first points on the board when quarterback Wayne Cook connected with Kevin Jordan on a 20-yard TD pass. It would be a big day for Jordan, who finished with seven catches for 129 yards. But his big-play teammate, All-American J.J. Stokes, was on the sidelines — a persistent leg problem had led to questions about his playing status all week.

Cook and Jordan still were able to take advantage of an inexperienced Husker secondary that was shuffling players to try to recover from the loss of safety Mike Minter. The defensive quarterback had suffered a season-ending knee injury against Texas Tech the game before.

It appeared to be a game of offenses for a while — UCLA moved the ball well through the air, while Nebraska ran over, around and through the Bruins.

Frazier countered again for Nebraska. This time, he went in himself from 12 yards out and added a two-point conversion run off the option for a 19-7 lead.

Backup I-back Damon Benning capped the next Husker drive with a 2-yard touchdown run. Frazier again ran successfully for the two-point conversion. Nebraska led 28-7 at the half.

"They are far and away the most difficult offense we face," Donahue said. "No one is nearly as difficult to defend when they have good players in their offense, as they do now. I was concerned all week about our defense's ability to match up. That proved to be an accurate assessment."

Even their big guys can move — 285-pounder Christian Peter (55) is all over a Bruin punt.

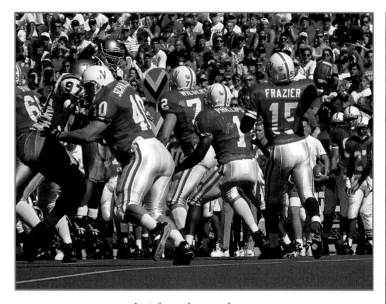

*Just for a change of pace,
Frazier (15) took to the air 11 times for 59 yards.*

UCLA's own offense was a handful as well. With Cook and Jordan getting much of the attention, tailback Sharmon Shah ran 3 yards for a Bruin touchdown about 2:30 into the second half. It was a 28-14 game.

Then Phillips broke loose on his sprint down the sideline to ignite Nebraska once more. Backup I-back Clinton Childs, who had runs of 25 and 22 yards in Frazier's earlier touchdown march, capped off that drive with an 8-yard touchdown run with 2:23 to go in the third period.

Frazier then gave coach Osborne reason to relax. He hit Brendan Holbein on a 9-yard touchdown pass just five seconds into the fourth quarter.

"There was a period of time where we just weren't stopping them very well," Osborne said. "Sometimes I would rather be on the sidelines and sputter offensively if our defense is dominating."

"Against West Virginia, I didn't feel uneasy at all. Today, I felt uneasy until there was 10 or 12 minutes left because they moved the ball with regularity."

The Bruins finished with 285 passing yards and 129 more on the ground. Cook, who hit 15 of 28 passes for 217 yards, could have made things worse had he not been sacked twice and intercepted twice under the pressure of the Nebraska pass rush.

(Right) Lawrence Phillips (1) – always tough to catch – ran 19 times for 178 yards against his home state school.

"Our execution, pursuit and aggressiveness were there when it needed to be," said Nebraska defensive end Dwayne Harris.

Shah gained 91 yards to lead the Bruin rushers, who were unable to repeat the 192-yard day they had had behind Skip Hicks' 148-yard effort against the Huskers the year before in Pasadena.

Frazier came out of the game early in the fourth quarter with 5-of-11 passing for 59 yards and two touchdowns. He also ran for 29 yards, one TD and two extra points.

"I think Frazier is one of the premier players in the country," Donahue said. "I think of the players I've seen in the country over the last couple of years, [and] I think Tommie Frazier is certainly in the upper echelon of those players.

"Real good teams have three, four or five difference-makers on them. A couple on defense and a couple on offense. The rest of the guys are good, solid football players, but they're just not difference-makers.

"Frazier, obviously, is clearly a difference-maker. J.J. Stokes is a difference-maker. We're a different team with J.J. Stokes than we are without Stokes in the game."

Frazier's backup, Brook Berringer, also got some playing time, capping a scoring drive of his own with a 1-yard run with 11:32 to play. Unfortunately, James Milliner recorded an 11-yard TD run for the Bruins against Husker reserves down the stretch.

Linebackers Ed Stewart and Troy Dumas and cornerback Kareem Moss each were credited with 10 tackles for the Husker defense, and Clint Brown and safety Tony Veland, who had made his first start for the injured Minter, had the interceptions.

The Huskers admitted after the game that they, too, had had something to prove to UCLA after last year's

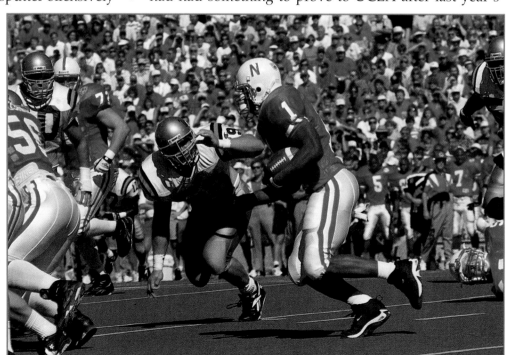

close game in California. They wanted to show the Bruins that they hadn't gotten Nebraska's best when the Huskers committed four turnovers in Pasadena in 1993.

"They did more talking than they did preparing for us," Frazier said. "They talked all week about how good they are and how they shouldn't have lost to us, and that we were lucky last year. You can't come out and say things like that."

Nebraska ended the game with more points than any Husker team had ever scored in 10 meetings with UCLA. The 49 points also were the most given up by a Terry Donahue-coached Bruin team in his 19 years at the school.

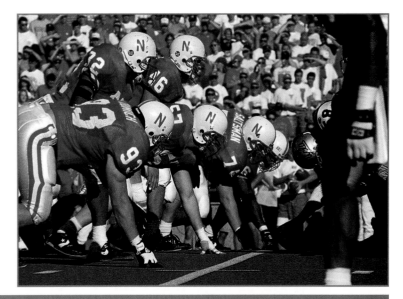

The Nebraska defense blitzes against a Bruin offense that was intercepted twice on the day.

Scoring Summary

	1st Quarter	2nd Quarter	3rd Quarter	4th Quarter	Final
Nebraska	12	16	7	14	49
UCLA	0	7	7	7	21

NU - Eric Alford 23-yard pass from Tommie Frazier (kick blocked), 9:09, Qtr. #1.
NU - Lawrence Phillips 1-yard run (pass failed), :11, Qtr. #1.
UCLA - Kevin Jordan 20-yard pass from Wayne Cook (Bjorn Merten kick), 13:23, Qtr. #2.
NU - Frazier 12-yard run (Frazier run), 9:34, Qtr. #2.
NU - Damon Benning 2-yard run (Frazier run), 3:33, Qtr. #2.
UCLA - Sharmon Shah 3-yard run (Merten kick), 12:30, Qtr. #3.
NU - Clinton Childs 8-yard run (Tom Sieler kick), 2:23, Qtr. #3.
NU - Brendan Holbein 9-yard pass from Frazier (Sieler kick), 14:55, Qtr. #4.
NU - Brook Berringer 1-yard run (Sieler kick), 11:32, Qtr. #4.
UCLA - James Milliner 11-yard run (Merten kick), 8:07, Qtr. #4.

Team Statistics

	NU	UCLA
First downs	31	24
Rushing att.-yards	65-484	35-129
Passes	6-12-0	21-35-2
Passing yards	71	285
Total att.-yards	77-555	70-414
Returns-yards	5-17	2-13
Sacks by	2-13	0
Punts-average	3-47.0	4-40.5
Fumbles-lost	2-1	0-0
Penalties-yards	7-65	4-25
Time of poss.	32:05	27:55

Individual Leaders

Rushing:
NU: Lawrence Phillips 19-178-1; Clinton Childs 7-78-1; Cory Schlesinger 7-50-1; Jeff Makovicka 7-50-0.
UCLA: Sharmon Shah 18-91-1; James Milliner 7-38-1; Derek Ayers 4-15-0.
Passing:
NU: Frazier 5-11-0-59; Berringer 1-1-0-12.
UCLA: Wayne Cook 15-28-2-217.
Receiving:
NU: Eric Alford 2-35-1; Brendan Holbein 2-14-1; Abdul Muhammad 1-15-0; Childs 1-7-0.
UCLA: Kevin Jordan 7-129-1; Daron Washington 4-39-0.
Interceptions:
NU: Clint Brown 1-4-0; Tony Veland 1-0-0.
Tackles (UT-AT-TT):
NU: Troy Dumas 5-5-10; Kareem Moss 5-5-10; Ed Stewart 4-6-10; Dwayne Harris 3-3-6.
UCLA: Abdul McCullough 6-6-12; Shane Jasper 2-9-11; Paul Guidry 2-7-9.
Sacks:
NU: Harris 1.5-9; Terry Connealy 0.5-4.
UCLA: None

Nebraska
Pacific

70
21

Berringer (18) made his presence known when he came off the bench against Pacific: He threw for three touchdowns.

For both No. 1-2 Nebraska and an obviously outmanned Pacific team (coached by longtime Tom Osborne acquaintance Chuck Shelton), this was the money game on the schedule. Osborne spent much of the week prior to the game explaining how a team like Pacific could find its way onto the schedule of such a powerhouse football program.

Shelton defended Osborne by commenting that it was the type of game both types of programs needed at least once a year.

For Osborne, it was a home game which guaranteed home-game ticket and concessions sales. Those sales, he explained, were worth somewhere in the $1 million neighborhood for Nebraska. Plus, Pacific had been willing to play in Lincoln and had not required a home-and-home series, so Osborne had been able to schedule an additional home game for the following season.

For Shelton, this game was the source of a good percentage of his school's athletic budget — a guaranteed paycheck of about $425,000.

"We get two-thirds of our income on the football budget from three games," the former Utah State and Drake coach said. "This is the major one. It is a must for us. I appreciate the opportunity."

And to Coach Shelton's credit, his Big West Conference team wasn't bad. Pacific came to Lincoln with a 2-1 record; it had played nationally ranked Arizona, at Arizona, in its money game of 1993 and lost by only three (16-13).

Shelton explained that his teams also had played the likes of Washington and Texas Tech on the road. He was building a program and needed such opportunities.

(Right) Frazier (15), over center for what would be the last time in the regular season,
played in only two series in Nebraska's fourth game of the season.

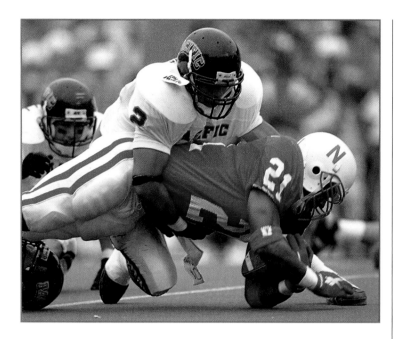

Backup I-back Damon Benning (21) scrambles for some of his 87 yards.

There also was the experience factor. His kids would get to play in front of 75,000 people in a first-class stadium. But Shelton wasn't coming to Lincoln blind, either.

"I would say that the ease with which they were able to dominate UCLA's defense shocked me," he said of the Huskers. "Surprise would be mild. I thought they would win the football game because they're a better football team. But they really handled UCLA."

On the other side, Osborne wanted his team to play sharp. It still needed to build on the UCLA win and fix a few things that were not up to No. 1 standards. And he knew Shelton would bring a team that was ready to play.

"I've always had a great deal of respect for Chuck Shelton," Osborne said. "When he was over at Drake, I thought he did a great job.

"We played him when he was at Utah State, and I thought he always got the most out of his players. I think they will be well-organized, well-prepared."

Nebraska, despite its 3-0 start, still was trying to get its secondary organized. It was shuffling players around in an attempt to find a formula that would make up for the loss of injured Mike Minter. Osborne also wanted more consistency from his offense.

"I'm hopeful we'll become a better football team this week than we were last week," Osborne said. "I think it's always important to have some movement in a positive direction."

Lawrence Phillips, off to the races, breaks free for a 74-yard TD run.

Not long after the kickoff, that "movement" was well underway. Osborne started substituting liberally after I-back Damon Benning scored the first touchdown early in the game on a 1-yard run. 12:45 remained in the first quarter.

Quarterback Tommie Frazier was at the controls, and he marched the Huskers right down the field on the next possession. I-back Lawrence Phillips provided the final 74 yards less than five minutes into the game.

At that point, Frazier came out and backup Brook Berringer took over. After the game, Osborne explained that Frazier had had some tightness in his right leg which was thought to have resulted from a hit or bruise suffered during the game against UCLA. It later turned out to be much more than a bruise.

But with Berringer at the controls, the Huskers didn't miss a beat. Fullback Cory Schlesinger scored the next two touchdowns, the first on an 8-yard run and the second on a 39-yard trap play. Prior to the end of the first quarter, the score was 28-0.

"How in the world do you stop those people?" Shelton asked. "I don't have an idea. Once you have a plan, you're committed to it. If it doesn't work, there's not much you can do about it."

Berringer ran 6 yards for Nebraska's first score of the second quarter, then threw touchdown passes of 15 yards (to Clester Johnson) and 46 yards (to tight end Eric Alford) for a 49-0 halftime advantage.

Nebraska tackle Zach Wiegert said later that the Huskers had been mentally ready for this game. That can sometimes be tough to do when your opponent is supposed to be a breather.

Wiegert said that, in his mind, he was preparing for a big-time California university team instead of the Stockton, Calif., school of 4,000 students.

"A lot of times, as far as linemen are concerned, when people think these teams aren't so great, they are hurting at the skilled positions," Wiegert said. "But a lot of

times, they have some good defensive linemen, so you can't underestimate them if you're a lineman."

And the NU line dominated. There was little Pacific could do to stop the bleeding.

Phillips rushed for 138 yards on just nine carries. Benning added 87 on 10 carries. A third I-back, Clinton Childs, had 64 on 10 tries, and backup fullback Jeff Makovicka added 59 yards on three carries.

"We could have beat Pacific 100-whatever," said kicker Tom Sieler. But, as Wiegert pointed out, the final score was not the issue — getting better was. It couldn't hurt to have lots of players play and get game experience — just in case they were needed somewhere down the schedule.

Berringer made his third touchdown pass of the day less than five minutes into the second half. This time, he found wingback Abdul Muhammad from 18 yards away.

Berringer ended with 8-of-15 passing for 120 yards and three touchdowns. He also gave opponents a glimpse of what would become another dangerous weapon for Nebraska's offense in the upcoming weeks: an accurate passing arm.

As the Husker starters cheered on their reserve teammates from the sidelines, Pacific finally managed to get on the scoreboard.

Craig Whelihan hit Joe Abdullah for a 17-yard score. After Childs ran 1 yard for another Nebraska TD, Abdullah scored again, this time on a 2-yard run.

In the fourth quarter, quarterback Matt Turman, third on the depth chart, drove the Huskers down the field and hit Jeff Lake on a 24-yard touchdown pass.

Pacific's Damon Bowers made the last score of the day with a 9-yard pass from Nick Sellers.

Nebraska's final statistics included 510 rushing yards. The Pacific matchup was the third-straight game in which Nebraska covered over 400 yards on the ground. The 699 yards in total offense were the third-most in school history.

The defense had Pacific immobilized until the reserves came in. The Tigers finished with only 84 yards rushing, and they had to pass 51 times. Pacific completed 27 with two interceptions. Leslie Dennis returned one of those pick-offs 48 yards. Tyrone Williams had the other.

Pacific even had trouble punting; Barron Miles blocked two kicks. Miles now had three for the season. Trampis Wrice, a sophomore cornerback, blocked a third one for Nebraska.

In all, the Huskers used more than 100 players in the game. Included in that list were backup quarterbacks Adam Kucera and Ryan Held. Kucera began the season as a student manager, but the freshman from Lake Havasu, Ariz., was asked to assume his old high school position of quarterback so the Huskers would have enough quarterbacks for practice. Held was converted from split end for the same reason.

Kucera and Held were moved out of necessity; after several players transferred over the summer and during preseason, Frazier and Berringer were the only two scholarship quarterbacks left on the squad. An injury to walk-on freshman Monte Christo further depleted the numbers.

But just about everyone who suited up (and wasn't redshirted) had a chance to play against Pacific.

Reserve Darren Schmadeke was Nebraska's leading tackler with eight. Freshman cornerback Octavious McFarlin added seven, and freshman outside linebacker Grant Wistrom garnered five.

Osborne was almost apologetic after the game. He was asked about Pacific returning to Lincoln for a rematch in 1995. Both the 1994 and 1995 games with the Tigers were fill-ins; the Tigers had been approached after Utah State, a school Shelton had brought to Nebraska a few years previous, asked to be released from its contracts.

"Who are you going to get?" Osborne asked about

Mr. Steady, Tom Sieler, boots another PAT.

(Left) Reggie Baul (7) breaks loose after one of his two pass catches.

(Right) Brenden Stai (66) appears ready to unload on a Pacific defender. The line cleared the way for 510 yards in rushing for the day.

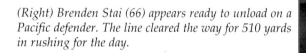

(Left) Abdul Muhammad (27) slips by a defender on his 18-yard TD catch and run.

replacement teams. "It's so difficult to replace a team on one year's notice.

"I looked at the top 100 power ratings, and I'm not a gambler or anything like that, but of 106 teams in Division I, there are probably better than 20 or 30 teams that are rated lower than Pacific."

Shelton had known his hands were full.

"I talked to the officials about calling the second half off," he said. "They wouldn't."

Co-captains Wiegert and defensive tackle Terry Connealy were glad they didn't. It gave them a chance to watch some of their teammates in action.

"I saw some of the guys who back up my position at right tackle, and I was impressed with the blocking and execution," Wiegert said.

"Getting all those guys in the game will be something that will make us better as a team," Connealy said. "The first game is a feeling you can't substitute. And now we've all got something to talk about in the locker room."

Talk soon changed to another subject, however. The day after the game, Frazier checked into a Lincoln hospital and was diagnosed with a blood clot behind his right knee. It was uncertain how lengthy the healing process would be, but doctors were confident they could dissolve the clot.

Osborne labeled the Heisman Trophy contender questionable for the upcoming game against Wyoming as doctors administered blood thinners. Everyone tried to take a wait-and-see attitude — everyone, that is, except Berringer. He had to prepare as though he were about to make his first career start. It proved to be a smart decision – the Wyoming game would be just that.

Scoring Summary

	1st Quarter	2nd Quarter	3rd Quarter	4th Quarter	Final
Nebraska	28	21	14	7	70
Pacific	0	0	14	7	21

NU - Damon Benning 1-yard run (Tom Sieler kick), 12:45, Qtr. #1.
NU - Lawrence Phillips 74-yard run (Sieler kick), 9:02, Qtr. #1.
NU - Cory Schlesinger 8-yard run (Sieler kick), 5:50, Qtr. #1.
NU - Schlesinger 39-yard run (Sieler kick), 3:58, Qtr. #1.
NU - Brook Berringer 6-yard run (Sieler kick), 14:31, Qtr. #2.
NU - Clester Johnson 15-yard pass from Berringer (Darin Erstad kick), 11:02, Qtr. #2.
NU - Eric Alford 46-yard pass from Berringer (Erstad kick), 6:22, Qtr. #2.
NU - Abdul Muhammad 18-yard pass from Berringer (Erstad kick), 11:06, Qtr. #3.
PAC - Joe Abdullah 17-yard pass from Craig Whelihan (Roger Fleenor kick), 8:05, Qtr. #3.
NU - Clinton Childs 1-yard run (Ted Retzlaff kick), 5:30, Qtr. #3.
PAC - Abdullah 2-yard run (Fleenor kick), 2:11, Qtr. #3.
NU - Jeff Lake 24-yard pass from Matt Turman (Retzlaff kick), 8:12, Qtr. #4.
PAC - Damon Bowers 9-yard pass from Nick Sellers (Fleenor kick), 5:28, Qtr. #4.

Team Statistics

	NU	PAC
First downs	32	20
Rushing att.-yards	59-510	25-84
Passes	12-22-0	27-51-2
Passing yards	189	290
Total att.-yards	81-699	76-374
Returns-yards	8-99	1-(-2)
Sacks by	1-4	1-5
Punts-average	1-45.0	7-29.0
Fumbles-lost	2-1	1-0
Penalties-yards	8-90	5-37
Time of poss.	31:38	28:22

Individual Leaders

Rushing:
NU: Lawrence Phillips 9-138-1; Damon Benning 10-87-1; Clinton Childs 10-64-1; Jeff Makovicka 3-59-0.
PAC: Yasin Reeder 4-34-0; Joe Abdullah 9-20-1; Stanley Green 4-17-0.
Passing:
NU: Brook Berringer 8-15-120-0; Matt Turman 3-4-43-0.
PAC: Craig Whelihan 25-49-279-2.
Receiving:
NU: Reggie Baul 2-26-0; Eric Alford 1-46-1; Childs 1-26-0; Jeff Lake 1-24-1.
PAC: Tyrone Watley 7-126-0; Eric Atkins 4-29-0; Kerry Brown 4-28-0.
Interceptions:
NU: Leslie Dennis 1-48-0; Tyrone Williams 1-6-0.
PAC: None
Tackles (UT-AT-TT):
NU: Darren Schmadeke 7-1-8; Octavious McFarlin 4-3-7; Grant Wistrom 3-2-5.
PAC: Jeff Russell 11-4-15; Vince Bruno 4-6-10; Nathan Young 3-5-8.
Sacks:
NU: Terry Connealy 1-4.
PAC: Ed Tatola 1-5.

Nebraska
Wyoming

42
32

And he can run, too! Berringer recorded three rushing touchdowns against the Cowboys.

When the Huskers — ranked first and second in the polls — played Wyoming, it was their first game without star quarterback Tommie Frazier, and all eyes were locked on backup Brook Berringer. The general consensus across the country was that it was too bad Nebraska's championship hopes had been lost to something as mortal as blood clots.

Frazier had been hospitalized the previous week after he was diagnosed with a blood clot behind his right knee. Berringer, who had never started a game for the Big Red, was being pushed into action as a starter against Wyoming.

He was the only other scholarship quarterback in coach Tom Osborne's stable of players, and he had to be the man to step up. There was little other choice.

"We have full confidence in Brook," Osborne said. "He's a very good player and has been in our system long enough that he knows what he's doing."

Wyoming coach Joe Tiller didn't anticipate much of a difference with Berringer at quarterback instead of Frazier.

"We think with Brook Berringer going, really it's the same offense, which I think is a great tribute to the Nebraska coaching staff and Nebraska program," Tiller said. "Over the years, the plays haven't changed. The players have."

The Husker players also lined up in support of Berringer.

"Everybody is pretty confident in Brook," I-back Lawrence Phillips said. "He did well in spring ball and practice up to this point and in the last game. We're pretty confident with what he can do. At least now he won't be thrown into a game. He played a lot last Saturday, and I think he's prepared to play. He doesn't seem too dazed that he'll be going

(Right) Wyoming freshman Jeremy Dombek (11) was one of the few quarterbacks to have a big day against the Husker Blackshirts.

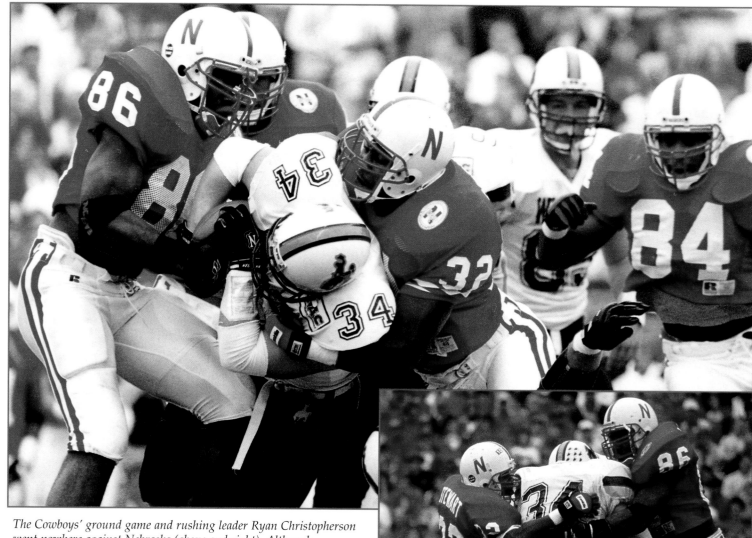

The Cowboys' ground game and rushing leader Ryan Christopherson went nowhere against Nebraska (above and right). Although Christopherson was one of the nation's leading rushers, he had zero net yards against the Blackshirts.

in as the starter. He's prepared, and he's ready."

And indeed, Berringer did just fine in his first career start. It's a good thing, too, considering how a fired-up Wyoming team played.

The Cowboys, who came to Lincoln with a 2-2 mark and a number of Nebraska natives on the squad, took advantage of their good fortune when a Husker defender fell down on two separate occasions in the first quarter. Wyoming scored on a 39-yard pass from Jeremy Dombek to Marcus Harris and a 6-yarder from Dombek to Jeremy Gilstrap.

The Huskers found themselves down 14-0 by quarter's end. They had been intercepted, suffered through five penalties in a span of six plays and generally looked miserable.

"We struggled early in the game, and some of that was caused by Wyoming. Sometimes we even missed a block, and sometimes we just didn't make the play when we needed to," Osborne said. "As the game went along, we seemed to get on track."

Berringer sparked the offense in the second quarter,

driving toward the end zone to allow Phillips the carry for the final yard and Nebraska's first score — just 5:25 before the half.

Wyoming countered: Terry Hendricks scored from 1 yard out. The clock read 2:12.

Then Berringer demonstrated why he was considered Nebraska's best passer. He hit seven straight passes to cover 59 yards and ran the final 5 yards to the end zone. Twelve seconds remained in the half; the two-minute drill seldom had been run better at Nebraska.

Berringer took a hard hit on that touchdown run, but he didn't realize how hard it had been until after the game. He later discovered that one of his lungs had partially collapsed.

"When you watched the film, you could tell after the hit that I was a little stunned," Berringer said. "I knew right away something was wrong. When the guys helped me and I stood up, I got excited about the touchdown.

"When I got to the sidelines, I had some pain in the ribs. At the time, I thought I had some bruised ribs and didn't think much about it. But the shortness of breath was, I thought, just the wind knocked out of me. I couldn't catch my breath."

He recalled that he still was short of breath during the halftime break, but the pain wasn't "all that severe."

The trainers tried to rig some sort of rib padding, thinking the quarterback had bruised his ribs.

"I've never had bruised ribs or cracked ribs," Berringer said. "I thought it was something along those lines. The collapsed lung was something that never entered my mind. But it was pretty sore."

Berringer's backup was walk-on sophomore Matt Turman, another player with limited time on the field and no starting experience.

But Berringer would come out to play in the second half.

Nebraska headed for the lockers down 21-14; it was the first time the Huskers trailed at halftime in a regular-season game since a 7-0 deficit to Oklahoma State in 1993, and the first time it had done so at home since Oklahoma led 14-3 in 1991.

The halftime deficit, however, was quickly overcome. Berringer scored on a run of 24 yards just three minutes into the second half to tie the game. Phillips added a 40-yard TD run, and Berringer scored again from 11 yards on an option. Wyoming could manage only a 40-yard field goal late in the period.

The Huskers entered the final 15 minutes up 35-24.

Berringer ended with 12 carries for 74 yards and three touchdowns. He also hit 15 of 22 passes for 131 yards.

"There wasn't a whole lot I could fault him on," Osborne said.

"I was happy I got to finish the game," Berringer said. "I felt I came out and did some things to get the job done the second half. I was happy about that. I was concerned about the game, and I wanted to make sure we'd come out with the win."

He later found himself in the hospital. A tube was placed in his chest to reinflate his injured lung. The development was, needless to say, a concern for Osborne.

"It's been an unbelievable set of circumstances," Osborne said. "Going into the year, the two thinnest spots were free safety and quarterback, and we've had

some guys go down at those positions. But it doesn't mean we can't play. It's a little tougher right now because we're not absolutely certain of Brook's status."

Phillips, who was about to be called upon to carry Nebraska's offensive load, also ended with three touchdowns against the Cowboys. He got his third on an 8-yard run and put the game away with 5:28 to go. He improved on his third-ranked rushing average of 154 yards per game with a 27-carry, 168-yard day.

"Nebraska is Nebraska when it comes to offense," Tiller said. "They've got tools, and they're going to bring the ball at you. You don't lead the nation in rushing for 10 years in a row by accident."

Dwayne Harris (86) just missed Dombek this time, but later, he made the day's only sack.

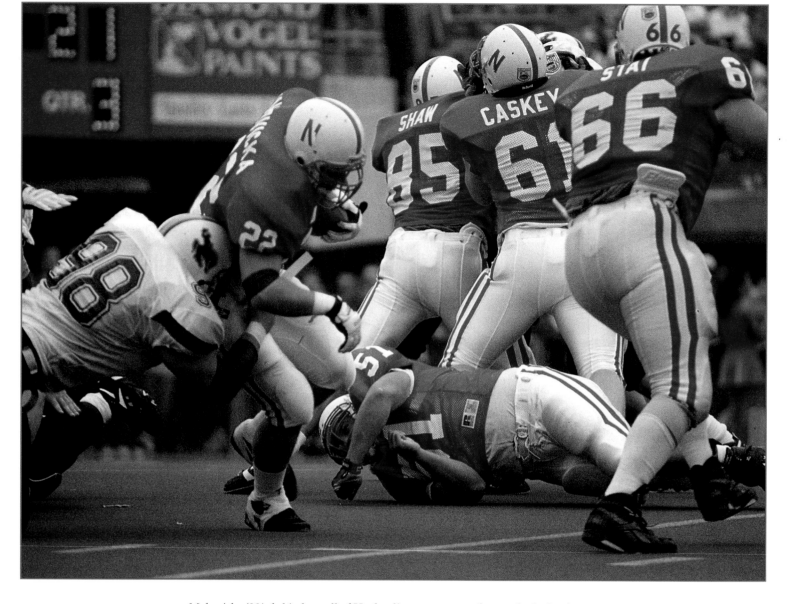

Makovicka (22), behind a wall of Husker linemen, earns a few yards the hard way.

Actually, Nebraska had spent only five of 10 years as national rushing leader heading into 1994, but the Huskers have been among the top three nationally in rushing annually since 1978.

The final touchdown was the result of a bobbled punt by Wyoming's Je'Ney Jackson. Damon Benning recovered the punt for Nebraska.

"We had our backs to the wall a little bit," Osborne said. "If it wasn't for the fumbled punt at the end, it might have been anybody's ballgame right down to the wire."

On the other side of the ball, the Nebraska defense had targeted the Cowboy rushing game, led by Wyoming's Ryan Christopherson, the nation's fifth-leading rusher with a 152-yard average. He had zero net yards on 12 carries for the day, and Wyoming managed only 36 yards as a team.

"We geared up to shut down the run and make them throw the ball," Barron Miles said.

However, redshirt freshman Dombek, who also made his first start for Wyoming, threw two touchdown passes in his 17-of-35, 264-yard day. Also, Harris and Eddie Pratt had eight catches each for 149 and 129 yards.

"It is always important — who can put some points on the board first," Dombek said. "That built my confidence, and it built our team's confidence."

But Dombek also threw three interceptions, which Nebraska converted to three touchdowns.

"The turnovers really hurt us," Tiller said. "It was a good football game ... for a while there anyway."

Dombek took a hard hit early in the fourth quarter and was replaced by senior John Gustin, who hit 8 of 11 passes for another 80 yards. A 2-yard TD pass to Gilstrap with 9:09 to play made it a 35-32 game.

Jackson's fumbled punt at his own 10 and Benning's

recovery at the 8 let Nebraska escape with a 10-point cushion that was not indicative of how well Wyoming stayed in the game.

"It was really a long day," Nebraska linebacker Ed Stewart said. "It was not due to the absence of Tommie Frazier. It was because the defense had to adjust, and we weren't adjusting quickly enough.

"It was an average day for me and an average day for the secondary. We got an average result: 32 points. Hope it doesn't happen again."

NU defensive coordinator Charlie McBride convinced his players it had better not happen again during his halftime speech, which, he later admitted, wasn't for family audiences.

"I told them we should play the third quarter like we always do," McBride said. "I have never seen so many guys falling down, tripping and zigging and zagging."

McBride was particularly unhappy with the pass defense, and for good reason — Chad May of Kansas State and Kordell Stewart of Colorado were coming in the weeks ahead.

McBride said his colorful halftime talk was an attempt to waken his Husker defenders, who gave up 21 points and 185 passing yards in the first half.

"We call it getting yelled at," Miles explained about McBride's message.

But the message apparently found its mark: Nebraska rallied to win.

Scoring Summary

	1st Quarter	2nd Quarter	3rd Quarter	4th Quarter	Final
Nebraska	0	14	21	7	42
Wyoming	14	7	3	8	32

WYO - Marcus Harris 39-yard pass from Jeremy Dombek (Taylor Sorenson kick), 8:30, Qtr. #1.
WYO - Jeremy Gilstrap 6-yard pass from Dombek (Sorenson kick), :25, Qtr. #1.
NU - Lawrence Phillips 1-yard run (Tom Sieler kick), 5:25, Qtr. #2.
WYO - Terry Hendricks 1-yard run (Sorenson kick), 2:12, Qtr. #2.
NU - Brook Berringer 5-yard run (Sieler kick), :12, Qtr. #2.
NU - Berringer 24-yard run (Sieler kick), 12:05, Qtr. #3.
NU - Phillips 40-yard run (Sieler kick), 11:36, Qtr. #3.
NU - Berringer 11-yard run (Sieler kick), 8:11, Qtr. #3.
WYO - Sorenson 40-yard field goal, :31, Qtr. #3.
WYO - Gilstrap 2-yard pass from John Gustin (Gilstrap pass from Gustin), 9:09, Qtr. #4.
NU - Phillips 8-yard run (Sieler kick), 5:28, Qtr. #4.

Team Statistics

	NU	WYO
First downs	24	18
Rushing att.-yards	56-322	21-36
Passes	15-22-1	25-46-3
Passing yards	131	344
Total att.-yards	78-453	67-380
Returns-yards	7-53	4-5
Sacks by	1-3	0
Punts-average	8-42.4	7-41.6
Fumbles-lost	3-1	2-1
Penalties-yards	9-91	6-30
Time of poss.	34:20	25:40

Individual Leaders

Rushing:
NU: Lawrence Phillips 27-168-3; Brook Berringer 12-74-3; Damon Benning 6-46-0.
WYO: Terry Hendricks 4-34-1; John Gustin 2-9-0; Ryan Christopherson 12-0-0.

Passing:
NU: Berringer 15-22-131-1.
WYO: Jeremy Dombek 17-35-264-3; Gustin 8-11-80-0.

Receiving:
NU: Mark Gilman 4-48-0; Abdul Muhammad 4-30-0; Phillips 3-22-0.
WYO: Marcus Harris 8-149-1; Eddie Pratt 8-126-0; Jeremy Gilstrap 3-25-2.

Interceptions:
NU: Barron Miles 2-1-0; Tyrone Williams 1-28-0.
WYO: Lee Vaughn 1-10-0.

Tackles (UT-AT-TT):
NU: Ed Stewart 5-7-12; Doug Colman 3-5-8; Kareem Moss 5-1-6; Troy Dumas 3-3-6.
WYO: Lee Vaughn 4-9-13; John Burrough 5-5-10; Jim Talich 4-6-10.

Sacks:
NU: Dwayne Harris 1-3.
WYO: None.

Nebraska
Oklahoma State 3

32 oSu

No sacks for OSU today. But the Cowboys shouldn't feel too badly; Zach Wiegert (72) allowed no sacks all year in the process of earning the Outland Trophy for the nation's top lineman.

Nebraska began Big Eight Conference play with a lot of questions. Would Tommie Frazier be able to return before the end of the season? Would Brook Berringer's partially collapsed lung heal enough for him to continue?

Would a defense struggling from the loss of safety Mike Minter be able to come together in time to cause passing game problems for the likes of Kansas State's Chad May and Colorado's Kordell Stewart?

Coach Tom Osborne remained in fairly good spirits despite all of his injury questions.

"I read in the paper where Pat Jones said he doesn't trust anybody at Nebraska except Bob Devaney, Danny Nee and Bill Byrne," Osborne joked about Jones' assessment of Frazier's injury and playing status.

"My feelings are really hurt," Osborne said. "If you can't make that list, you're not very trustworthy."

In Stillwater, Okla., Jones said that he would prepare for this game as though Frazier had never been hurt and was expected to play.

"We're preparing for the best, and they aren't going to run any different plays without him," Jones said of Frazier. He noted that Berringer, or any other NU quarterback, could run the Husker offense, too. "Frazier just does it a little bit faster."

Osborne proved to be trustworthy, as Frazier was not available to play. Berringer had been cleared to practice but only without contact. He still had to protect the lung that had partially collapsed after he was hit hard in the previous week's game against Wyoming.

(Right) Matt Turman (11) got plenty of playing time in the second half, and he led Nebraska to win No. 6 with three touchdown drives.

The OSU ground game found the going tough against the quick Huskers.
Unfortunately for the Cowboys, the passing yards were just as hard to come by.

The defense also was slowed by injuries to cornerback Barron Miles, Sam backer Troy Dumas and safety Tony Veland, who also was taking a few snaps at his old position of quarterback.

Against the Cowboys, the Huskers again started slow. But Nebraska's lethargic start against OSU wasn't quite as dramatic as the previous week's struggle, during which the Huskers fell behind 14-0 against Wyoming.

Oklahoma State, which has frequently thrown defensive challenges in Nebraska's path with Jones as coach, held NU scoreless in the first quarter; it was the second-straight week the Huskers hadn't scored in the first quarter. And, following a Husker turnover, the Cowboys put up three points themselves with Lawson Vaughn's 27-yard field goal, five minutes into the game.

Nebraska played a conservative game, trying to protect Berringer's injured lung. The option game was not necessarily an option.

It was Berringer's second career start, and after his injury the week before, he expected Oklahoma State's defense to try to put more pressure on him.

"I'm sure they're going to blitz quite a bit," Berringer said. "They're going to try to do everything they can to get at us, but we're going to do everything we can to win the game."

I-back Lawrence Phillips would be the workhorse for the day — it was his 2-yard touchdown run, two minutes into the second quarter, that gave Nebraska its lead, which it would hold for good.

Phillips carried 33 times, gaining 221 yards and scoring three touchdowns for the second-straight game.

Darin Erstad added a 48-yard field goal before halftime, and the lead at intermission was 9-3.

Then things got interesting for Osborne and his staff.

A precautionary X-ray had been scheduled for Berringer at halftime to see how his lung was holding up. The X-ray showed that the lung had begun to deflate again. Berringer would not be able to return.

"It was a shock to all of a sudden get a phone call and be told Brook can't play any more," Osborne said. "We're going to go by what the doctors say. That's what we always do around here. The team reacted well, and I was pleased."

Turman, a walk-on from Wahoo, stepped to the front of the shortening line of Husker quarterbacks. The last time Turman, whose teammates affectionately call the 5-11, 165-pounder "The Terminator," had played anything close to a significant role in a game was the spring scrimmage. Against an outside opponent, his last real action was in the state high school playoffs, when the prep senior quarterbacked Wahoo Neumann for his father, Tim, the coach.

"Coach Turner Gill told me to get in there, call the play, line up and take a deep breath and pretend like it was just another scrimmage," Turman recalled.

The way he played, no one, not even Osborne, could tell Turman was nervous. He directed two scoring drives on his first three possessions.

"Matt Turman went in and did well under the circumstances," Osborne said. "I thought the offensive line picked up the pace and did a good job. He wasn't excited. He went out there and performed."

The sophomore and his Husker teammates scored three second-half touchdowns: another 2-yard run by Phillips, a 7-yard run by Phillips and a 7-yard run by backup I-back Clinton Childs.

When Phillips heard that Berringer wouldn't return, he knew that he would have his hands on the ball more. That proved to be just fine with him. The sophomore from West Covina, Calif., set career highs in carries and yards.

Phillips also exceeded the 1,000-yard mark just six games into the season. With his sixth-straight 100-yard game, the youngster had already amassed 1,006 yards for the season.

"We thought we might be running a lot, just to start off so Matt could settle in," Phillips said. "We were ready for the challenge."

"With No. 11 (Turman) in there, it became an inside run drill," OSU's Jones said. "They just lined up and whipped us."

Turman also rolled out to pass to tight end Eric Alford for a two-point conversion after Phillips' second 2-yard score.

"The two-point conversion was a big boost to me," said Turman. He had to throw only four passes; he completed one for 23 yards.

"Turman played well," Osborne said. "The offensive line picked up the pace. The running backs did a nice job. The defense stepped it up a notch."

The boost Turman received from his two-point conversion was nothing compared to the rush he got when he saw the offensive line in action. Tackles Zach Wiegert and Rob Zatechka were leading a charge that flattened the Cowboys.

"We may have lost a championship quarterback, but we've got guys like Brook and Matt who can come in and step up and still allow us to be a championship team," Zatechka said. "And Matt's not a bad quarterback. Anybody who pays attention can tell from the scrimmages and times he's gotten into games that he's played well."

"When I saw the offensive line just blowing people off the ball and the defense play an incredible game, I felt pretty comfortable," Turman admitted.

The running game also made Turman feel more at home.

"I think our team has taken everything in stride and stepped up offensively and defensively," Phillips said. "Obviously, people are worried about our quarterback

This close-knit group of Husker Blackshirts doesn't let much come between them — opposing offenses in particular.

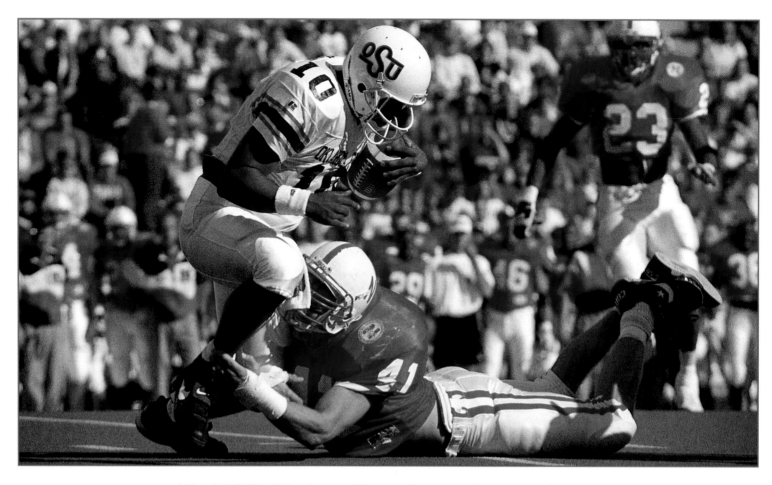

(Above) Phil Ellis (41) makes one of his six tackles against OSU in a superb showing.

(Below) Turman counted on the ground game; this time, Clinton Childs (26) got the call.

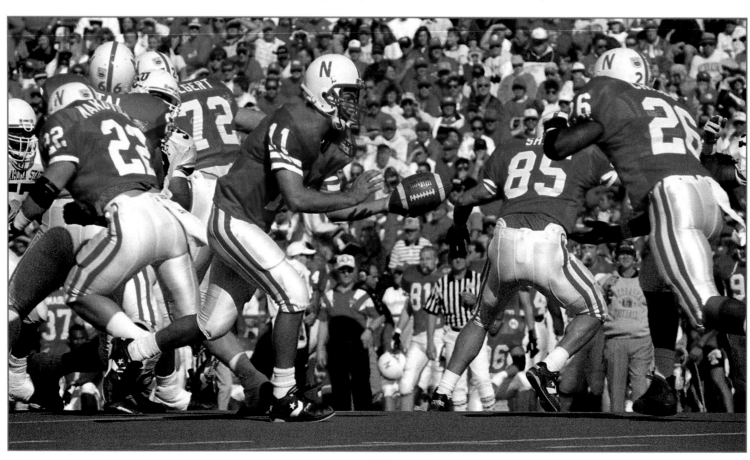

position. But Brook can cut it up and run, and he's a good passer. If it's not Brook, Turman can get the job done, too."

"They can win ballgames with the defense and kicking game if they have to," Jones added.

His Cowboys simply were stuffed in the second half. Oklahoma State managed only 40 yards rushing and 96 yards passing in the ballgame and covered just 24 total yards after intermission.

"When you can't run the ball some, it's awfully, awfully hard on us," the OSU coach said. "We knew it would be hard to sustain anything against them. We weren't under any false illusions as far as being able to come up here and drill these guys running."

"We know the offense can do whatever it wants," said Nebraska defensive tackle Christian Peter, who had one of NU's three quarterback sacks. "Whoever's in there will get the job done. We just have to come through on defense and keep shutting people down."

This game may have been the defensive turning point of the season, too. The Husker Blackshirts knew that because the quarterbacking situation was so fragile, they had to step up and dominate games. The theme that would drive them to the end of the season — "If they can't score, they can't win" — was coming into play.

Co-captain Ed Stewart could sense it.

"I think we came out and played hard, like we're capable of playing," said the Chicago senior, who led NU with 10 tackles. "I do not know if we came out angry, but we came out more focused. Since I came here, the defense has been abused, and we are here to change that."

Scoring Summary

	1st Quarter	2nd Quarter	3rd Quarter	4th Quarter	Final
Nebraska	0	9	16	7	32
OSU	3	0	0	0	3

OSU - Lawson Vaughn 27-yard field goal, 10:11, Qtr. #1.
NU - Lawrence Phillips 2-yard run (kick failed), 13:14, Qtr. #2.
NU - Darin Erstad 48-yard field goal, :04, Qtr. #2.
NU - Phillips 2-yard run (Eric Alford pass from Matt Turman), 4:40, Qtr. #3.
NU - Phillips 7-yard run (Darin Erstad pass from Jon Vedral), 1:00, Qtr. #3.
NU - Clinton Childs 7-yard run (Erstad kick), 3:48, Qtr. #4.

Team Statistics

	NU	OSU
First downs	30	7
Rushing att.-yards	68-372	31-40
Passes	12-20-0	6-20-1
Passing yards	103	96
Total att.-yards	88-475	51-136
Returns-yards	5-68	1-5
Sacks by	3-23	0
Punts-average	2-34.5	9-41.3
Fumbles-lost	4-3	2-1
Penalties-yards	5-49	3-31
Time of poss.	36:55	23:05

Individual Leaders

Rushing:
NU: Lawrence Phillips 33-221-3; Clinton Childs 6-45-1; Damon Benning 7-42-0.
OSU: David Thompson 11-35-0; Joe Jefferson 5-15-0.
Passing:
NU: Brook Berringer 10-15-75-0; Matt Turman 1-4-23-0.
OSU: Tone' Jones 6-20-96-1.
Receiving:
NU: Abdul Muhammad 4-53-0; Childs 2-22-0; Reggie Baul 2-5-0.
OSU: Derek Jones 2-33-0; Rafael Denson 1-34-0.
Interceptions:
NU: Moss 1-0-0.
OSU: None
Tackles (UT-AT-TT):
NU: Ed Stewart 3-7-10; Christian Peter 3-6-9; Phil Ellis 2-4-6; Clint Brown 2-3-5.
OSU: James Elliott 6-8-14; Jeroid Johnson 4-8-12; Eric Hobbs 1-11-12; Louis Adams 3-8-11.
Sacks:
NU: Terry Connealy 1-9; Jason Pesterfield 1-8; Peter 1-6.
OSU: None

Nebraska
Kansas State

17
6

Running the ground game between the tackles was Nebraska's bread and butter against Kansas State. Here, Makovicka gets one of the team's 10 fullback carries and scores the clinching touchdown.

According to Kansas State, ranked 11th and 16th in the two national polls, this was the year the Wildcats finally had Nebraska's number. The second-ranked Huskers were struggling with a shortage of quarterbacks: No. 3 Matt Turman would get the start this week. Tommie Frazier was out with recurring blood clots in his right leg. His backup, Brook Berringer, had suffered a partially collapsed lung two weeks in a row. Turman would be Nebraska's third starter in seven weeks.

And Nebraska (6-0) would play at Manhattan, Kan., where K-State (4-0) had been building a winning tradition under coach Bill Snyder.

There was plenty of talk prior to this game, mostly from Manhattan. Wildcat fans already were talking about ending Nebraska's 25-game win streak against K-State, as well as how a win this week would propel K-State to the Orange Bowl as Big Eight champions.

But quarterback Chad May was anxious. He had thrown for a Big Eight record 489 yards against the Huskers in a 45-28 loss at Lincoln the year before, and NU wasn't supposed to be able to stop May and returnees J.J. Smith, Kevin Lockett and company any better this time.

Even coach Tom Osborne believed that K-State had closed the talent gap within the league. The Wildcats were nearing the championship level.

"I think with Chad May in there, they're real close," Osborne said. "Coming down here, I wasn't sure that they weren't better. They're a good football team. Coming down here, I thought it was a 50-50 proposition. I thought it was anybody's ballgame."

(Right) A Wildcat defender gets a hand on Damon Benning (21) or rather, Benning's shirttail.

At the start of this regionally televised game, there was little doubt that May gave K-State the quarterback edge.

But Nebraska defensive coordinator Charlie McBride and linebacker co-captain Ed Stewart said the 1993 game, not May, was their inspiration for the '94 meeting. The NU Blackshirts had taken enough heat about that game and NU's leaky pass defense. They weren't about to take any more such talk.

Besides, with Turman starting at quarterback and with only a questionable Brook Berringer to back him up, the defense needed to carry this game for Nebraska.

That's pretty much how it unfolded.

Turman, the sophomore walk-on from Wahoo, came out and played like a veteran. On their second possession, he drove the Huskers in for a first-quarter touchdown, capped by Lawrence Phillips' 2-yard run, two-thirds of the way through the opening period.

May, who found this year's Husker pass rush even more nerve-wracking than that of a year ago, managed to get the touchdown back in the second quarter when he hit Mitch Running on a 29-yard TD pass. But Troy Dumas blocked the extra point, so Nebraska rolled into half-time with a 7-6 lead.

"I think Chad May is as good a thrower as we've seen in a long time," Osborne said. "We tried to keep Chad May off-balance by showing blitz and not coming all the time. I thought our defensive staff did a great job."

Can you find the QB in this picture? Turman (11) is surrounded by a mountain of linemen in a huddle during the game against nationally ranked Kansas State. The K-State game was Turman's first career start.

May had been sacked just seven times in his previous four games. But in the game against Nebraska, May was sacked six times. Freshman outside linebacker Grant Wistrom had two, and Stewart had another, one of his team-leading nine tackles.

The pressure caused May to miss on 26 of his 48 passes, one of which was intercepted by Dumas.

"They tried to get pressure on me, and some guys came untouched," May said. "When they're pushing up field and guys are in your face, it's kind of hard to throw. Sometimes I couldn't see where I was throwing the ball."

The teams also were playing on a field wet with morning rain, which didn't help May, either.

"I don't want to make excuses or anything, but there were a few times where the ball was slipping out of my hand. I had some guys open a few times, but the ball slipped out of my hand," he said.

Stewart credited the defense with much of May's frustration.

"There were a lot of times when they were throwing the ball and there was no one there, so I think we did fluster them a little bit," Stewart said. "I think our coaches did an excellent job of putting together a package. We gave them a lot of different looks and kept pressure on them at the line. I don't think they knew exactly what defense we were playing most of the time."

Osborne brought Berringer in for the last drive of the first half and started him the second half. But it was basic offense. To protect the junior as much as possible, Berringer was ordered to pass only in drop-back situations, run no options and not call any option plays on audibles.

Besides throwing, he was allowed to hand off to the I-backs and fullbacks.

"Offensively, of course, we were handicapped a little bit in what we wanted to do," Osborne said. "They knew when Turman was in there we weren't going to throw very much, and when Berringer was in there we weren't going to run the option very much. They're smart, and they adjusted accordingly."

Turman, who has small hands, also was handicapped somewhat by the slick ball. He still managed to complete two of his four passes for 15 yards and added 10 yards rushing on four carries before he took the bench.

Berringer, who played with a special flak jacket to protect his injured lung, sputtered when he first got the call to play.

"I thought Brook did well as the game went along," Osborne said. "He was out of sync a little bit there at first. I think above all, the thing we wanted to do was get Brook through a game without that lung collapsing again. We were kind of holding our breath that he wouldn't get hit hard. Our offensive line did a great job of protecting him."

And the line did a great job of allowing the rushing game to operate. Nebraska's game plan was almost a "call-the-play-out-loud-and-you-try-to-stop-it" format. Forty of Nebraska's 60 plays were runs inside the tackles.

Even given that statistic, Phillips carried 31 times and

A jarring tackle (one of many; see also inset) by Donta Jones sends its victim's ball and mouthpiece flying. NU shut down the K-State offense in a 17-6 win.

ground out 117 yards. Despite playing with a badly sprained thumb, he collected his seventh 100-yard game of the season and caught two passes for 15 yards.

"Phillips is a great player. He's pretty special, and he's got a lot of help," Snyder said. "I don't think we played bad defensively. Our defense played well. Their offensive line played well, but Phillips kept fighting and made some plays."

The Wildcats blanked the Huskers in the third period, but the Blackshirts returned the favor for K-State. Field position helped; Darin Erstad provided some exceptional punts that pinned K-State deep in its own territory.

"We have moved the ball against Nebraska and made big plays in recent years," Snyder said. "But not today. We had no big plays at all, and we needed them because we were working out of the shadow of the goal line."

And the Wildcats were their own worst enemies. They were penalized 12 times for 102 yards.

"We took more snaps than they did and had enough TV time-outs, so I think we were well-rested," Snyder said. "We held the ball longer but got no movement in our offense. We shot ourselves in the foot with near-misses and penalties."

Nebraska entered the fourth quarter with a one-point

(Above) Barron Miles shadows his man in coverage and tips the ball away from K-State star Kevin Lockett (83) for an incompletion in the end zone. (Left) This was just one of Miles' six school-record pass break-ups on the day.

lead and again claimed the final 15 minutes for itself.

"We try to play the first three quarters so we can be the strongest team in the fourth," Osborne said. "We play a physical style of football, and I was really pleased with the fourth-quarter performance."

Nebraska put together an 11-play scoring drive, which was capped by backup fullback Jeff Makovicka's 15-yard touchdown run with 11:01 to play.

"It was a good place to have it," Makovicka

said of his touchdown. "I give all the credit to the offensive line. They sealed it off perfect. All I had to do was follow them in."

The Huskers then put together a 12-play drive that used up most of the time remaining in the game and ended with Erstad's 24-yard field goal with 1:32 to go.

"There with seven minutes left, I was thinking to myself [that] we did the same thing to Kansas last week," May said of a come-from-behind win on the road at Kansas. "We were down by eight and had a chance to score and tie the game. When we got down by 11 (against Nebraska), we had to score twice and just ran out of time.

"We went into this game with a lot of confidence and expected to win," May said. "We didn't play well, and

they played a good game."

"Last year, we had a couple of breakdowns in coverage," NU cornerback Barron Miles said. "This year, we had like one breakdown early. We got a hold of ourselves and came back and played hard. We played a gang of man-to-man today. We proved to the nation that we can cover and that our defense is probably the No. 1 defense in the nation." Miles had a school-record six pass break-ups during the game.

K-State ended with 289 yards passing but had minus 7 yards rushing.

"Until they get beat, they should be right up there, and they deserve it," Snyder said of the Huskers' ranking. "They miss Frazier, but they're still a great, great football team."

Scoring Summary

	1st Quarter	2nd Quarter	3rd Quarter	4th Quarter	Final
Nebraska	7	0	0	10	17
Kansas State	0	6	0	0	6

NU - Lawrence Phillips 2-yard run (Darin Erstad kick), 6:12, Qtr. #1.
KSU - Mitch Running 29-yard pass from Chad May (kick blocked), 14:55, Qtr. #2.
NU - Jeff Makovicka 15-yard run (Erstad kick), 11:01, Qtr. #4.
NU - Erstad 24-yard field goal, 1:32, Qtr. #4.

Team Statistics

	NU	KSU
First downs	16	17
Rushing att.-yards	50-210	23-(-7)
Passes	4-11-0	22-48-1
Passing yards	52	249
Total att.-yards	61-262	71-242
Returns-yards	4-74	3-17
Sacks by	6-53	0
Punts-average	7-37.3	8-36.0
Fumbles-lost	2-1	2-0
Penalties-yards	9-70	12-102
Time of poss.	31:26	28:34

Individual Leaders

Rushing:
NU:Lawrence Phillips 31-117-1; Jeff Makovicka 7-56-1; Cory Schlesinger 3-24-0.
KSU: J.J. Smith 14-29-0; Chad May 9-(-36)-0.
Passing:
NU: Brook Berringer 2-7-37-0; Matt Turman 2-4-15-0.
KSU: May 22-48-249-1.
Receiving:
NU: Phillips 2-15-0; Abdul Muhammad 1-34-0.
KSU: J.J. Smith 6-29-0; Mitch Running 5-79-1; Kevin Lockett 5-78-0.
Interceptions:
NU: Troy Dumas 1-54-0.
KSU: None
Tackles (UT-AT-TT):
NU: Ed Stewart 4-5-9; Christian Peter 5-3-8; Troy Dumas 4-3-7; Donta Jones 3-4-7.
KSU: Chuck Marlowe 3-13-16; Tim Colston 4-8-12; DeShawn Fogle 0-8-8.
Sacks:
NU: Grant Wistrom 2-24; Donta Jones 1-10; Ed Stewart 1-8; Terry Connealy 1-6; Christian Peter 1-5.
KSU: None

Nebraska
Missouri

42

7

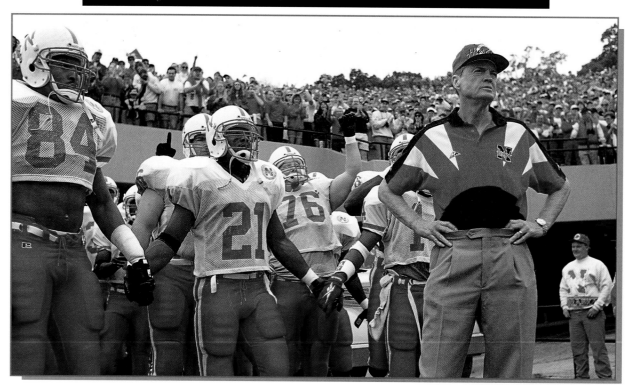

Poised and ready to hand a licking to Missouri, Osborne and his players await the signal to enter Faurot Field.

A week prior to his team's long-anticipated showdown with No. 2 Colorado, Nebraska coach Tom Osborne took his third-ranked Huskers to Columbia, Mo., to face a struggling Missouri Tiger team and first-year head coach Larry Smith.

Osborne's offense faced a struggle of its own: returning to good health. Brook Berringer's lung was still considered too fragile to withstand many hits, so the option game was again put on the back burner to minimize the possibility of reinjury to Nebraska's only available scholarship quarterback. After all, one of the season's biggest games was only a week away.

And although Osborne did want to ensure that the entire arsenal of weapons was ready, there wouldn't be many options called in this one. Aside from his quarterback's delicate lung and the matter of the slick artificial turf in Columbia, Mo., Osborne knew that the Huskers could move the ball just fine without Berringer having to run.

Osborne wasn't especially thrilled with what he had to do, but the results — a 42-7 whipping of the outmanned 2-5 Tigers — would ease his mind.

"This is more like a pro offense, and I never have liked professional football because I feel like you're fighting with one hand tied behind your back," said Osborne, whose team stayed with basic football for the third-straight game.

"You're standing there without any options. That's what the pro people do every day, and that's what we've done the last two weeks. Basically, we've stood there like a pro team."

(Right) Muscle football again was Nebraska's game plan. Phillips' carries were designed to protect Berringer's injured lung one more week.

Berringer had survived two games without reinjuring his lung (which had partially collapsed in the game against Wyoming on Oct. 1 and then re-deflated on Oct. 8), but he again was reduced to handing off to his stable of talented running backs. No risk there. He did get in a few bootlegs and rollouts but never took a solid hit.

He also indicated that NU's running game wasn't the only weapon about which Colorado would have to worry. The Goodland, Kan., junior hit 9 of 13 passes for 153 yards and three touchdowns, all in the second half. Those were his only completions of the half on just a handful of tosses.

"We've got a heck of a passing game," Berringer said. "Sometimes we don't get to it as much as we'd like. They gave us opportunities, and we took them."

Berringer also ran for 23 yards on five carries and wasn't sacked. He said he'd be 100 percent for the game against No. 2 Colorado, which greatly pleased Husker fans from Omaha to Scottsbluff.

"Brook can do it all," Osborne said. "Next week, he'll have to do it all. I wanted to try to get Berringer through

122

(Center) Linebacker Ellis (41) and company swarmed everywhere Missouri went. Hard hits by Harris (far left) and Stewart (above) limited the Tigers to 48 rushing yards.

today without getting hit, and I don't think he took any bad blows. Obviously, we can't sit on anything now."

"I didn't want to take any unnecessary hits," Berringer said. "If I had a chance to get out of bounds, that's what I had in mind. I came out of it all right."

Osborne wished everyone had.

Berringer's backup, Matt Turman, sprained his right shoulder while running the option in the fourth quarter. At first, the injury appeared to be a separation. It was later determined to be a sprain, so although it would be painful, it probably wouldn't keep Turman from emergency duty, if needed, against Colorado.

"We just get out of the woods with Brook getting healthy, and we're back in them with Matt's injury," Osborne said.

Third-stringer Monte Christo, a walk-on freshman

Muhammad on the loose, once again, after one of his two catches from Berringer.

In the past three games, opponents had scored a total of only 13 points.

Cornerback Barron Miles had another big game. He foiled a Missouri scoring opportunity when he forced Joe Freeman to fumble into the end zone from the 1. Miles also returned an interception 27 yards to set up a Nebraska score.

"It was real pivotal, the key point of the game," Smith said of Freeman's fumble. "If you turn something like that into seven points, it gives us momentum and motivation."

The Tigers' field position for that play was practically a gift from Nebraska: An errant pitch by Berringer was recovered by Mizzou at the Husker 10. Brock Olivio ran 9 yards to the 1, but then, on the next play, Freeman coughed up the ball after a hard hit by Miles. Ed Stewart recovered for Nebraska in the end zone.

"We were a little lucky on that Missouri fumble during the beginning of the second half," Coach Osborne said. "Eventually though, I think as the game went along, we wore them down a little bit."

"Defensively, you can't play a team like Nebraska all day long," said Tiger defensive tackle Damon Simon. "I think we came out excited in the first half. I don't think their size was a factor. They were just more prepared. I felt we could beat Nebraska, but things didn't go our way. Things just fell apart. You can't make the mistakes we made against them and expect to win."

Nebraska's defense sacked Missouri quarterback Jeff Handy three times and limited the Tigers to 48 yards rushing. Handy hit 19 of 29 passes for 150 yards and was picked off once.

Handy prevented a shutout, however, when he completed a 34-yard touchdown pass to Rahsetnu Jenkins with 7:34 to play. Jenkins finished with eight catches for 90 yards — one of the few bright spots in the Tigers' afternoon.

Smith wasn't at all happy with his team's play.

"I'm angry and disappointed," Smith said. "The last three touchdowns should not have been scored. I'm angry that we let ourselves get in that position. Some people thought the game was over. It's something that can be turned around, but we can't play like we did in the fourth quarter."

And Nebraska never gave the Tigers a break.

Berringer found Reggie Baul on a 43-yard scoring pass with six minutes to go in the game. Benning's second touchdown capped the scoring with 1:23 to go.

"I was pleased with our effort," Osborne said. "In some games like this, there is a temptation to let up. But we didn't and played well throughout the game."

from Kearney who had intended to redshirt, had to finish the game.

"I didn't want to do it very bad, but I didn't want to play Berringer any more either," Osborne said of pulling the redshirt label off Christo. In fact, the youngster was just coming off the injured list himself. He had suffered a thumb injury in the fall and had had his hand in a cast.

Nebraska's main weapon against the Tigers was again the I-back. Lawrence Phillips rushed for 110 yards and a touchdown on 22 carries, and Damon Benning also scored twice.

Nebraska failed to score in the first quarter but picked up a 5-yard TD from Phillips and a 9-yard touchdown from Benning in the second quarter.

"Missouri is a competitive football team," Osborne said. "They fought hard with great effort and played tough defense, particularly in the beginning of the ballgame. We weren't sure we would ever get on track."

Tight end Mark Gilman caught a 1-yard pass from Berringer just over 10 minutes into the third quarter, and Berringer hooked up with split end Brendan Holbein on a 30-yard pass play for another score in the third.

For the third-straight week, the defense dominated.

With its victory, Nebraska continued a 16-game winning streak against Missouri as well as a streak of wins dating back to 1973 against the Tigers in Faurot Field.

Nebraska ended with 330 yards rushing — its seventh game over 300 for the season — and more than 40 points for the fifth time in 1994.

Berringer's passing total gave NU 482 yards total offense.

"We didn't run the full gamut of our offense today," Berringer said. "But we came out and threw the ball well."

"Brook executed well. It takes a while to get used to a new quarterback," Osborne said. "We used most of our offense, but we were not able to run the option very much because of Berringer's condition."

Berringer admitted he took few chances when he was running.

"It was nice to run the bootleg with those guys in red in front of you knocking the Missouri guys down," he said. He also said he didn't want to risk getting yelled at, so when he had a chance to run out of bounds before getting hit, he did so.

Meanwhile, the defense again played nearly flawless football.

"We had one mistake that went for a touchdown, but this was a great game for our defense," said defensive coordinator Charlie McBride.

Miles was also obviously tickled with the Blackshirts.

"We were kind of upset not getting a shutout, but it was only seven points, and we still won the game," said the Nebraska senior who got his fourth interception of the season against Missouri quarterback Jeff Handy and returned it for a career-long 27 yards.

Scoring Summary

	1st Quarter	2nd Quarter	3rd Quarter	4th Quarter	Final
Nebraska	0	14	14	14	42
Missouri	0	0	0	7	7

NU - Lawrence Phillips 5-yard run (Tom Sieler kick), 11:15, Qtr. #2.
NU - Damon Benning 9-yard run (Sieler kick), 8:00, Qtr. #2.
NU - Mark Gilman 1-yard pass from Brook Berringer (Darin Erstad kick), 4:56, Qtr. #3.
NU - Brendan Holbein 30-yard pass from Berringer (Erstad kick), 1:36, Qtr. #3.
MU - Rahsetnu Jenkins 34-yard pass from Jeff Handy (Kyle Pooler kick), 7:36, Qtr. #4.
NU - Reggie Baul 43-yard pass from Berringer (Erstad kick), 6:00, Qtr. #4.
NU - Benning 2-yard run (Erstad kick), 1:23, Qtr. #4.

Team Statistics

	NU	MU
First downs	23	13
Rushing att.-yards	58-330	29-48
Passes	9-13-0	19-32-1
Passing yards	152	150
Total att.-yards	71-482	61-198
Returns-yards	7-71	2-1
Sacks by	3-23	0
Punts-average	4-42.3	9-39.8
Fumbles-lost	2-1	3-1
Penalties-yards	9-75	5-50
Time of poss.	31:31	28:29

Individual Leaders

Rushing:
NU: Lawrence Phillips 22-110-1; Clinton Childs 6-65-0; Damon Benning 10-39-2; Cory Schlesinger 5-35-0.
MU: Brock Olivo 11-37-0; Joe Freeman 11-26-0.
Passing:
NU: Brook Berringer 9-13-152-0.
MU: Jeff Handy 19-29-150-1.
Receiving:
NU: Abdul Mahammad 2-23-0; Benning 2-20-0; Mark Gilman 2-7-1; Reggie Baul 1-43-1; Brendan Holbein 1-30-1; Eric Alford 1-29-0.
MU: Rahsetnu Jenkins 8-90-1; Brian Sallee 5-38-0; Frank Jones 2-15-0.
Interceptions:
NU: Barron Miles 1-27; MU: None.
Tackles (UT-AT-TT):
NU: Ed Stewart 3-5-8; Troy Dumas 2-6-8; Kareem Moss 4-3-7; Doug Colman 3-4-7; Christian Peter 3-4-7.
MU: Travis McDonald 4-12-16; Darryl Chatman 2-10-12; DeMontie Cross 5-6-11; Andre White 2-7-9.
Sacks:
NU: Jason Pesterfield 1-13; Dwayne Harris 1-7; Ellis 1-3.
MU: None.

Nebraska
Colorado

24
7

The final handshake? Colorado's head coach, Bill McCartney (left), resigned at the end of the season after providing Osborne with many tough battles on the field.

Finally, the game marked in capital red letters on Colorado's schedule and at the center of an invisible target on Nebraska's had arrived. This was supposed to be the Big Eight Conference game of the year, perhaps the national game of the year.

The two big boys of the conference, unbeaten and sharing the No. 2 and 3 spots in both major polls, would face off to decide not only bragging rights for the year but who gets the inside track to the Orange Bowl. And it was all on national television.

Bill McCartney made this game his special project after he was named head coach at Colorado. He gave traditional power Nebraska the label of "rival." Then he set out to earn respect for the Buffaloes by trying his best to beat Nebraska.

Tom Osborne didn't take kindly to the term "rival." He still doesn't. He elected to designate the Colorado matchup a big game, just like any other game that is important if your team hopes to play for a national championship at the end of the year. Both of these teams figured to do just that.

Colorado entered with a 7-0 record and had already bumped off the likes of Michigan and Texas on the road. The Buffs had an offense that averaged nearly 503 yards and 40 points per game.

Osborne compared Colorado's weapons — quarterback Kordell Stewart, running back Rashaan Salaam and receiver Michael Westbrook — with the 1983 Nebraska offense that had All-Americans Turner Gill at quarterback, Heisman Trophy winner Mike Rozier at I-back and Irving Fryar at split end.

(Right) Berringer is poised to unload. He hit 12 of 17 passes, mostly to his tight ends, and kept Colorado off balance.

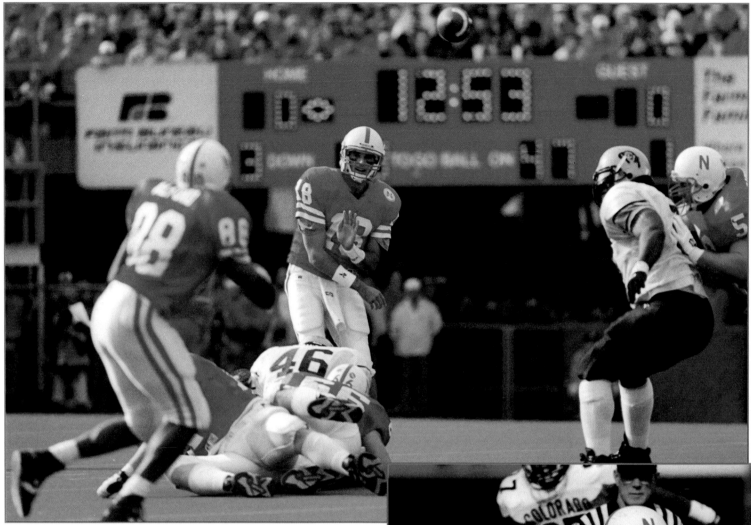

It was a quick-strike offense with lots of weapons, a good tight end, a strong and veteran line, and everything to gain by beating Nebraska at home.

Nebraska — despite its 8-0 start, wins over three previously ranked opponents and the waiting 200th consecutive home sellout crowd at homecoming — was actually an underdog in the pregame point spread. It was only the sixth time in Osborne's 22 years of coaching that one of his teams was not favored to win at home.

A win would give Osborne his 22nd-straight nine-win season and extend Nebraska's NCAA record of such seasons to 26. But few people gave the Huskers much of a chance, due to their struggles to keep quarterbacks healthy, a defensive secondary which included first-year safety Tony Veland and several other youngsters, and the awesome-looking Buffaloes.

Osborne finally had a healthy Brook Berringer to quarterback his team again. Berringer's fragile lung, partially collapsed in his first career start against Wyoming back on Oct. 1, was considered to be 100 percent once more.

But Berringer had never played in a game of this magnitude. How would the junior from Goodland, Kan., fill the shoes of two-year veteran Tommie Frazier against CU? Frazier always seemed to play big in big games.

Could the option game turn the corner after it had been put on the shelf for three games while Berringer was on the mend? And would Berringer hold up if Colorado forced him to scramble or play the option?

"I've seen Brook step it up a little bit in terms of focus of preparation," Osborne said. "I think he's always been pretty good about it, but when you know you're going to be carrying the load, you tend to pay closer attention to it. You tend to pick up the pace in practice, and I think he's done that."

It showed in this game.

Nebraska wasted no time turning what had promised to be a nail-biting, claw-to-the-end type of game into a nightmare, once again, for Kordell Stewart and his teammates.

Tight end Alford (88) zooms in for one of his career-high five catches (top left). (Below) Schlesinger (40) cuts wide on this 14-yard scoring play to put Nebraska on the board. (Right) Sieler (12) is good from 24 yards out for a 17-0 halftime lead.

Stewart, who had managed only an 8-of-28 passing performance (with three interceptions) in a 21-17 loss at Boulder in 1993, again was rattled by the Husker defense's harassment.

The Blackshirts played one of their most complete games of the year as they attacked everything Colorado had.

Offensively, Nebraska scored on four of its first six possessions. In doing so, the Huskers silenced the voices of critics who had said NU wouldn't be able to move the ball in this game as it had against the likes of Oklahoma State, Kansas State and Missouri.

The option game was back, running as though it had never missed a beat. The powerful Husker line added a few wrinkles to knock Colorado's exceptional defensive tackles off the ball. And Berringer's passing was on target and so well-timed that the Buffalo defense was kept guessing all afternoon.

Fullback Cory Schlesinger put the first points on the board for Nebraska in the opening drive; he ran the final 14 yards with 5:47 to play in the first quarter.

Tom Sieler kicked a 24-yard field goal six minutes into the second quarter. Clinton Childs covered the final 2 yards on a drive that ended with a touchdown 36 seconds before halftime. Berringer set up that score with three passes of 15, 15 and 16 yards to the tight ends and a 12-yarder to wingback Abdul Muhammad. In all, NU covered 73 yards to score.

Joel Wilks (76) was the unsung hero in Nebraska's '94 offensive line. This time, he disables one of the talented Buffaloes to make a hole for Phillips (1) on one of his 24 carries (103 yards).

The Husker Blackshirts have all the holes plugged even before Heisman Trophy winner Rashaan Salaam (19) can get the handoff from Colorado quarterback Kordell Stewart. Salaam still managed 134 yards (96 in the second half); he was the only back to get 100 yards against NU all year.

By halftime, Nebraska had a 17-0 lead and had out-yarded Colorado's powerful offense 234-89.

Kordell Stewart and company were struggling, due in large part to the lightning-quick defense they were facing. But Darin Erstad's punts were also a factor. He had the Buffaloes in the hole all game.

"The punt exchanges generally favored us quite a bit," Osborne said. "Field position, largely because of the kicking game, favored us. So when Colorado had to drive a long way, which they normally did, usually 80 or 85 yards against a good defense, they had a tough time doing it."

Stewart managed only 12-of-28 passing for 150 yards. No pass play covered more than 22 yards — the Huskers' speed closed any gaps in a hurry. Not that there were many gaps. Generally, every time a Buffalo offensive star headed downfield, he had a Nebraska defender in his pocket.

Stewart had few passing options and even fewer chances to pick out one of his gifted receivers.

"I think he was scared all day," NU linebacker Phil Ellis said of the Buffaloes' quarterback. "He was looking around a lot, and he didn't like what he saw. For three years, he hasn't done anything against us. This year, he was talking about how it was going to be different. We took that personally."

Nebraska didn't let Colorado convert on any of its 11 third-down plays nor any of its four tries on fourth down.

Defensive coordinator Charlie McBride said he was proud of the way his defense dominated; the defense held Colorado to its lowest point total since a 52-7 loss to Nebraska in 1992. He said it reminded him of the old Georgia "Junkyard Dogs" who had led that team to a national championship in 1980 on the strength of their dominating defense.

McBride said some of the pregame press clippings from Colorado had helped inspire his team. He said the fire in his players' eyes reminded him of when former Oklahoma State All-America running back Thurman Thomas boarded the NU bus before the Cowboys were to meet the Huskers and proclaimed that no one in the country could stop him.

"He got 7 yards that day," McBride beamed. "Kids don't like that very much."

Nebraska cornerback Barron Miles said that was true.

"Our defense was fed up with everyone saying we couldn't stop them," he said. "Colorado did everything we expected, but we were well-prepared."

The defense was developing into possibly the best Osborne had ever had as head coach. Although they allowed Wyoming to escape with 32 points on Oct. 1, in the four games that followed, Oklahoma State, Kansas State, Missouri and Colorado had combined for only 23.

(Above) Donta Jones (84) and Dwayne Harris (86) celebrate yet another sack of Kordell Stewart. Each got to the Colorado QB once, and Terry Connealy sacked him twice.

(Right) There is no doubt as to where Harris believes the Huskers should be ranked after their win over Colorado.

"For the last four games, it's played certainly right at that level," Osborne said of the best defense at Nebraska. "In 1984, we had a great defensive team. I think last year, down the stretch, we developed into a very, very good defensive team. Last year's team and this year's team kind of parallel each other in that we seem to get better as we go along on defense."

"We pounded away and punished them from the first snap until the last," linebacker Troy Dumas said.

He wasn't getting any argument from Colorado.

"They are a real tough defense," Salaam said. "They just play hard-nosed football."

Salaam, the nation's rushing leader, did become the first back to gain 100 yards on Nebraska this season when his 22 carries totaled 134. But then, he also went on to win the Heisman Trophy and top 2,000 yards for the year.

The Huskers showed new wrinkles for this game on defense, too. Two new blitzes and a few alignment changes helped keep the Buffaloes off guard.

"We put in quite a bit of new stuff," Osborne admitted. "Some we had worked on for a couple of weeks. Some we put in on Monday. We thought we had to change up some. They have pretty good people. We didn't want to come in with a pat hand."

Add in the speed factor of Nebraska's fastest defense ever, and Colorado had a problem, according to its coach.

"We didn't block the blitzes. We practiced for the things they were going to do, but maybe the speed was something we couldn't prepare for," McCartney said.

On the other side of the football for Nebraska, Berringer had his team prepared and moving behind the powerful offensive line.

Five minutes into the third quarter, he found tight end

Eric Alford on a 30-yard touchdown pass. It was 24-0.

"They found a way to make us look bad,"said Colorado defensive tackle Darius Holland. "They kicked us."

Although Colorado's defense obviously was geared to shut down the run, Berringer found his tight ends open all afternoon. Alford had five catches for 78 yards, Mark Gilman had four catches for another 46 and Muhammad added two catches from his wingback spot for 14 yards.

Alford later joked that he kept having to look at his jersey to see if he was playing for the right team —

Berringer called the tight ends' numbers on several pass plays.

"I had the same kind of reaction," Gilman said later with a laugh. "They just kept calling those plays for us. The coaches saw a characteristic of the Colorado defense. We thought, if the tight ends could get behind them, we could find a soft spot to sit down and, with Brook's throwing ability, to get us the ball. Fortunately, it worked well."

Thanks to his ball-control passing game, Berringer ended with 12 completions in 17 throws for 142 yards. He had one pass picked off, which led to Colorado's lone touchdown, a 6-yard run by Salaam with 1:06 left in the third quarter. Osborne and Berringer both admitted it was a bad read, the result of not picking up a defender in the area. But that's about all the young quarterback did wrong.

Nebraska also controlled the clock. By game's end, Nebraska had close to a 17-minute advantage in time of possession.

Colorado did hold the Nebraska running game to a season-low 203 total yards, although Lawrence Phillips covered over 100 yards for the ninth-straight game. He ended with 103 on 24 carries. Schlesinger added 65 yards on just eight tries.

But what pleased Nebraska most was showing the country that it was capable of winning big games without quarterback Tommie Frazier. There was more to this team than one big-play man. There were a bunch of them.

"I hope everyone is convinced now," Berringer said. "I think that I've put all doubts — if there were any left — aside. It doesn't seem like anything we've done so far has impressed anyone. But this was a big game, and we played so well. So it should help."

"It certainly was a satisfying win," Osborne said. "I think there were many who didn't think we would be able to do it. I'm sure there were very few who thought we would be able to beat Colorado by a fairly convincing margin. And frankly, I didn't either. I thought we could win. I expected to win. But I thought it would be close."

The convincing nature of the victory led to postgame interviews in which a fired-up bunch of Nebraska players announced exactly where they thought the Huskers should move in the national rankings.

"In my mind, considering the way we played, we deserve to be No. 1," said NU linebacker Donta Jones, who earned ABC Player-of-the-Game honors for NU with his seven tackles and a sack. "I know we've got a lot more believers now."

Linebacker Ed Stewart said there should no longer be any doubts. Nebraska should be ranked at the top.

Indeed, Nebraska jumped to No. 1 in *The Associated Press* poll and was a close second to Penn State in the *USA Today-CNN* coaches' poll.

"It just confirms what I've always said, that sportswriters know a lot

The goal posts came down in a jubilant post-game celebration. The excitement confirmed the importance of this matchup: Even the fans thought this game was BIG.

more than coaches," Osborne joked about the ratings. Earlier, he had commented that coaches might have a better handle on the polls because they see a lot of game films and likely study more teams as a result.

Then the coach had a little more fun, poking a good-natured barb at ESPN commentator Lee Corso, who had switched allegiance more than once while discussing his favorite teams during the season.

"I sound like Lee Corso," Osborne said with a chuckle. "I can flip-flop on this."

Osborne actually had been downplaying the importance of the polls all season and wasn't about to start jockeying for votes even after this win. He said he refused to lobby and would much prefer to win every-

one's approval with Nebraska's play.

"I guess the thing that is important is we're in position now that if we continue to play well, we have some things in our own hands," he said. "You'd like to be in a position where you could play for the whole thing at the end, or at least have a chance to. We're pleased that people have that much confidence in us."

But he wasn't going to be made nor broken by a No. 1 ranking, even at the end of the year.

"All we want to do is play well," Osborne said. "If people think we deserve to be No. 1, great. If not, then we've done all we can. The most important thing to me is [that] our team play well, and I feel good about how our team plays. That's the honest truth."

Scoring Summary

	1st Quarter	2nd Quarter	3rd Quarter	4th Quarter	Final
Nebraska	7	10	7	0	24
Colorado	0	0	7	0	7

NU - Cory Schlesinger 14-yard run (Tom Sieler kick), 5:47, Qtr. #1.
NU - Sieler 24-yard field goal, 9:01, Qtr. #2.
NU - Clinton Childs 2-yard run (Sieler kick), :36, Qtr. #2.
NU - Eric Alford 30-yard pass from Brook Berringer (Sieler kick), 10:42, Qtr. #3.
CU - Rashaan Salaam 6-yard run (Neil Voskeritchian kick), 1:06, Qtr. #3.

Team Statistics

	NU	CU
First downs	20	18
Rushing att.-yards	53-203	37-155
Passes	12-17-1	13-30-0
Passing yards	142	159
Total att.-yards	70-345	67-314
Returns-yards	1-9	3-7
Sacks by	4-28	0
Punts-average	6-38.3	6-38.3
Fumbles-lost	1-0	0-0
Penalties-yards	6-41	4-30
Time of poss.	38:24	21:36

Individual Leaders

Rushing:
NU: Lawrence Phillips 24-103-0; Cory Schlesinger 8-65-1; Clinton Childs 5-14-1.
CU: Rashaan Salaam 22-134-1; Kordell Stewart 14-24-0.
Passing:
NU: Brook Berringer 12-17-142-1.
CU: Stewart 12-28-150-0; Koy Detmer 1-2-9-0.
Receiving:
NU: Eric Alford 5-78-1; Mark Gilman 4-46-0; Abdul Muhammad 2-14-0.
CU: Michael Westbrook 6-80-0; Rae Carruth 2-28-0; Salaam 2-24-0.
Interceptions:
NU: None.
CU: Dalton Simmons 1-0.
Tackles (UT-AT-TT):
NU: Troy Dumas 8-3-11; Kareem Moss 6-1-7; Ed Stewart 3-4-7; Donta Jones 3-4-7; Doug Colman 2-5-7; Christian Peter 2-5-7.
CU: Matt Russell 5-13-18; Ted Johnson 6-10-16; T.J. Cunningham 5-2-7; Greg Jones 4-3-7.
Sacks:
NU: Terry Connealy 2-9; Dwayne Harris 1-12; Jones 1-7.
CU: None.

Nebraska
Kansas

45
17

The Blackshirts didn't let Osborne down — take it from KU quarterback Mark Williams.

Refocus. That was the primary objective on coach Tom Osborne's mind a week after the big win over Colorado. Now that Nebraska was ranked No. 1 in *The Associated Press* poll and second only to Penn State in the *USA Today-CNN* coaches' poll, the nation's focus was back on the Huskers (9-0). Could they continue to play winning football without Tommie Frazier, as they had done since the star quarterback was sidelined with blood clots after the Pacific game (Sept. 24)?

Luckily, Brook Berringer had suffered no ills in the game against Colorado and had played well while guiding the offense. His fragile lung, which had partially collapsed twice in the two games after he was given the quarterbacking duties, apparently had had time to heal. He was a whole man again for the first time since Oct. 1.

The convincing win against Colorado concerned Osborne, however. Coming back to earth was essential. Kansas had a good football team.

"We did talk," he said of the coaches and players. "We've still got several games to play, and you don't want to make any proclamation because things could change in a hurry.

"We played a fine defensive game against Colorado last year, and then down at Kansas, they banged us around pretty good. We just about didn't get the job done on either side of the ball," Osborne said.

In last season's Kansas-Nebraska matchup, unbeaten Nebraska barely escaped from Lawrence, Kan., with a 21-20 win. Frazier's 10-yard touchdown pass to tight end Gerald Armstrong with 8:20 remaining had enabled the Huskers to take the tenuous lead, and a two-point conversion pass attempt was foiled with 52 seconds left in the game.

(Right) Berringer shone against Kansas with 13-of-18 passing for 267 yards — one of the best passing performances in school history.

The Husker defense halts a very good Kansas ground attack. Very few opponents succeeded in running up the middle against the Blackshirts.

Osborne didn't want his team to fall into that trap again.

Berringer said the players didn't need the reminder. The Kansas escape wasn't so far back that anyone had trouble remembering. And, of course, they also recalled the upset at Iowa State in 1992, which had occurred after Nebraska walloped nationally ranked Colorado and Kansas on successive weekends.

No, the Huskers knew where their focus was, and it was on Kansas.

Berringer also was inspired by the comments of Colorado coach Bill McCartney. He had questioned Berringer's ability to throw to his wide receivers after the Husker junior threw nine times to tight ends in the 24-7 victory.

"He said we had to throw to our wide receivers, so that's what we did," Berringer said, grinning after he threw for 267 yards against the Jayhawks. He was 13-for-18 passing for the day, and six of those went to his wide receivers.

The passing yardage was the seventh-best in Husker history and was only 30 yards short of David Humm's school record of 297. It was the best individual Husker performance in 21 years.

"I was surprised they threw the ball as well as they did," Kansas coach Glen Mason said. "If you are able to stop the run, they are going to go to Berringer throwing the ball."

Osborne was surprised that Kansas hadn't picked up on the fact that Berringer could throw and throw well. Most defenses would have allowed for that, the coach said.

"You would have thought so, but Kansas came out and did some things. They were just keying on the running game," Osborne said. "There were several times when we were in certain formations, they were coming with an eight-man front and bringing a lot of people. With the speed we have at receiver, that's kind of hard to get away with."

Reggie Baul hauled in a 51-yard touchdown strike from Berringer just five minutes into the game. Tom Sieler had kicked a 35-yard field goal to begin Nebraska's scoring less than two minutes earlier.

Nebraska didn't score on its first possession but did on its next six. Big plays were the rule of the day.

Before the first quarter ended, Cory Schlesinger had stung the Jayhawks with a 40-yard TD jaunt.

"When the defense has to watch for our quarterback,

our I-back, our tight end and our wide receivers, things are going to be open for the fullback," Schlesinger said after he broke a tackle at the line and scampered to the end zone.

Then, in the second quarter, backup fullback Jeff Makovicka scored on an 8-yard run, and Lawrence Phillips ran in from 4 yards out. Berringer also hooked up with Clester Johnson on a 64-yard touchdown pass.

"With eight men on the line of scrimmage, we knew we were going to get some big plays deep," Berringer said.

Berringer had 249 yards passing by halftime.

Not bad considering how Osborne had felt when he brought his team out of the tunnel to start the game.

"I didn't have the feeling before the game [that] we were real focused," Osborne admitted. "I was a little worried. It's just a little hard to play a game like Colorado, when everybody's focused on it nationally for TV, then come out the next week. I thought Kansas had enough horses [that] they could beat us."

Kansas did, too, until Berringer lit it up in the air.

"I don't think this is the type of team that will let down," Berringer said. "We're on a mission, and we'll do whatever it takes to win. Every game is the national championship for us, and we're playing with that attitude."

Osborne said it was important to get off to a good start.

"Had we given them a lot of daylight and let them feel they could win, it might have been tough," he said.

Kansas, after all, had returned tailback June Henley, who rushed for 148 yards against Nebraska in 1993, and quarterback Asheiki Preston, who, in that one-point loss to NU, hit 13 of 19 passes for 118 yards without an interception. This was a team, Osborne figured, that had the potential to make an afternoon miserable.

But Berringer made his coach feel more comfortable. He also added bounce to his receivers' steps. They were

So many Huskers, so few Jayhawks. The swarming Blackshirts showed the nation what a speedy defense can do.

Kareem Moss (29) had a big day with 11 tackles, including one sack.

expecting the ball in the air.

"We had a stronger option game with Tommie. Now it's a passing game," said Baul. The quick-hitting potential is still there. It just comes from a different source.

"I think it's almost the same, except now it's through the air instead of Tommie making the long run," Baul said. "(Defenses) have to play a little more honest. They can't just worry about bringing 10 people up to the line of scrimmage. Now, they're going to have to play everybody more honestly. We can do more things offensively by getting them off our backs."

Even Osborne was beginning to enjoy this passing game.

"I feel very comfortable that if we had to go out and throw it 35 or 40 times, we'd be pretty effective," said the coach who had cooked up a steady diet of option football during the past 15 years. "I don't want to do that if we can help it because I don't think, in the long haul, we'd be quite as effective as doing what we're doing. But if we had to, I think we could do it pretty well."

Kansas tried to play catch-up after a dismal offensive start. Safety Tony Veland and cornerback Tyrone Williams intercepted passes on the Jayhawks' first three offensive plays. Veland's led to Sieler's field goal. Williams' interception gave NU the ball for a drive that ended with the Baul touchdown catch.

Then KU (5-4) seemed to settle down somewhat.

Jeff McCord kicked a 41-yard field goal in the first quarter, and June Henley scored on a 6-yard run in the second. But Kansas still found itself down 38-10 by intermission.

"We gave up way too many big plays," Mason said. "Obviously, when you go against a team averaging 370 yards rushing, you have to stack it up against them. When you do that, you leave yourself vulnerable in other areas. They hit a couple of big plays that really hurt us."

Nebraska hadn't seen long passing like this since the days of All-Americans David Humm and Vince Ferragamo. Those were the throwing days of Osborne's balanced offenses. Since the late-1970s, option has been king at NU.

But, as Osborne observed, Kansas was just setting the table for Berringer.

"They crowded the run," the coach said. "Their secondary was really supporting quickly, so we thought we had to get them off our backs. We threw the ball long a little more than usual and generally threw it effectively."

Berringer was effective enough that Mason and his assistant coaches tried to make some adjustments in the second half. That's when Nebraska's ground game took over.

The Huskers rolled up 201 yards rushing in the second half.

Held to 35 yards on 11 carries in the first two quarters, Phillips broke loose for 118 yards and his second touchdown in the third quarter alone. He had one big run that didn't end in the end zone and a 22-yarder that did. After the TD, the score was 45-10 with 6:32

remaining in the period.

Phillips ended with 153 yards on 21 carries, his 10th-straight 100-yard game. He also had enough yardage to break Bobby Reynolds' sophomore rushing record for Nebraska. Reynolds, an All-American, ran for 1,342 yards in 1950.

By this time, Mason was scratching his head.

"Just because you commit extra guys to the run doesn't mean you are going to stop it against these guys. They are awfully good, but when haven't they been good?" he asked. "You don't average 370 yards a game rushing unless you have an awfully good offensive line. They have an army of guys that look good."

Scoring Summary

	1st Quarter	2nd Quarter	3rd Quarter	4th Quarter	Final
Nebraska	24	14	7	0	45
Kansas	3	7	0	7	17

NU - Tom Sieler 35-yard field goal, 11:53, Qtr. #1.
NU - Reggie Baul 51-yard pass from Brook Berringer (Sieler kick), 10:19, Qtr. #1.
KU - Jeff McCord 41-yard field goal, 8:11, Qtr. #1.
NU - Lawrence Phillips 4-yard run (Sieler kick), 6:00, Qtr. #1.
NU - Cory Schlesinger 40-yard run (Sieler kick), 2:24, Qtr. #1.
NU - Jeff Makovicka 8-yard run (Sieler kick), 11:07, Qtr. #2.
KU - June Henley 6-yard run (McCord kick), 6:32, Qtr. #2.
NU - Clester Johnson 64-yard pass from Berringer (Sieler kick), 3:41, Qtr. #2.
NU - Phillips 22-yard run (Sieler kick), 6:32, Qtr. #3.
KU - L.T. Levine 1-yard run (McCord kick), 7:01, Qtr. #4.

Team Statistics

	NU	KU
First downs	24	12
Rushing att.-yards	49-336	45-141
Passes	13-18-0	8-23-2
Passing yards	267	129
Total att.-yards	67-603	68-270
Returns-yards	7-39	1-26
Sacks by	3-18	2-16
Punts-average	3-49.0	6-39.5
Fumbles-lost	2-1	2-0
Penalties-yards	4-26	2-11
Time of poss.	28:44	31:16

Individual Leaders

Rushing:
NU: Lawrence Phillips 21-153-2; Cory Schlesinger 4-49-1; Damon Benning 6-45-0; Brian Schuster 3-25-0.
KU: June Henley 16-86-1; L.T. Levine 13-42-1; Van Davis 1-13-0.
Passing:
NU: Brook Berringer 13-18-267-0.
KU: Asheiki Preston 7-18-107-2; Mark Williams 1-4-22-0.
Receiving:
NU: Phillips 4-11-0; Reggie Baul 3-106-1; Brendan Holbein 2-12-0; Clester Johnson 1-64-1.
KU: Hosea Friday 4-60-0; Rodney Harris 1-43-0.
Interceptions:
NU: Tony Veland 1-0-0; Tyrone Williams 1-0-0.
KU: None.
Tackles (UT-AT-TT):
NU: Kareem Moss 5-6-11; Ryan Terwilliger 1-6-7; Phil Ellis 3-3-6; Grant Wistrom 2-4-6.
KU: Gerald McBurrows 4-6-10; Don Davis 3-5-8; Sylvester Wright 3-5-8.
Sacks:
NU: Wistrom 1-8; Moss 1-5; Doug Colman 1-5.
KU: Brett McGraw 1-11; Wright 1-5.

Nebraska
Iowa State

28
12

Iowa State

He was tense, yes, but he had no reason to panic.
Berringer threw for nearly 200 yards against a fired-up Cyclone squad.

Nebraska coach Tom Osborne, whose team was now No. 1 in both *The Associated Press* and *USA Today-CNN* polls, couldn't have created a better ambush himself than what awaited his 10-0 team in Ames, Iowa. The attention his team was receiving as the No. 1 squad in the nation was bad enough. Now, Iowa State was being portrayed as the patsy of the week. Worse yet, the Cyclones somewhat fit the picture: In nine games, they had recorded no wins and appeared to have little chance of claiming any.

The 0-8-1 Cyclone defense ranked 105th out of 107 Division I-A teams against the run, 101st in passing efficiency defense and 96th in scoring. That defense would be expected to put a lid on Nebraska's offense, one which led the nation in rushing; featured Brook Berringer, the quarterback with the best efficiency rating in the Big Eight; was third in the nation in total offense and scored an average of 39.4 points per game.

On paper, it seemed that this would be an ugly game.

But coach Jim Walden, under pressure, announced his resignation at the beginning of the week. And that sentiment-filled development was icing on the ready-made emotions of the team's geographic makeup: There were 18 Nebraskans on that Iowa State squad.

"They've got nine or 10 or 11 Nebraska players who have played key roles for them," Osborne said. "I'm sure those guys are certainly going to give it everything they've got. They always do. There's a little pride at stake here."

Plus, there was evidence of strong Cyclone efforts in the past. In 21 years, only Oklahoma and Missouri have beaten Osborne-coached teams more than Iowa State, which owned three wins versus NU, the same number as Colorado.

(Right) Harris fights through a block — an example of how the defense worked to shut down the Iowa State running game.

(Above) Phillips (1) breaks loose for a 21-yard TD run to clinch the win. (Right) Ellis (41) catches up with ISU receiver Geoff Turner.

But there was pride at stake for Nebraska, too. Many players vividly remembered the 1992 game. A confident Husker team, ranked No. 7 and fresh from demolishing nationally ranked Colorado and Kansas on successive weekends, had rolled casually into Ames. But the Huskers had come crashing back to earth when a lightly regarded Iowa State team handed them a 19-10 Cyclone upset.

It was the first and only time an Osborne-coached team had lost to a team that finished the regular season with a losing record.

But this year's setup sounded all too familiar.

Nebraska opened the game as expected. The Huskers used their time-consuming ground attack to grind out an 80-yard, 7:26-minute drive, capped by Lawrence Phillips' 1-yard run.

But a pair of Husker turnovers helped Iowa State rally; the Cyclones fought back to 7-6 with a pair of Ty Stewart field goals. Stewart, one of the native Nebraskans, scored on kicks from 35 and 37 yards out.

A 38-yard touchdown pass from Brook Berringer to Abdul Muhammad with 57 seconds on the clock made it 14-6 at the half.

Nebraska was not overpowering on the scoreboard,

but the score was deceiving when the statistics were considered. Nebraska had 202 total yards; Iowa State had only 55.

Still, only eight points separated the nation's No. 1 team from a team that had yet to win.

"It's hard to keep 1992 out of your mind," Berringer said. He had not been a member of that traveling squad two years ago, but he remembered what he'd heard as he listened to the game on the radio.

"I think I was out quail hunting, listening to the game," Berringer recalled. "I just remember getting back in the truck and being a little surprised by the score."

The halftime score this year was a surprise, too. Even more unnerving was the score at the end of the third quarter.

Quarterback Todd Doxzon, another Nebraska product, threw a 58-yard pass to Calvin Branch just over 11 minutes into the third quarter. His run attempt on the extra point conversion failed, but the Cyclones were down just 14-12 heading into the fourth quarter.

"Two points and we had confidence," Doxzon said.

"I thought we were in the game going into the fourth quarter," said Branch. "I don't think they were expect-

ing to be up [by only] two that late in the game."

"You could see our confidence grow as the game went on," said ISU linebacker Matt Nitchie, another of the Nebraska imports. "After we cut it to two, everybody was real excited. It reminded me of two years ago. I don't think Nebraska overlooked us. I just don't think they expected us to play that hard for four quarters."

"I was thinking about 1992 all week," Nebraska defensive tackle and co-captain Terry Connealy said. "I had a real good feeling after that first drive. We need to give (the Cyclones) a lot of credit. It was obvious they remembered 1992. They were real pumped."

Damon Benning damaged that Iowa State confidence, however,

when he scored on a 6-yard run following a 28-yard option by Berringer.

Benning admitted that he wasn't thinking about 1992. He was thinking about Florida State in Miami.

"I think the only flashback I had was to not get beat, and that flashback came from the Orange Bowl. We didn't want to let anybody take anything away from us that we worked so hard for," he said.

It would have been easy for Nebraska to wilt under the pressure of being No. 1, as well as the overwhelming favorite, and allow Iowa State to grasp the momentum for the fourth quarter. But Berringer would have nothing to do with that.

"I think the biggest thing for me in this situation was to just show the rest of the team poise and leadership," he said. "It's easy for some people to go into a game like this and start to panic when it gets as close as it was."

Benning's TD made it a 21-12 game with 12:09 to play. But Iowa State wasn't quite finished.

Doxzon hit Geoff Turner for a 32-yard touchdown, but the play was called back by a holding penalty. Iowa State never came close to scoring again.

"One big play could have changed this game dramatically," Doxzon said. "I think that was the one. We

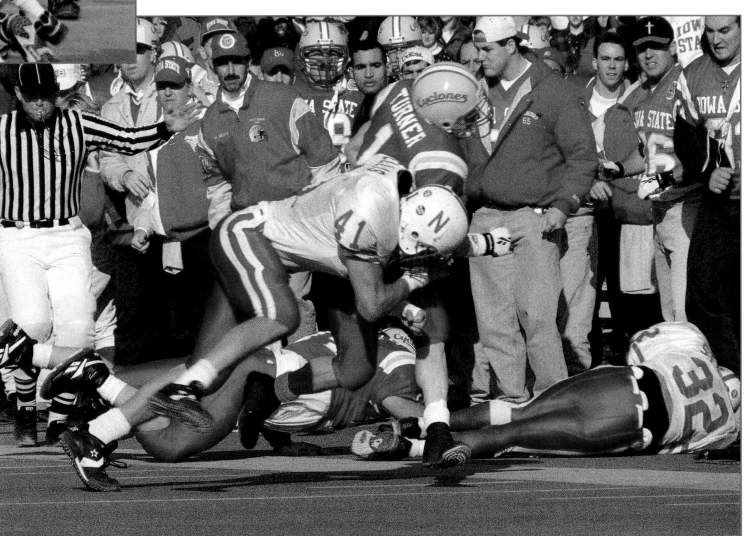

didn't have the gas to hold up much after that."

"The biggest play for us was calling the touchdown back," Walden said. "Who knows whether it was right or wrong, but it hurt. We were running out of energy. When you run out of energy against that team, they run you over."

Phillips, who was held to 63 yards on 27 carries through three quarters, rushed for 120 in the fourth quarter on nine tries. The sophomore I-back credited much of his success to a change of shoes. He had slipped four times on the artificial surface before he borrowed reserve lineman Bryan Pruitt's shoes for the final 15 minutes.

"I wanted to stick to my other shoes because they're more comfortable," Phillips said. "But coach wanted me to change them, so I did. They seemed to do the job."

Phillips broke loose on a 61-yard run to Iowa State's 6-yard line midway through the fourth quarter only to have Nitchie catch him and strip the ball. The ball rolled into the end zone, and the Cyclones recovered for a touchback.

Outside linebackers Dwayne Harris and Donta Jones then recorded two of Nebraska's six sacks, throwing Doxzon for losses of 7 and 8 yards and forcing a punt.

The Huskers marched down the field on their next possession, and Phillips got the final 21 yards for a touchdown with 1:25 to play.

Nebraska finished with 478 yards of offense.

"We should be able to go out and blow people off the ball right from the get-go, and I'm not really sure why we didn't do it," Berringer said. "The main thing was that we stayed with it. Nobody panicked, and nobody gave up."

Berringer ended with 11-of-18 passing for 193 yards. He also had 61 yards rushing on nine carries.

Phillips, however, was again the workhorse with 36 carries for 183 yards. His first carry gave him 2,000 career yards rushing for NU. He was also the leading receiver with four catches for 40 yards.

"I was trying a little too much early in the game," he said. "Once we started passing, it opened their defense up. They were hyped up. They weren't going to give up after that first seven."

"I guess you could say this was our bowl game, and we played

148

like that," ISU linebacker Marc Lillibridge said. "I think we showed this team has fight and spirit, and that this team can play with the big boys."

Osborne said that if Iowa State had played like that against everyone, they wouldn't have been 0-9-1.

"It was a very emotional situation," Osborne said. "It doesn't surprise me that Iowa State played a very good football game. Looking at film, I saw Iowa State has become a much better football team in the last couple of weeks."

One of the reasons for that improvement was a healthy Doxzon, a quick-footed sophomore who had missed several games or parts of games with a variety of injuries. Several other Cyclones also returned for the Nebraska game.

But the Walden situation had provided a lot of emotion, too. He had not only submitted his resignation, effective at the end of the season, but was suspended by the Big Eight office for the Cyclones' last scheduled game at Colorado the following week.

"I'm tired," said Walden, who was a former assistant coach with Osborne at Nebraska under Bob Devaney. "It's been an emotional roller coaster this year."

The Nebraska game was almost a great going-away present from his team.

"That is really a good football team," Walden said of Nebraska. "I am proud of the way that we played against that good football team. When you play a team that demands as much as they do, you must have everyone out there working hard. We played well."

Scoring Summary

	1st Quarter	2nd Quarter	3rd Quarter	4th Quarter	Final
Nebraska	7	7	0	14	28
Iowa State	3	3	6	0	12

NU - Lawrence Phillips 1-yard run (Tom Sieler kick), 7:34, Qtr. #1.
ISU - Ty Stewart 35-yard field goal, 4:04, Qtr. #1.
ISU - Stewart 37-yard field goal, 12:04, Qtr. #2.
NU - Abdul Muhammad 38-yard pass from Brook Berringer (Sieler kick), :57, Qtr. #2.
ISU - Calvin Branch 58-yard pass from Todd Doxzon (run failed), 3:42, Qtr. #3.
NU - Damon Benning 6-yard run (Sieler kick), 12:09, Qtr. #4.
NU - Phillips 21-yard run (Sieler kick), 1:25, Qtr. #4.

Team Statistics

	NU	**ISU**
First downs	21	11
Rushing att.-yards	56-285	43-62
Passes	11-18-1	8-13-0
Passing yards	193	151
Total att.-yards	74-478	56-213
Returns-yards	3-3	4-7
Sacks by	6-33	0
Punts-average	5-41.6	8-45.1
Fumbles-lost	2-1	1-0
Penalties-yards	5-55	5-50
Time of poss.	33:35	26:25

Individual Leaders

Rushing:
NU: Lawrence Phillips 36-183-2; Brook Berringer 9-61-0; Cory Schlesinger 7-24-0.
ISU: Rodney Guggenheim 6-32-0; Troy Davis 4-10-0.
Passing:
NU: Berringer 11-18-193-1.
ISU: Todd Doxzon 8-13-151-0.
Receiving:
NU: Phillips 4-40-0; Reggie Baul 3-49-0; Abdul Muhammad 2-52-1.
ISU: Geoff Turner 3-31-0; Calvin Branch 2-63-1.
Interceptions:
NU: None.
ISU: Cedric Linwood 1-0-0.
Tackles (UT-AT-TT):
NU: Terry Connealy 4-9-13; Ed Stewart 7-6-13; Christian Peter 4-7-11; Kareem Moss 4-3-7.
ISU: Matt Nitchie 1-17-18; Troy Petersen 3-11-14; Tim Sanders 0-14-14; Michael Cooper 0-12-12.
Sacks:
NU: Stewart 2-9; Donta Jones 1-8; Dwayne Harris 1-7; Connealy 1-6; Peter 1-3.
ISU: None.

Nebraska
Oklahoma

13
3

Graham (54) snaps to Berringer and searches for his blocking assignment.
Rushing yardage would not come easily for Nebraska today.

A trip to Norman, Okla., the day after Thanksgiving for the traditional meeting of Oklahoma and Nebraska generally culminates in an all-out effort from two powerful and proud football teams. The emotional levels are always at a peak. But the sentiment reading for this game may have soared off the chart when Gary Gibbs announced that he was resigning his position as Sooner coach.

It was the second consecutive game in which Nebraska would meet a team that was playing its final game for its head coach and also its last home game for its seniors.

"We know [that] going down to Oklahoma is going to be a tough game," said Husker Ed Stewart, one of three finalists for the Butkus Award for the nation's top linebacker. "I can remember my last home game, how much of an emotional game it was for us seniors, so I expect it to be the same for them."

"Generally speaking, players are loyal to their coach and want to do well for him," NU coach Tom Osborne said. "The last thing they can do for Gary Gibbs is play well Friday, and I think they will. I think it was the same way with the Iowa State players. Even though they had another game to play, I thought our game over there was kind of their deal, a salute to Jim (Walden) or however you want to put it. They gave great effort."

Osborne expected the same from the Sooners. Besides, this was the Oklahoma-Nebraska game.

Perhaps NU linebacker coach Kevin Steele put it best.

"I think the people who really know football, know the Alabama-Tennessee, the Florida-Florida State, the Nebraska-Oklahoma, that's big-time football," Steele said. "The recruits, when you talk to them on the phone, it's rather ironic. There may be people who ask 'Coach, who you got this week?' even in some of the bigger weeks.

(Right) NU tackle Zatechka locks horns with a Sooner defender in the battle for line dominance.

150

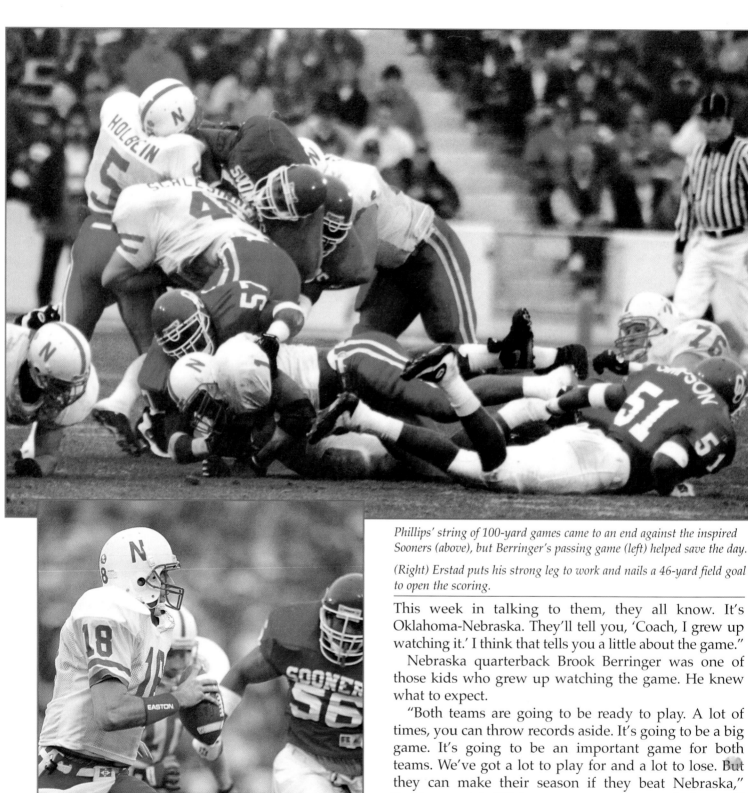

Phillips' string of 100-yard games came to an end against the inspired Sooners (above), but Berringer's passing game (left) helped save the day.

(Right) Erstad puts his strong leg to work and nails a 46-yard field goal to open the scoring.

This week in talking to them, they all know. It's Oklahoma-Nebraska. They'll tell you, 'Coach, I grew up watching it.' I think that tells you a little about the game."

Nebraska quarterback Brook Berringer was one of those kids who grew up watching the game. He knew what to expect.

"Both teams are going to be ready to play. A lot of times, you can throw records aside. It's going to be a big game. It's going to be an important game for both teams. We've got a lot to play for and a lot to lose. But they can make their season if they beat Nebraska," Berringer said. "We've got to come out and play well and finish up with the Big Eight championship to go on to the national championship."

Berringer wasn't expecting anything less than the best from the Sooners, particularly in light of the Gibbs situation.

"I think they'll be a team that's more inspired, kind of like Iowa State was," he said. "That's the way we expect them to come out. We think they'll come out and play hard and try to win one for the coach, with that attitude. We'll run into their best effort."

Berringer cuts back behind a Wiegert block on one of his 15 carries. His 1-yard TD clinched the game in the fourth quarter.

The Sooners found the Blackshirts to be worthy foes. Dumas (4), here in hot pursuit, was one of the reasons why OU gained just 108 total yards. After the half, the Sooners managed just 47 yards.

Nebraska (11-0) was inspired, too. Although ranked No. 1 in both polls and the owner of an uncontested fourth-straight Big Eight championship as well as another trip to the Orange Bowl, the national championship still was hanging in the balance. A loss to a 6-4 Sooner team would dash every dream the NU players had built since they started working out the day after last season's heartbreaking 18-16 loss to No. 1 Florida State in the Orange Bowl.

Yes, there was plenty to play for when two of the nation's top defenses took the field to stop two of the country's most solid offenses.

The teams played a scoreless first quarter and traded field goals in the second. Husker Darin Erstad scored first on a 46-yarder about a minute into the period.

"Colorado obviously had a good defense. We did some things that hurt them. We were prepared to do the same things against Oklahoma, but they're definitely one of the best defenses we've played this year," Berringer said.

The Sooners were stuffing the Nebraska running game. The Huskers lost 10 yards in the second quarter. And Oklahoma's pass rush was finding a way to Berringer; they sacked him twice. At halftime, NU's total offensive output was just 63 yards.

"We felt coming in that the strong part of Oklahoma's team was its defense," Osborne said. "We were worried about moving the ball because their tackles and inside linebackers were outstanding.

"Oklahoma has some good players. They were smoked up with emotion," Osborne said. "They gave great effort. Gary Gibbs is a good defensive coach, and I am sure he had a lot to do with the way their defense played today. His preparation today was outstanding."

Oklahoma's Scott Blanton tied the game at 3-3 with a 25-yarder just 2:19 before the half. It was Blanton's second field goal try of the quarter. Earlier, he had had one blocked by Nebraska cornerback Barron Miles. That was Miles' fourth block of the season.

The Huskers also had a pretty good defense; they allowed Oklahoma just 132 yards in total offense in the first half.

Sooner fullback Jerald Moore, who had returned to the squad from the injured list and had a big game the week prior to the Nebraska matchup, was now finding the running yards tough to come by. And OU quarterback Garrick McGee was having just as tough a time as Berringer. Kareem Moss intercepted one of McGee's passes on the Sooners' second play of the game.

Oklahoma succeeded in driving inside the Husker 10-yard line once in the half but had to settle for Blanton's field goal.

Regrouping at halftime provided some relief for the Nebraska offense. It remained tough going, but Tom Sieler put the Huskers ahead with his 26-yard field goal with 7:03 left in the period.

Then Berringer marched NU downfield late in the quarter and carried the final yard for the game's only touchdown with 13:25 to play.

He then turned Nebraska's offense up a notch. After completing only 4 of 11 passes for 23 yards and rushing for only 2 yards more in the first half, the junior from Goodland, Kan., hit 9 of 12 passes for 143 yards and had 46 yards rushing on nine carries.

"There were a lot of breakdowns in the first half," Berringer said. "And I'll take full credit for them. But other than the interception at the end, I think I did better the second half."

His improvement was crucial because the running game was going nowhere.

Nebraska's rushing attack, the best in the nation, was the target of the Sooner defense. The Huskers managed only 136 yards rushing for the game. I-back Lawrence Phillips' 11-game string of 100-yard efforts was snapped. He ended with just 50 yards on 21 carries.

"As far as what they do, they are the best," said Sooner defender David Campbell. "We did what we had to do to stop the running game, but it was the passing that hurt us."

Berringer ran 28 yards on an option and hit wingback Abdul Muhammad on a 24-yard pass to get Nebraska into position for Sieler's field goal. Berringer and Muhammad teamed up again for 44 yards that were key to an 82-yard drive that ended with Berringer's TD run.

"We were frustrated on not moving the ball," Nebraska All-American tackle and Outland Trophy winner Zach Wiegert said. "They've got great personnel and a great defense. They gave 100 percent all day long, and you have to give them credit."

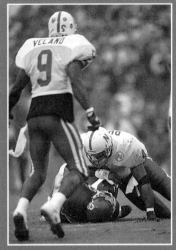

The Defense Rises

For years, the most dominant aspect of coach Tom Osborne's football teams has been the offense. But after Nebraska's 13-3 win over Oklahoma, Osborne could finally lean back and declare that his defense was capable of winning a national championship.

"I was real proud of our defense," Osborne said. "I thought they carried the day."

Of course, Oklahoma played an inspired defensive game of its own — as it always seems to against Nebraska. Even the powerful Husker offensive line couldn't bully the Sooners. NU managed just 136 yards on 50 rushing plays, and I-back Lawrence Phillips failed to get 100 yards for the first time all season. The Sooners had snapped Phillips' streak of 100-yard games at 11.

But the Blackshirt defense was a sight to see. Oklahoma managed just 47 total yards the second half and only minus 5 in the fourth quarter. OU quarterback Garrick McGee was sacked three times and intercepted once.

Linebacker Ed Stewart and tackle Terry Connealy, the co-captains on defense, made the most of their motto — If an opponent can't score, it can't win — in the Oklahoma game. But throughout the season, they did their best to ensure that their opponent never scored — particularly if the game was on the line.

In the end, the Sooners experienced what many other teams before them had when faced with these Nebraska defenders: They were unable to score in the fourth quarter. Of all the Big Eight teams, only Kansas and Missouri managed to score against the Husker defense. And those scores hardly counted, considering the fact that both games had been blowouts until Nebraska sent in its reserves to finish the games. Overall, the Husker defense never allowed any foe more than eight points in the final 15 minutes.

Nebraska had served notice: The fourth quarter belonged to the Big Red.

Even Miami couldn't argue with that.

*Wiegert (72) is more than a handful for David Campbell (59) and opposing defenders,
but the Sooners had a big day, too. NU gained only 136 rushing yards.*

"Brook's a good passer, and we knew he could help out," Wiegert said.

But the Huskers had Tommie Frazier suited up on the sidelines, just in case. The junior star quarterback had been cleared to play after nine weeks on medication. A blood-thinning medication was used to rid him of the recurring blood clots that had put him on the sidelines since late September.

Osborne admitted that he had looked at Frazier a few times. But he stuck with Berringer.

"It wasn't Brook's problem," the coach said of the offense's struggles. "He was doing a good job."

So was the Husker defense. The Sooners managed just 47 total yards in the second half and only minus 5 yards in the fourth quarter. McGee was sacked three

times, and Miles picked off another of his passes.

"I was real proud of our defense," Osborne said. "I thought they carried the day."

"It was a true defensive struggle," said Nebraska linebacker Troy Dumas, who had a team-leading 12 tackles. "The best defense was going to win the game."

"We felt we had to win the game on defense," teammate Stewart added. "We knew if we could hold them, our offense could score and we could come out on top."

"A game like this comes down to a few good plays, and Nebraska is the one who made those plays," Gibbs said. "We played them well. We knew it had to be low-scoring. You have to credit Nebraska because they controlled the ball so well."

One would have thought that clinching a fourth-straight trip to the Orange Bowl as Big Eight champs would have resulted in bedlam in the Nebraska locker room. Instead, there was surprising calm.

"It's not time to cut loose yet," Dumas explained. "All the work we've been doing has been toward one goal, the national championship."

"Sure, we're happy to be Big Eight champions," Wiegert added. "But this is our fourth Big Eight championship in a row. We're looking for more."

Concentration. Osborne always closely watches every move from the sidelines.

Scoring Summary

	1st Quarter	2nd Quarter	3rd Quarter	4th Quarter	Final
Nebraska	0	3	3	7	13
Oklahoma	0	3	0	0	3

NU-Darin Erstad 46-yard field goal, 14:11, Qtr. #2.
OU-Scott Blanton 25-yard field goal, 2:19, Qtr. #2.
NU-Tom Sieler 26-yard field goal, 7:03, Qtr. #3.
NU-Brook Berringer 1-yard run (Sieler kick), 13:25, Qtr. #4.

Team Statistics

	NU	OU
First downs	18	10
Rushing att.-yards	50-136	32-108
Passes	13-23-1	6-18-2
Passing yards	166	71
Total att.-yards	73-302	50-179
Returns-yards	3-12	3-29
Sacks by	3-17	2-24
Punts-average	5-47.0	7-38.0
Fumbles-lost	2-0	0-0
Penalties-yards	4-28	5-35
Time of poss.	36:48	23:12

Individual Leaders

Rushing:
NU: Lawrence Phillips 21-50-0; Brook Berringer 15-48-1; Cory Schlesinger 3-11-0.
OU: Jerald Moore 15-71-0; Garrick McGee 5-20-0.
Passing:
NU: Berringer 13-23-166-1.
OU: McGee 6-18-71-2.
Receiving:
NU: Abdul Muhammad 5-98-0; Phillips 3-24-0; Mark Gilman 2-23-0.
OU: Albert Hall 3-51-0; Michael McDaniel 2-11-0.
Interceptions:
NU: Barron Miles 1-0-0; Kareem Moss 1-0-0.
OU: Wendell Davis 1-20-0.
Tackles (UT-AT-TT):
NU: Troy Dumas 9-3-12; Christian Peter 5-4-9; Donta Jones 6-2-8; Phil Ellis 3-5-8; Dwayne Harris 1-5-6.
OU: Tyrell Peters 7-2-9; Anthony Fogle 5-2-7; Broderick Simpson 5-2-7.
Sacks:
NU: Peter 1-9; Terry Connealy 1-5; Jones 1-3.
OU: Peters 1-12; Davis 1-12.

Nebraska
Miami

24
17

MIAMI

Frazier, back at the controls after an eight-game absence, gets the Husker option attack going full speed.

Miami wasn't the only team to show up for the Orange Bowl on New Year's night with an attitude. The third-ranked Hurricanes were their normal brash and abrasive selves, ran through their pregame smoke with helmets held high, elicited screams from their partisan crowd and played confidently at home.

Miami had lost only once in this stadium in more than 60 games. The singular disappointment occurred when Washington stunned the Canes 38-20 in the third game of the '94 season. The loss snapped a Miami home winning streak that had stretched back 58 games.

Nebraska had quite a different "stadium" story to tell. Its history against Miami in the Orange Bowl was not good: three meetings, three losses. The first was on Jan. 1, 1984, in a setting similar to that of the '94 championship game.

A 12-0 Nebraska team entered that game ranked No. 1 and favored to win against a No. 5 Miami team coached by Howard Schnellenberger. Everyone figured it was coach Tom Osborne's year to win the title. After all, he had Heisman Trophy-winning I-back Mike Rozier, Lombardi- and Outland-winning guard Dean Steinkuhler and All-Americans Turner Gill at quarterback and Irving Fryar at wide receiver. The Huskers, despite rewriting NU and NCAA record books with their offensive talents, came up short 31-30 in that one.

But this Husker team was different from any Miami had seen before. It was a squad that had learned in an 18-16 heartbreaking loss to national champion Florida State in the Orange Bowl the year before that it could play with the Florida big boys on their own turf.

(Right) Connealy led the defense by example, and tackles such as this one shut Miami down when it counted.

Phillips (1) skillfully picks his way through the nation's No. 1 defense as Wiegert slows a trio of Hurricanes.

The 1994 edition of yet another top-ranked Husker squad entered this Orange Bowl with its own attitude, inspiring music that created heart-pounding anticipation for the home crowds in Lincoln during the season, and a belief that it was the better team.

Still on their backs was the weight of a seven-game losing streak in the bowls and media skepticism about whether Nebraska could get over the hump and win a big bowl game in the South against a homestate team. But they were irritated by pre-bowl talk and reminders of the biggest point spread of any bowl (which favored the talented Florida State team a year ago), and the Big Red players knew they could clench their teeth and play with anybody. There was no backing off, not with these guys.

It was the first time in recent bowl history that the Huskers were favored slightly to win. The near miss against Florida State served notice that the Huskers had returned to the national championship levels that had been their normal perch through much of the 1970s and '80s.

Byron Bennett's field goal try in the final seconds of the 1994 Orange Bowl (it sailed wide left) nearly gave Osborne his first national title. Instead, Bobby Bowden won his first after so many close calls at Florida State.

But the loss changed Nebraska's attitude. The Big Red was done being pushed around by the likes of Miami

and Florida State in bowl games. The Huskers now could match those teams with speed and power.

A 12-0 Nebraska team took the field that Sunday night against 10-1 Miami with the nation watching. Tommie Frazier had returned to start at quarterback, his first action since blood clots in his leg had sidelined him on Sept. 24. Backup Brook Berringer, who guided the team to a 7-0 record in games he started as Frazier's backup, was waiting in the wings. He, too, would play. Osborne had promised.

The much-debated quarterbacking situation was not finalized for the public until a few days before the game, when Osborne said Frazier's performance in the last pre-bowl scrimmage had proved he was back at full stride. He would need to be against the nation's top defense.

Miami's defense had proved fatal before in the Orange Bowl. The No. 2 Canes stopped the sixth-ranked Huskers 23-3 in the 1989 game. No. 1 Miami then blanked an 11th-ranked Nebraska team 22-0 in the 1992 Orange Bowl.

This time, the Canes were No. 1 in the nation against the pass, tops in total defense and points allowed and No. 7 against the run. The longest run Miami had allowed all season was 21 yards.

Nebraska's offense was tops in the nation in rushing, No. 5 in total offense and No. 6 in scoring. A huge offensive line combined speed and power to open gaping holes for a trio of gifted running backs, led by All-Big Eight I-back Lawrence Phillips and fullback Cory Schlesinger.

Cane tackle Warren Sapp — a first-team All-American, Heisman Trophy finalist and Lombardi Trophy winner — was a force with which to reckon. But he wasn't the only one. Everybody who slipped on those orange, green and white jerseys could run.

"Nebraska hasn't seen a defense like ours before," cornerback Chad Wilson bragged before the game.

"Speed rules, baby," added strong safety Malcolm Pearson, who rattled off the list of players who ran 40-yard dashes with sprinter speed.

But this time, as Osborne and his staff noted, Nebraska had a defense with speed of its own. That fact was not lost on Miami coach Dennis Erickson, who said this squad was unlike any Husker team he had seen before.

Unfortunately, the game didn't start as Nebraska had hoped. The Huskers found themselves trailing 10-0 in the first quarter after the Canes came up with big plays. Dane Prewitt kicked a 44-yard field goal about eight

minutes into the contest. The Husker ground attack started marching the ball back down the field, but Frazier, trying to catch the Cane defense napping, was intercepted throwing deep into double coverage.

"They had played tremendous defense all year, and we were moving the ball," Osborne said.

Five plays later, Frank Costa connected on the first of his two touchdown passes, a 35-yarder to Trent Jones, who outraced Husker defenders to the end zone.

"That guy was so quick, we just couldn't catch him," Osborne said.

"You don't play a whole game against a team that throws like Miami and not expect them to make some big plays," said NU cornerback Barron Miles. "Of course they're going to catch some passes on you. You can't hang your head because of that."

Berringer came off the bench to prove that the Huskers can throw (with a TD pass, right) and run (with a handoff fake to Phillips, below).

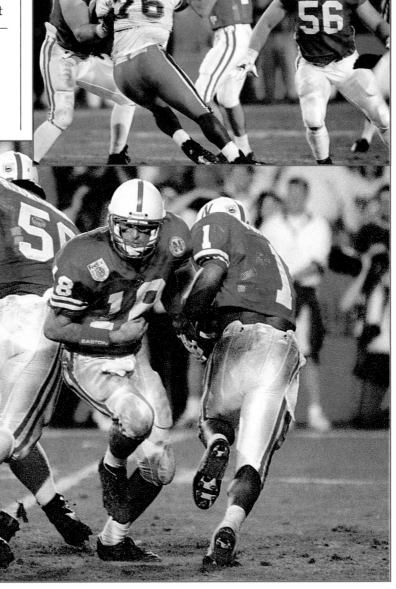

In the second quarter, Frazier was replaced by Berringer, whose passing arm had opened up the Husker running game during the season. The move to bring in the passer from Goodland, Kan., was predetermined.

Berringer kept the game close with a rollout pass to tight end Mark Gilman, who hauled in the touch pass over a Miami defender and tumbled into the end zone eight minutes into the second quarter.

But Costa made it 17-7 in the third quarter when he found Jonathan Harris on a 44-yard catch and run. Harris used his speed to break a few tackles, then he outran several Huskers to the end zone.

"It was frustrating," said defensive end Donta Jones. "We tried to put pressure on Costa to help out the defensive backs."

The Huskers just couldn't quite reach the Miami quarterback, however, until Dwayne Harris pulled Costa down for a safety late in the third quarter. That made it 17-9.

Then came the fourth quarter. Nebraska's players could see their destiny on the tired faces of their Miami opponents. The pounding of the mammoth offensive line, the harassment from the Husker defense and liberal substitution on both sides of the ball for Nebraska for three quarters was starting to pay off.

"We thought the factors against Miami that we had to exploit were we thought we had a little better depth, and we thought maybe we were better conditioned," Osborne said. "So we wanted to wear them down. We felt if we could stay close, come the fourth quarter we'd be the dominant team, and it worked out that way."

"It came to the fourth quarter, and we got the job done," Jones said.

"I think we were in better shape," said offensive guard Brenden Stai, who switched sides of the line to put his All-Big Eight 300-pound body on Sapp. "I think we caught them by surprise."

The Huskers let one big opportunity get away. A center snap went over the Miami punter's head early in the final period, and a bizarre turn of events followed. The punter kicked the ball out of the end zone rather than risk a Nebraska recovery. NU had the option of either taking the safety or taking the ball where it was kicked. The Huskers took the ball at the Hurricane 4-yard line.

Osborne said later that he was confident his team could score, but Berringer rolled out and, trying to throw the ball way through the end zone, was intercepted.

Osborne made the decision to return Frazier to the game. He called it a hunch, an instinctive move. And the decision to put the quick junior's fresh feet back in the game paid off.

"Everyone was very confident," said Frazier, who was named most valuable player of the game for the second-straight year. "We knew their defensive front was very tired. We knew that all we had to do was pound the ball inside, and since they were tired, we'd be able to drive them off the ball."

The Huskers did just that on offense, and the defense smothered Miami on the other side of the ball.

"Our defense did a tremendous job," Osborne said. "They were three plays and out four straight possessions. That won the game for us more than anything."

But the offense still needed eight points for a tie. A pitch to I-back Lawrence Phillips, sweeping the end, gained 22, and the Hurricanes were gasping for air. Then Schlesinger slipped through the middle on a trap play for a 15-yard score that pulled the Huskers within two. The clock read 7:22.

Nebraska went for the tie and got it when Frazier threw a bullet through the middle and tight end Eric Alford was there to pull it down. It was 17-all. Ironically, the maneuver was completed in the same end zone in which Gill's 1984 Orange Bowl two-point pass attempt to I-back Jeff Smith in the final 48 seconds was tipped away.

Gill was on the sidelines this time as the Nebraska quarterback coach. No, he didn't have any flashbacks when Frazier came over center. Gill said the circumstances were different. This wasn't win or lose like it was in 1984. This was for a tie, and there was plenty of time to come back and score again. Gill never doubted there would be another score.

"All along we felt we were going to win because we felt we were in better condition," he said.

And this time, Nebraska had a great defense.

The Huskers, who allowed Miami 143 yards in the first quarter, gave up only 134 yards in the other three. They stuffed Costa and company again and forced a punt.

Again the Huskers took over in good field position. This time, they were 58 yards away from a go-ahead score.

"We looked at each other when it was 17-17 and we said 'We'd been here, we worked too hard, too long,'" said wide receiver Brendan Holbein. "It was all from the heart. We came through."

(Right) ESPN analysts Craig James (right) and Lee Corso (center) predict that fullback Schlesinger (40) will be key to Nebraska's running success.

(Below) Schlesinger fulfills the media's game-day prophesy with a run for the winning TD, his second fourth-quarter touchdown of the night.

Frazier ran an option inside the 30. Phillips gained 7 on the next play, and Frazier cut in on an option to the 14. That set up another trap play. Schlesinger sliced through the middle nearly untouched to tumble into the end zone with the go-ahead score. The extra point by Tom Sieler made it 24-17, and Nebraska had no doubts about who was in control with less than three minutes to play.

"We knew that they were tired," Frazier said. "Our line started to drive them off the ball. We like to give it to Cory at the end of the game because he's so reliable."

"I may have been the one scoring the touchdowns, but I couldn't have done anything without the line blocking," Schlesinger said. "There were just huge holes for me to run through. And the receivers did a great job of blocking on the last touchdown."

Among the key blocks was one thrown by tiny Abdul Muhammad (5-foot-9, 160 pounds). Consider it payback for what happened to him a year ago in this same stadium.

After catching a ball against Florida State, Muhammad was hit hard: He suffered cracked ribs and a lacerated liver. He nearly decided to redshirt the 1994 season, his senior year, because of the pain he experienced all summer. But two-a-day contact led him to believe he could play.

Not only did he throw the block that helped Schlesinger score the winning touchdown, he caught

four passes for 60 yards to lead the Huskers in receiving for the game.

Back in Lincoln, Schlesinger told a Bob Devaney Sports Center crowd of nearly 15,000 that the touchdown put an end to the cries of all those doubters who had refused to give Nebraska respect. Among them were several Miami players.

"No one gives Nebraska respect, and that can really tear at a person. They were doing a lot of talking before, during and even after the game," said the big fullback from tiny Duncan, Neb. "We just let our actions on the field do the talking.

"Our motto this year was 'Unfinished Business.' We came in this year with the idea of unfinished business from last year's game, and we were going to come in here and finish our business. That's what we did."

The defense put the finishing touches on Miami in the closing minutes. Costa was sacked by a swarming Terry Connealy, Jones and Harris. The team's confidence on the defensive side of the ball was showing. Connealy said one of his line teammates told everyone to meet at the quarterback. They did.

Then Kareem Moss picked off a fourth-down pass. Frazier had only to kneel twice to run out the clock.

"At 17-9, we had a lot of opportunities and couldn't take advantage of them, so we've got to give them credit for that," Miami coach Dennis Erickson said. "They came out when they had to, they ran the football

In the fourth quarter, Frazier's fresh legs were just too quick, even for Miami's speedy defense.

and ran the option at the end to make some plays.

"We were out there too long on defense, and they hit us with the trap play for two touchdowns. It was kind of two different halves. We dominated the first half but couldn't take advantage of the opportunities we had in the second half."

The Hurricanes were flagged for penalties 11 times for 92 yards. Several were key to stopping their drives or sustaining drives for Nebraska.

The Miami rushing attack managed only 29 yards in the fourth quarter. And even with the two big scoring plays, the Cane passing attack managed less than 14 yards per completion.

Nebraska, meanwhile, ran the ball 46 times to get 199 yards — 96 from Phillips on 19 carries and 48 from Schlesinger on just six tries. The Huskers also held the ball 32:32, more than five minutes longer than Miami. That extra possession time proved fatal for the Hurricanes down the stretch when the game was on the line.

"We were swarming to the ball until the end of the game," said Sapp. "And then we didn't make some tackles. You have to make plays to win. They made the plays in the end, and we didn't."

A relieved Tom Osborne showed his emotions with a beaming smile as he was hoisted onto the shoulders of his players.

"The scary thing to me all week was knowing how much this game meant to the people in Nebraska," Osborne said. "All I could do was prepare a football team, but I just knew if we didn't win there was going to be huge disappointment and despondency, and to have that on your shoulders is uncomfortable.

"I knew the players were going to play hard and give it all we had. But if we'd lost, it would have been another failure ... it would have been a bad scene."

Instead, there was jubilation. Most of the nearly 20,000 Big Red backers in the stadium (which had held 81,753 for the battle) stayed for an hour after the game. Players and coaches returned after a short stop in the locker room to thank them and to collect hugs from friends and family.

"I know everybody left it all on the field," said All-America linebacker Ed Stewart. "We kicked Miami's butt in Miami, and we're No. 1."

"My best day on earth," sighed an elated Connealy.

"We hung in there, and we did it," added offensive tackle Rob Zatechka.

"The old saying goes ... hard work pays off," Outland Trophy-winning tackle Zach Wiegert said. "We worked harder all year than they did. It's very deserving of this program to win it all."

Even Osborne's wife, Nancy, came out of the stands for post-game interviews. She was elated for her husband and had had a hunch that this was the year.

"Before the game started, I really had a feeling we were going to win, so I wasn't as nervous as I sometimes am," she admitted. "I just really feel good about it."

"I wish you would have told me," her husband countered with a big smile.

The weight of so many near-misses finally had been relieved. Osborne's 1982 team finished 12-1 and third in the final polls. The 1983 team also ended 12-1, finishing second in both polls after its loss to Miami.

The Huskers were fourth with a 10-2 record in 1984. Two more 10-2 teams finished in the top 10 in 1986 and 1987, but the string of bowl losses had soured poll voters in recent years, keeping Nebraska out of the final top 10 until last year's No. 3 finish.

Cover man Barron Miles (14) is the only one who made a catch on this play.

Many players were happier for their coach than for themselves. It was Osborne's first title in 22 years as the head man in Lincoln.

"When I came here, I really wanted to win a national championship," Frazier said. "Last year it avoided us, but this year we were able to get it done. He's the type of coach who really doesn't show his emotions much, but I'm sure that once he's had a chance to think about it, he'll shed a couple of tears and get pretty excited about it."

(Above) Orange Bowl MVP Frazier prepares to throw.

(Below) Moss (29) holds up the reward from his game-clinching interception in the final minute.

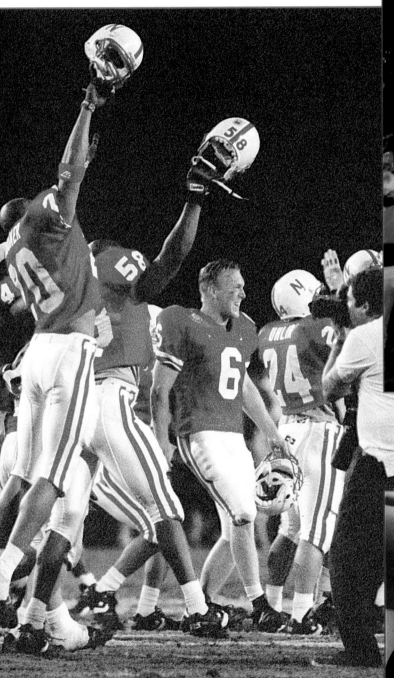

There's more than one way to celebrate! (Above) Wilks (76) frames the final score on the Orange Bowl scoreboard.

(Below) Two Husker veterans, trainer George Sullivan (left) and retired athletic director and coach Bob Devaney, shake hands in celebration of the long-awaited national championship.

Make no mistake — the Orange Bowl trophy gets top billing! The national championship prize is loaded onto the plane ahead of the team that won it.

During the post-Orange Bowl conference, MVP Tommie Frazier commented that the national championship trophy sitting on the table was the reason he came to Nebraska. He was more than happy to help Coach Osborne win his first.

Scoring Summary

	1st Quarter	2nd Quarter	3rd Quarter	4th Quarter	Final
Nebraska	0	7	2	15	24
Miami	10	0	7	0	17

UM - Dane Prewitt 44-yard field goal, 7:54, Qtr. #1.
UM - Trent Jones 35-yard pass from Frank Costa (Prewitt kick), :04, Qtr. #1.
NU - Mark Gilman 19-yard pass from Brook Berringer (Tom Sieler kick), 7:54, Qtr. #2.
UM - Jonathan Harris 44-yard pass from Costa (Prewitt kick), 13:19, Qtr. #3.
NU - Safety Dwayne Harris tackles Costa in end zone, 11:35, Qtr. #4.
NU - Cory Schlesinger 15-yard run (Eric Alford pass from Tommie Frazier), 7:38, Qtr. #4.
NU - Schlesinger 14-yard run (Sieler kick), 2:46, Qtr. #4.

Team Statistics

	NU	UM
First downs	20	14
Rushing att.-yards	46-199	28-29
Passes	11-20-2	18-35-1
Passing yards	106	248
Total att.-yards	66-305	63-277
Returns-yards	9-106	4-34
Sacks by	5-24	3-20
Punts-average	7-41.1	7-39.7
Fumbles-lost	2-1	2-0
Penalties-yards	3-20	11-92
Time of poss.	32:32	27:28

Individual Leaders

Rushing:
NU: Lawrence Phillips 19-96-0; Cory Schlesinger 6-48-2; Tommie Frazier 7-31-0; Damon Benning 3-18-0.
UM: James Stewart 17-72-0; Jonathan Harris 1-6-0; Larry Jones 1-2-0.
Passing:
NU: Frazier 3-5-25-1; Brook Berringer 8-15-81-1.
UM: Frank Costa 18-35-248-1.
Receiving:
NU: Abdul Muhammad 4-60-0; Mark Gilman 1-19-0; Phillips 4-13-0.
UM: C.T. Jones 6-63-0; A.C. Tellison 2-53-0; Derrick Harris 1-44-1; Trent Jones 1-35-1; Jammi German 3-22-0; Marcus Wimberly 2-18-0.
Interceptions:
NU: Moss 1-0-0.
UM: Carlos Jones 1-0-0; Earl Little 1-0-0.
Tackles (UT-AT-TT):
NU: Barron Miles 9-3-12; Tony Veland 4-2-6; Ed Stewart 2-3-5; Phil Ellis 3-3-6.
UM: Ray Lewis 8-5-13; C.J. Richardson 7-3-10; Marvin Davis 9-0-9; Warren Sapp 5-1-6; Kenny Holmes 4-1-5.
Sacks:
NU: Dwayne Harris 3-11; Troy Dumas 1-5; Terry Connealy 1-8.
UM: Sapp 2-17; Kenard Lang 1-3.

The Celebration

The victorious Husker squad brought both the Orange Bowl trophy and the national championship home to over 15,000 fans. They are led into the Bob Devaney Sports Center by coach Tom Osborne (left) and Nebraska Chancellor Dr. Graham Spanier (right).

In the Bob Devaney Sports Center, Tom Osborne hands the microphone to I-Back Damon Benning during the victory celebration held in honor of the Huskers' first football national championship in 24 years.

Nebraska players (from left to right) Damon Benning, Tony Veland, Joel Wilks and Mike Minter and assistant coach Dan Young stand behind the crystal Sears Trophy and bask in the spotlight of their victory and the national championship.

Coach Osborne is greeted by the Nebraska faithful upon his arrival in Lincoln after the Huskers' Orange Bowl victory.

Season Statistics

(13-0-0 Overall / 7-0-0 in Big Eight, Conference Champions, National Champions)
(Does not include 1995 Orange Bowl)

Team Stats

	Nebraska	Opponents
Total First Downs	293	176
By Rush	215	68
By Pass	66	89
By Penalty	12	19
Total Offensive Yards	5,734	3,106
Avg. Per Game	477.8	258.8
Total Plays	897	765
Avg. Gain Per Play	6.4	4.1
Net Rushing Yards	4,080	951
Avg. Per Game	340.0	79.3
Rushing Attempts	687	401
Avg. Per Attempt	5.9	2.4
Yards Gained Rushing	4,356	1,359
Yards Lost Rushing	276	408
Net Passing Yards	1,654	2,155
Avg. Per Game	137.8	179.6
Avg. Per Attempt	7.9	5.9
Avg. Per Completion	13.8	12.5
Attempts	210	364
Completions	120	172
Completion Percent	57.1	47.3
NCAA Rating	140.2	96.7
Interceptions By	17	7
Yards Returned	218	34
Avg. Per Return	12.8	4.9
Touchdowns	0	0
Punting Avg.	42.6	41.4
Number of Punts	50	88
Yards	2,130	3,645
Had Blocked	0	3
Net Punting Avg.	41.2	36.7
Punt Returns	49	24
Yards Returned	419	69
Avg. Per Return	8.6	2.9
Touchdowns	0	0
Kickoff Returns	25	35
Yards Returned	571	636
Avg. Per Return	22.8	18.2
Touchdowns	0	0
Penalties/Yards	76/670	60/475
Avg. Yards Per Game	55.8	39.6
Fumbles Lost	27/13	18/4
Total Turnovers	20	21
3rd Down Conversions	74/164	50/174
Conversion Percent	45.1	28.7
4th Down Conversions	12/19	5/18
Conversion Percent	63.2	27.8
Sacks By/Yards Lost	43/263	6/54
Time of Possession	6:43:08	5:16:52
Touchdowns	59	18
By Rush	44	8
By Pass	15	10
By Return	0	0
PAT Kicks Made/Att.	52/54	14/15
PAT Run-Pass Made/Att.	4/5	1/3
Field Goals Made/Att.	7/14	7/11
Safeties	0	0
Total Points	435	145
Avg. Per Game	36.3	12.1

Rushing

	G/GS	Att.	Gain	Loss	Net	Avg./ Play	Avg./ Game Play	Long Play	TD
L. Phillips	12/12	286	1,785	63	1,722	6.0	143.5	74	16
C. Schlesinger	12/9	63	459	3	456	7.2	38.0	41	4
C. Childs	12/0	62	399	4	395	6.4	32.9	30	5
D. Benning	12/0	67	376	9	367	5.5	30.6	23	5
J. Makovicka	12/0	47	321	0	321	6.8	26.8	50	2
B. Berringer	12/7	71	409	130	279	3.9	23.3	28	6
T. Frazier	4/4	33	276	28	248	7.5	62.0	58	6
B. Schuster	12/0	13	99	1	98	7.5	8.2	33	0
M. Turman	11/1	19	94	14	80	4.2	7.3	24	0
A. Muhammad	12/11	5	39	7	32	6.4	2.7	30	0
T. Uhlir	5/0	6	27	0	27	4.5	5.4	10	0
S. Davenport	3/0	4	27	2	25	6.3	8.3	12	0
E. Alford	11/1	1	17	0	17	17.0	1.6	17	0
V. Jackson	3/0	3	12	0	12	4.0	4.0	8	0
C. Norris	3/0	2	7	0	7	3.5	2.3	5	0
R. Washington	11/0	1	5	0	5	5.0	.5	5	0
A. Kucera	1/0	1	4	0	4	4.0	4.0	4	0
C. Stanley	2/0	1	0	0	0	0.0	0.0	0	0
R. Held	1/0	1	0	0	0	0.0	0.0	0	0
Team	12/0	1	0	15	-15	-15.0	-15.0	0	0
Nebraska	**12**	**687**	**4,356**	**276**	**4,080**	**5.9**	**340.0**	**74**	**44**
Opponents	**12**	**401**	**1,359**	**408**	**951**	**2.4**	**79.3**	**41**	**8**

Receiving

	G/GS	Recpts.	Yards	Avg.	Long Play	TD
A. Muhammad	12/11	23	360	15.7	44	2
L. Phillips	12/12	22	172	7.8	27	0
R. Baul	12/8	17	300	17.7	51	3
M. Gilman	12/3	17	196	11.5	48	1
E. Alford	11/1	14	271	19.4	46	4
B. Holbein	12/5	9	88	9.8	30	2
D. Benning	12/0	5	68	13.6	37	0
C. Childs	12/0	5	58	11.6	26	0
C. Johnson	12/2	4	93	23.3	64	2
J. Lake	5/0	1	24	24.0	24	1
T. Carpenter	8/0	1	12	12.0	12	0
J. Vedral	12/0	1	7	7.0	7	0
J. Makovicka	12/0	1	5	5.0	5	0
Nebraska	**12**	**120**	**1,654**	**13.8**	**64**	**15**
Opponents	**12**	**172**	**2,155**	**12.5**	**58**	**10**

Passing

	Att.	Comp.	Pct.	Yds.	Avg./ Att.	Avg./ Game	Int.	TD	NCAA Rating
B. Berringer	151	94	.623	1,295	8.6	107.9	5	10	149.5
T. Frazier	44	19	.432	273	6.2	68.3	2	4	116.2
M. Turman	12	6	.500	81	6.8	7.4	0	1	134.2
J. Vedral	1	1	1.000	5	5.0	0.4	0	0	142.0
L. Phillips	1	0	.000	0	0.0	0.0	0	0	0.0
A. Kucera	1	0	.000	0	0.0	0.0	0	0	0.0
Nebraska	**210**	**120**	**.571**	**1,654**	**7.9**	**137.8**	**7**	**15**	**140.2**
Opponents	**364**	**172**	**.473**	**2,155**	**5.9**	**179.6**	**17**	**10**	**96.7**

Season Statistics

Score by Qtr.	1st Quarter	2nd Quarter	3rd Quarter	4th Quarter	Final
Nebraska	95	136	103	101	435
Opponents	23	36	43	43	145

Average	1st Quarter	2nd Quarter	3rd Quarter	4th Quarter	Final
Nebraska	7.9	11.3	8.6	8.4	36.3
Opponents	1.9	3.0	3.6	3.6	12.1

Total Offense

	G/GS	Plays	Rush	Pass	Total	Avg./Play	Avg./Game
L. Phillips	12/12	287	1,722	0	1,722	6.0	143.5
B. Berringer	12/7	222	279	1,295	1,574	7.1	131.2
T. Frazier	4/4	77	248	273	521	6.8	130.3
C. Schlesinger	12/9	63	456	0	456	7.2	38.0
C. Childs	12/0	62	395	0	395	6.4	32.9
D. Benning	12/0	67	367	0	367	5.5	30.6
J. Makovicka	12/0	47	321	0	321	6.8	26.8
Nebraska	12	897	4,080	1,654	5,734	6.4	477.8
Opponents	12	765	951	2,155	3,105	4.1	258.8

Kickoff Returns

	G/GS	Rets.	Yards	Avg.	Long Play	TD
D. Benning	12/0	12	308	25.7	58	0
C. Childs	12/0	9	190	21.1	34	0
T. Uhlir	5/0	1	30	30.0	30	0
J. Williams	10/0	1	17	17.0	17	0
C. Schlesinger	12/9	1	16	16.0	16	0
J. Makovicka	12/0	1	10	10.0	10	0
Nebraska	12	25	571	22.8	58	0
Opponents	12	38	683	18.0	37	0

Scoring

	G/GS	TD	PAT1	PAT2	FG	TP
L. Phillips	12/12	16	0	0	0	96
T. Sieler	11/11	0	40	0	4	52
T. Frazier	4/4	6	0	2	0	40
B. Berringer	12/7	6	0	0	0	36
D. Benning	12/0	5	0	0	0	30
C. Childs	12/0	5	0	0	0	30
E. Alford	11/1	4	0	1	0	26
C. Schlesinger	12/9	4	0	0	0	24
D. Erstad	12/12	0	10	1	3	21
R. Baul	12/8	3	0	0	0	18
B. Holbein	12/5	2	0	0	0	12
J. Makovicka	12/0	2	0	0	0	12
A. Muhammad	12/11	2	0	0	0	12
C. Johnson	12/2	2	0	0	0	12
M. Gilman	12/3	1	0	0	0	6
J. Lake	5/0	1	0	0	0	6
T. Retzlaff	1/0	0	2	0	0	2
Nebraska	12	59	52	4	7	435
Opponents	12	18	14	1	7	145

Field Goals

	Season	1-19	20-29	30-39	40-49	50+
T. Sieler	4-6	0-0	2-2	2-4	0-0	0-0
D. Erstad	3-8	0-0	1-1	0-1	2-6	0-0
Nebraska	7-14	0-0	3-3	2-5	2-6	0-0
Opponents	7-11	0-0	2-2	2-4	3-5	0-0

Punting

	G/GS	Punts	Yards	Avg.	Net. Avg.	Inside Opp. 20	Blk.	Long
D. Erstad	12/12	50	2,130	42.6	41.2	20	0	73
Nebraska	12	50	2,130	42.6	41.2	20	0	73
Opponents	12	88	3,645	41.4	36.7	18	3	90

Season Statistics

All-Purpose Leaders

	G/GS	Rush	Rec.	PR	KOR	Total
L. Phillips	12/12	1,722	172	0	0	1,894
D. Benning	12/0	367	68	0	308	743
C. Childs	12/0	395	58	3	190	646
C. Schlesinger	12/9	456	0	0	16	472
R. Baul	12/8	0	300	119	0	419
A. Muhammad	12/11	32	360	0	0	392
J. Makovicka	12/0	321	5	0	10	336
E. Alford	11/1	17	271	0	0	288
B. Berringer	12/7	279	0	0	0	279
T. Frazier	4/4	248	0	0	0	248
Nebraska	**12**	**4,080**	**1,654**	**419**	**571**	**6,274**
Opponents	**12**	**951**	**2,155**	**69**	**683**	**3,858**

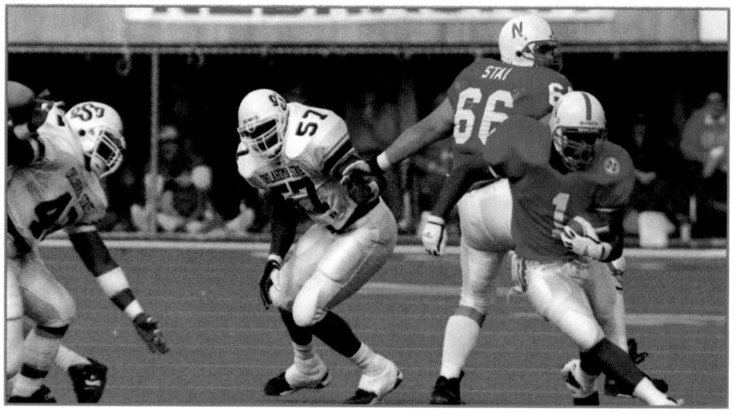

Lawrence Phillips, Nebraska's All-Purpose Yardage leader.

Interceptions

	G/GS	Int.	Yards	Avg.	Long Play	TD
B. Miles	12/12	5	35	7.0	27	0
T. Veland	12/10	3	35	11.7	35	0
T. Williams	11/11	3	34	11.3	28	0
K. Moss	12/12	2	0	0.0	0	0
T. Dumas	11/11	1	54	54.0	54	0
L. Dennis	12/1	1	48	48.0	48	0
S. Collins	1/0	1	8	8.0	8	0
C. Brown	11/1	1	4	4.0	4	0
Nebraska	**12**	**17**	**218**	**12.8**	**54**	**0**
Opponents	**12**	**7**	**34**	**4.9**	**20**	**0**

Punt Returns

	G/GS	Rets.	Yards	Avg.	Long Play	TD
K. Moss	12/12	31	234	7.6	28	0
R. Baul	12/8	11	119	10.8	22	0
T. Williams	11/11	4	42	10.5	18	0
B. Miles	12/12	1	21	21.0	21	0
C. Childs	12/0	1	3	3.0	3	0
T. Wrice	4/0	1	0	0.0	0	0
Nebraska	**12**	**49**	**419**	**8.6**	**28**	**0**
Opponents	**12**	**24**	**69**	**2.9**	**10**	**0**

Defensive Statistics

		(.................. Tackles			....................)		(... Fumbles	...)	Blocked	(.....Passes	.....)	QB	Int.
	G/GS	Solo	Assist.	Total	Sacks*	Loss	Csd.	Rec.	Kicks	BKUP	Int.	Hurry	Csd.
E. Stewart	12/12	41	55	96	3.5-18	5.5-23	0	1	0	1	0	18	0
C. Peter	12/12	32	39	71	7-31	14-45	0	0	0	2	0	20	0
T. Dumas	11/11	38	31	69	1-6	4-17	1	0	0	0	1	7	0
K. Moss	12/12	41	25	66	2-12	3-13	0	0	0	4	2	2	0
P. Ellis	12/4	24	34	58	0.5-2	7.5-21	0	0	0	0	0	2	0
D. Jones	12/12	23	29	52	5-31	10-52	1	0	0	2	0	22	0
D. Colman	12/8	17	34	51	2-15	3-16	1	1	0	1	0	4	0
D. Harris	12/12	15	28	43	5-38	10-48	1	0	0	4	0	19	1
T. Connealy	11/11	13	29	42	6.5-37	7.5-38	1	0	0	0	0	13	1
B. Miles	12/12	24	16	40	0	0	1	0	4	13	5	0	0
T. Williams	11/11	31	7	38	0	0	0	0	0	5	3	0	0
E. Stokes	12/0	12	24	36	0	0	0	0	0	2	0	0	0
G. Wistrom	12/0	14	22	36	4.5-49	6.5-55	0	0	0	0	0	11	0
T. Veland	12/10	13	13	26	0	0	0	0	0	1	3	0	0
J. Tomich	12/0	12	11	23	1-7	4-15	0	0	0	0	0	12	1
R. Terwilliger	12/0	8	11	19	2-8	3-14	0	0	0	0	0	2	0
C. Brown	11/1	8	10	18	0	1-1	0	1	0	0	1	1	0
L. Dennis	12/1	9	7	16	0	0	0	0	0	3	1	0	0
J. Pesterfield	12/1	9	6	15	3-26	5-33	0	0	0	1	0	9	0
O. McFarlin	8/0	6	9	15	0	0	0	0	0	1	0	0	0
J. Vedral	12/0	6	5	11	0	0	0	0	0	0	0	0	0
J. Hesse	12/0	5	6	11	0	2-2	0	0	0	0	0	1	0
D. Schmadeke	7/0	8	1	9	0	0	0	0	0	1	0	0	0
A. Penland	10/0	2	7	9	0	0	0	0	0	0	0	0	0
L. Hardin	6/0	4	5	9	0	0	0	0	0	0	0	2	0
L. Alexander	7/0	2	6	8	0	0	0	0	0	0	0	0	0
S. Saltsman	8/0	2	6	8	0	1-1	0	0	0	0	0	3	0
J. Peter	7/0	2	6	8	0	1-3	0	0	0	2	0	2	0
M. Minter	2/2	3	4	7	0	1-1	0	0	0	1	0	0	0
L. Townsend	10/0	2	4	6	0	1-3	0	0	0	0	0	2	0

* Sacks included in Tackles for Loss

1994 Highs and Lows

Nebraska	High	Low	Opponents High	Opponents Low
Points Scored	70 vs. Pacific	13 vs. Oklahoma	32 by Wyoming	0 by West Virginia
First Downs	32 vs. Pacific	16 vs. Kansas State	24 by UCLA	7 by Oklahoma State
Rushing Attempts	68 vs. Oklahoma State	49 vs. Kansas	45 by Kansas	21 by Wyoming
Rushing Yards	524 vs. Texas Tech	136 vs. Oklahoma	155 by Colorado	-7 by Kansas State
Passes Attempted	23 vs. Oklahoma	11 vs. Kansas State	51 by Pacific	13 by Iowa State
Passes Completed	15 vs. Wyoming	4 vs. Kansas State	27 by Pacific	6 by WVU, OSU, Oklahoma
Had Intercepted	2 vs. West Virginia	0 six games	3 by Wyoming	0 by Colorado, Iowa State
Passing Yards	267 vs. Kansas	52 vs. Kansas State	344 by Wyoming	71 by Oklahoma
Total Plays	88 vs. Oklahoma State	61 vs. Kansas State	76 by Pacific	50 by Oklahoma
Total Yards	699 vs. Pacific	262 vs. Kansas State	414 by UCLA	89 by West Virginia
Possession Time	38:24 vs. Colorado	28:44 vs. Kansas	31:16 by Kansas	21:36 by Colorado
Fumbles	4 vs. West Virginia, OSU	0 vs. Texas Tech	4 by West Virginia	0 by UCLA, CU, Oklahoma
Fumbles Lost	3 vs. West Virginia, OSU	0 vs. Texas Tech, CU, Oklahoma	1 four games	0 eight games
Turnovers	5 vs. West Virginia	1 six games	4 by Wyoming	0 by Colorado, Iowa State
Turnover Margin	+2 vs.Wyoming	-3 vs. West Virginia	+2 by West Virginia, ISU	-2 by Wyoming
Penalties	9 three games	4 vs. Kansas, vs. Oklahoma	12 by Kansas State	2 by Kansas
Yards Penalized	91 vs. Wyoming	26 vs. Kansas	102 by Kansas State	11 by Kansas
Sacks By	8 vs. West Virginia	1 vs. Pacific, Wyoming	2 by Kansas, Oklahoma	0 eight games

Individual Highs

Most Rushing Attempts: 36 (school record); Lawrence Phillips, vs. Iowa State
Most Net Rushing Yards: 221; Phillips, vs. Oklahoma State
Most Rushing TDs: 3; Tommie Frazier, vs. West Virginia; Phillips and Brook Berringer, vs. Wyoming; Phillips, vs. Oklahoma State
Longest Run: 74; Phillips, vs. Pacific (TD)
Most Pass Attempts: 23; Berringer, vs. Oklahoma
Most Completed Passes: 15; Berringer, vs. Wyoming
Most Passing Yards: 267; Berringer, vs. Kansas
Longest Pass: 64; Berringer to Clester Johnson, vs. Kansas (TD)
Most Pass Receptions: 5; Eric Alford, vs. Colorado; Abdul Muhammad, vs. Oklahoma
Most Receiving Yards: 106; Baul, vs. Kansas
Most Total-Offense Yards: 266; Berringer, vs. Kansas
Most All-Purpose Yards: 223; Phillips, vs. Iowa State
Most Touchdowns Scored: 3; Frazier, vs. West Virginia; Berringer and Phillips, vs. Wyoming; Phillips, vs. Oklahoma State
Most Field Goals Attempted: 2; Darin Erstad, vs. Texas Tech, vs. Kansas State; Tom Sieler, vs. Kansas
Most Field Goals Made: 1; Sieler, four times; Erstad, three times
Longest Field Goal: 48; Erstad, vs. Oklahoma State
Most Interceptions: 2; Barron Miles, vs. Wyoming
Longest Interception Return: 56; Troy Dumas, vs. Kansas State
Longest Punt Return: 28; Kareem Moss, vs. West Virginia; Moss, vs. Oklahoma State
Longest Kickoff Return: 58; Damon Benning, vs. Texas Tech
Highest Punting Average: 49.0; Erstad, vs. Kansas
Longest Punt: 73; Erstad, vs. Oklahoma
Most Total Tackles: 13; Ed Stewart and Terry Connealy, vs. Iowa State
Most Solo Tackles: 9; Troy Dumas, vs. Oklahoma
Most Assisted Tackles: 9; Connealy, vs. Iowa State
Most Tackles For Loss: 3; Stewart and Christian Peter, vs. Iowa State
Most Yards Lost: 24; Wistrom, vs. Kansas State
Most Quarterback Sacks: 2.5; Peter, vs. West Virginia

Opponents' Long Plays

Rush: 41; Rashaan Salaam, Colorado
Pass: 58; Calvin Branch from Todd Doxzon, Iowa State
Field Goal: 49; Jon Davis, Texas Tech
Punt return: 10; Rashaan Vanterpool, West Virginia
Kickoff return: 37; Ashaundai Smith, Kansas
Interception return: 20; Wendell Davis, Oklahoma
Punt: 90; Todd Sauerbrun, West Virginia

Season Statistics do not include Orange Bowl

1994 Nebraska Roster

No.	Ltrs.	Name	Position	Hgt.	Wgt.	Yr.	Hometown	High School
47		Aden, Matt	Rover	6-2	200	Fr.	Omaha, Neb.	Northwest
48		Alderman, Dave	Rover	5-10	180	So.	Omaha, Neb.	North
36		Alexander, Leonard	MLB	6-1	235	Sr.	Detroit, Mich.	Lutheran East
88	*	Alford, Eric	TE	6-2	225	Sr.	High Point, N.C.	Central
82		Allen, Jacques	WB	6-2	200	Jr.	Kansas City, Mo.	Raytown
25		Anderson, Darrell	FS	5-11	175	Fr.	Omaha, Neb.	Central
70		Anderson, Eric	OT	6-4	295	Fr.	Lincoln, Neb.	Southeast
23		Arnold, Larry	LB	6-4	220	So.	Copley, Ohio	Copley
7		Bailey, Dennis	FS	6-2	190	So.	St. Louis, Mo.	Beaumont
7	*	Baul, Reggie	SE	5-8	170	Jr.	Bellevue, Neb.	Papillion-LaVista
21	*	Benning, Damon	IB	5-11	205	So.	Omaha, Neb.	Northwest
18	**	Berringer, Brook	QB	6-4	210	Jr.	Goodland, Kan.	Goodland
11		Blahak, Chad	CB	5-10	190	So.	Lincoln, Neb.	Lincoln
20		Booker, Michael	DB	6-2	200	So.	Oceanside, Calif.	El Camino
9		Brouse, Chad	FS	5-11	195	So.	Lincoln, Neb.	East
45	*	Brown, Clint	SLB	6-1	215	Sr.	Arlington, Neb.	Arlington
81		Brown, Lance	WB	5-11	180	Fr.	Papillion, Neb.	Papillion-LaVista
87		Brummond, Darren	LB	6-2	210	Fr.	Englewood, Colo.	Cherry Creek
62		Butler, Ted	OG	6-1	240	Fr.	Lincoln, Neb.	Southeast
90		Carpenter, Tim	TE	6-2	225	Fr.	Columbus, Neb.	Columbus
61	**	Caskey, Brady	OT	6-4	290	Sr.	Stanton, Neb.	Stanton
48		Cheatham, Kenny	REC	6-4	195	Fr.	Phoenix, Ariz.	South Mountain
26	*	Childs, Clinton	IB	6-0	215	Jr.	Omaha, Neb.	North
9		Christo, Monte	QB	5-11	175	Fr.	Kearney, Neb.	Kearney
		Cobb, Josh	RB	5-11	218	Fr.	Wallace, Neb.	Wallace
46	**	Colman, Doug	MLB	6-3	240	Jr.	Ventnor, N.J.	Ocean City
99	***	Connealy, Terry	DT	6-5	275	Sr.	Hyannis, Neb.	Hyannis
3		Crayton, Tray	DB	6-2	195	Fr.	Oceanside, Calif.	El Camino
17		Davenport, Scott	IB	5-6	190	Sr.	Rye Brook, N.Y.	Port Chester
83		Davis, Aaron	SE	5-11	180	So.	Lincoln, Neb.	Lincoln
2		Dennis, Leslie	CB	5-8	165	Fr.	Bradenton, Fla.	Southeast
75	*	Dishman, Chris	OT	6-3	305	So.	Cozad, Neb.	Cozad
4	***	Dumas, Troy	SLB	6-4	220	Sr.	Cheyenne, Wyo.	East
63		Dumitrescu,Constantine	OL	6-5	300	Fr.	Hayward, Calif.	Moreau
41	**	Ellis, Phil	MLB	6-2	225	Jr.	Grand Island, Neb.	Grand Island
6		Erstad, Darin	P/PK	6-2	195	So.	Jamestown, N.D.	Jamestown
15	**	Frazier, Tommie	QB	6-2	205	Jr.	Bradenton, Fla.	Manatee
7		Foreman, Jay	DB	6-3	195	Fr.	Eden Prairie, Minn.	Eden Prairie
81		Gard, Sean	OLB	5-11	205	Fr.	Omaha, Neb.	Central
53		Gessford, Ben	OL	6-2	214	Fr.	Lincoln, Neb.	East
87	**	Gilman, Mark	TE	6-3	240	Jr.	Kalispell, Mont.	Flathead
54	**	Graham, Aaron	C	6-3	280	Jr.	Denton, Texas	Denton
81		Haafke, Billy	WR	5-11	176	Fr.	South Sioux City, Neb.	South Sioux City
58	**	Hardin, Luther	OLB	6-2	230	Jr.	O'Fallon, Ill.	Althoff Catholic
86	**	Harris, Dwayne	OLB	6-2	225	Sr.	Bessemer, Ala.	Jess Lanier
10		Held, Ryan	QB	6-1	175	Fr.	Overland Park, Kan.	Blue Valley North
		Herron, Chris	DB	6-0	180	Fr.	Scottsbluff, Neb.	Scottsbluff
59		Heskew, Josh	C	6-3	250	Fr.	Yukon, Okla.	Mustang
44		Hesse, Jon	MLB	6-4	225	So.	Lincoln, Neb.	Southeast
92	**	Higman, Jerad	OLB	6-1	230	Sr.	Akron, Iowa	Akron-Westfield
59		Hoffman, Michael	DT	5-10	230	Fr.	Spencer, Neb.	Spencer-Naper
40		Hogrefe, Quint	LB	5-11	185	Fr.	Auburn, Neb.	Auburn
5	*	Holbein, Brendan	SE	5-9	180	So.	Cozad, Neb.	Cozad
92		Horst, Joe	TE	6-1	245	Fr.	Wood River, Neb.	Wood River
62		Hoskinson, Matt	OG	6-1	275	Fr.	Battle Creek, Neb.	Battle Creek
51	**	Humphrey, Bill	C	6-2	265	Sr.	Libertyville, Ill.	Libertyville
38		Hunting, Matt	WLB	6-3	210	Fr.	Cozad, Neb.	Cozad
5		Jackson, Jai	DB	5-10	160	Fr.	Lincoln, Neb.	Northeast
84		Jackson, Sheldon	REC	6-3	205	Fr.	Diamond Bar, Calif.	Damien
34		Jackson, Vershan	FB	6-0	225	Fr.	Omaha, Neb.	South
96		Jenkins, Jason	DT	6-5	265	Jr.	Hammonton, N.J.	Oakcrest
33	*	Johnson, Clester	WB	5-11	210	Jr.	Bellevue, Neb.	West
84	***	Jones, Donta	OLB	6-2	220	Sr.	La Plata, Md.	Pomfret McDonough
19		Kosch, Jesse	P	6-0	180	Fr.	Columbus, Neb.	Scotus
30		Knuckles, Brian	IB	5-11	195	Jr.	Charlotte, N.C.	West
8		Kucera, Adam	QB	5-8	180	Fr.	Lake Havasu, Ariz.	Lake Havasu
89		Lake, Jeff	SE	6-4	205	Fr.	Columbus, Neb.	Lakeview
		Lafleur, Bill	P/PK	6-0	187	Fr.	Norfolk, Neb.	Catholic
54		Leece, Charlie	LB	6-0	210	Fr.	Grand Island, Neb.	Grand Island
		Lesser, Mike	OG	6-4	265	Fr.	Pierce, Neb.	Pierce
2		Livingston, John	SE	6-0	170	Jr.	San Marcos, Calif.	Hemet

No.		Name	Pos.	Ht.	Wt.	Yr.	Hometown	High School
13		Macken, Casey	LB	6-0	205	Fr.	Cozad, Neb.	Cozad
05		McFarlin, Octavious	DB	6-0	180	Fr.	Bastrop, Texas	Bastrop
		McGrane, Josh	TE	6-2	230	Fr.	Lincoln, Neb.	Lincoln
22	**	Makovicka, Jeff	FB	5-10	210	Jr.	Brainard, Neb.	East Butler
38		Makovicka, Joel	RB-LB	5-10	195	Fr.	Brainard, Neb.	East Butler
49		Martin, John	OLB	6-2	245	Sr.	Wahoo, Neb.	Neumann
78		Mikos, Kory	OT	6-5	260	So.	Seward, Neb.	Seward
14	**	Miles, Barron	LCB	5-8	165	Sr.	Roselle, N.J.	Abraham Clark
39		Miller, Andy	WR	5-10	162	Fr.	Papillion, Neb.	Papillion-La Vista
83		Miller, Bryce	OLB	6-5	210	So.	Elmwood, Neb.	Elmwood-Murdock
10	*	Minter, Mike	FS/ROV	5-10	175	So.	Lawton, Okla.	Lawton
		Mitchell, Ian	WLB	5-11	190	So.	Lincoln, Neb.	Northeast/Neb. Wesleyan
6		Morro, Brian	P/PK	5-9	170	Fr.	Middletown, N.J.	South
42		Morrow, Ed	OLB	6-4	230	So.	Ferguson, Mo.	St.Louis McCluer
29	**	Moss, Kareem	ROVER	5-10	190	Sr.	Spartanburg, S.C.	Garden City
27	***	Muhammad, Abdul	WB	5-9	160	Sr.	Compton, Calif.	Carson
80		Nelson, Erik	DL/OL	6-4	250	Fr.	Iowa City, Iowa	Iowa City
38		Norris, Chris	FB	5-10	235	Jr.	Papillion, Neb.	Papillion-LaVista
43		Noster, Sean	SLB	6-3	215	Fr.	San Antonio, Texas	John Marshall
63		Nunns, Brian	OT	6-2	280	Jr.	Lincoln, Neb.	Lincoln
97		Ogard, Jeff	DT	6-6	290	So.	St. Paul, Neb.	St. Paul
69	**	Ott, Steve	OG	6-4	275	Jr.	Henderson, Neb.	Henderson
52	**	Penland, Aaron	WLB	6-1	215	Jr.	Jacksonville, Fla.	University Christian
57	**	Pesterfield, Jason	DT	6-3	260	Sr.	Pauls Valley, Okla.	Pauls Valley
55	*	Peter, Christian	DT	6-2	285	Jr.	Locust, N.J.	Middletown South
95		Peter, Jason	DT	6-4	275	Fr.	Locust, N.J.	Milford Academy
1	*	Phillips, Lawrence	IB	6-0	200	So.	West Covina, Calif	Baldwin Park
73		Pollack, Fred	OT	6-4	305	Fr.	Omaha, Neb.	Creighton Prep
80	**	Popplewell, Brett	SE	6-0	205	Jr.	Melbourne, Aust.	Carey Grammar
65	*	Pruitt, Bryan	OG	6-1	255	Sr.	Midlothian, Ill.	St. Laurence
34		Reddick, David	REC	5-10	175	Fr.	Camden, N.J.	Woodrow Wilson
13		Retzlaff, Ted	PK	5-11	180	Fr.	Waverly, Neb.	Waverly
39		Roberts, Mike	ROVER	6-1	175	So.	Omaha, Neb.	Central
86		Roy, Dorrick	REC	6-4	220	Fr.	Inglewood, Calif	Montclair Prep
82		Rucker, Mike	LB	6-6	225	Fr.	St. Joseph, Mo.	Benton
35		Sakalosky, Jeff	MLB	5-11	210	Fr.	Omaha, Neb.	Gross
74		Saltsman, Scott	DT	6-2	255	So.	Wichita Falls, Texas	Rider
13		Schlake, Trent	QB	6-1	170	Fr.	Gothenburg, Neb.	Gothenburg
40	**	Schlesinger, Cory	FB	6-0	230	Sr.	Duncan, Neb.	Columbus
37	*	Schmadeke, Darren	RCB	5-8	180	Jr.	Albion, Neb.	Albion
58		Schmode, Anthony	OL	6-2	225	Fr.	Battle Creek, Neb.	Battle Creek
28		Schuster, Brian	FB	5-11	210	So.	Fullerton, Neb.	Fullerton
85	**	Shaw, Matt	TE	6-3	235	Sr.	Lincoln, Neb.	Northeast
12	***	Sieler, Tom	PK	6-5	205	Sr.	Las Vegas, Nev.	Chaparral
		Skoda, Adam	MLB	6-1	225	Fr.	Lincoln, Neb.	Lincoln
49		Smith, Larry	WR	6-0	190	Fr.	Lincoln, Neb.	Southeast
		Smith, Mike	FB	6-2	230	So.	Dunning, Neb.	Sandhills
31		Stanley, Chad	FB	5-11	215	Jr.	Lebanon, Kan.	Smith-Center
66	***	Stai, Brenden	OG	6-4	300	Sr.	Yorba Linda, Calif.	Anaheim Esperanza
32	***	Stewart, Ed	WLB	6-1	215	Sr.	Chicago, Ill.	Mount Carmel
16	*	Stokes, Eric	FS	5-11	175	So	Lincoln, Neb.	East
67		Taylor, Aaron	OG	6-1	290	Fr.	Wichita Falls, Texas	Rider
91	*	Terwilliger, Ryan	WLB	6-5	220	So.	Grant, Neb.	Grant
64		Tessendorf, Ross	OLB	6-3	235	Fr.	Columbus, Neb.	Lakeview
83		Toline, Travis	LB	6-4	220	Fr.	Wahoo, Neb.	Wahoo
93		Tomich, Jared	OLB	6-2	250	So.	St. John, Ind.	Lake Central
94		Townsend, Larry	DT	6-4	285	So.	San Jose, Calif.	Yerba Buena
77		Treu, Adam	OT	6-6	290	So.	Lincoln, Neb.	Pius X
		Tully, Kyle	OL	6-3	250	Fr.	Jefferson, Wisc.	Jefferson
11		Turman, Matt	QB	5-11	165	So.	Wahoo, Neb.	Neumann
23		Uhlir, Todd	IB	5-10	210	Fr.	Battle Creek, Neb.	Battle Creek
59		Van Cleave, Mike	OG	6-2	270	Fr.	Huffman, Texas	Hargrave
25		Vedral, Jon	WB	5-11	195	So.	Gregory, S.D.	Gregory
9	**	Veland, Tony	FS	6-2	200	Jr.	Omaha, Neb.	Benson
68		Volin, Steve	OG	6-2	275	Jr.	Wahoo, Neb.	Wahoo
53		Vrzal, Matt	C	6-1	290	So.	Grand Island, Neb.	Grand Island
74		Wade, Brandt	OL	6-3	275	Fr.	Springfield, Neb.	Platteview
26		Walther, Eric	DB	5-11	185	Fr.	Junita, Neb.	Hastings Adams Central
3		Washington, Riley	SE	5-9	170	So.	Chula Vista, Calif.	San Diego SW
72	***	Wiegert, Zach	OT	6-5	300	Sr.	Fremont, Neb.	Bergan
23		Wieting, Sean	WB	5-9	190	Fr.	Tulatin, Ore.	Tigard
76	**	Wilks, Joel	OG	6-3	280	Sr.	Hastings, Neb.	Hastings
28		Williams, Jamel	LB	6-2	195	So.	Merrillville, Ind.	Merrillville
8	*	Williams, Tyrone	RCB	6-0	185	Jr.	Palmetto, Fla.	Manatee
68		Wiltz, Jason	DL	6-4	280	Fr.	New Orleans, La.	St. Augustine
82		Winder, Shalis	OLB	6-4	220	So.	Scottsbluff, Neb.	Scottsbluff
98		Wistrom, Grant	LB	6-5	230	Fr.	Webb City, Mo.	Webb City
22		Wrice, Trampis	CB	5-9	170	So.	Valdosta, Ga.	Valdosta
64		Zatechka, Jon	OT	6-2	280	Fr.	Lincoln, Neb.	East
56	***	Zatechka, Rob	OT	6-5	315	Sr.	Lincoln, Neb.	East

Final Football Polls

USA Today/CNN

Rank	School	Record	Points
1.	Nebraska (54)	13-0-0	1,542
2.	Penn State (8)	12-0-0	1,496
3.	Colorado	11-1-0	1,382
4.	Alabama	12-1-0	1,344
5.	Florida State	10-1-1	1,329
6.	Miami (FL)	10-2-0	1,229
7.	Florida	10-2-1	1,186
8.	Utah	10-2-0	1,029
9.	Ohio State	9-4-0	842
10.	Brigham Young	10-3-0	832
11.	Oregon	9-4-0	831
12.	Michigan	8-4-0	787
13.	Virginia	9-3-0	765
14.	Colorado State	10-2-0	681
15.	Southern Cal	8-3-1	670
16.	Kansas State	9-3-0	661
17.	North Carolina State	9-3-0	626
18.	Tennessee	8-4-0	520
19.	Washington State	8-4-0	449
20.	Arizona	8-4-0	405
21.	North Carolina	8-4-0	313
22.	Boston College	7-4-1	304
23.	Texas	8-4-0	244
24.	Virginia Tech	8-4-0	189
25.	Mississippi State	8-4-0	158

Associated Press

Rank	School	Record	Points
1.	Nebraska (51 ½)	13-0-0	1,539 ½
2.	Penn State (10 ½)	12-0-0	1,497 ½
3.	Colorado	11-1-0	1,410
4.	Florida State	10-1-1	1,320
5.	Alabama	12-1-0	1,312
6.	Miami (FL)	10-2-0	1,249
7.	Florida	10-2-1	1,153
8.	Texas A&M	10-0-1	1,117
9.	Auburn	9-1-1	1,110
10.	Utah	10-2-0	955
11.	Oregon	9-4-0	810
12.	Michigan	8-4-0	732
13.	Southern Cal	8-3-1	691
14.	Ohio State	9-4-0	672
15.	Virginia	9-3-0	648
16.	Colorado State	10-2-0	630
17.	North Carolina State	9-3-0	511
18.	Brigham Young	10-3-0	500
19.	Kansas State	9-3-0	496
20.	Arizona	8-4-0	364
21.	Washington State	8-4-0	344
22.	Tennessee	8-4-0	303
23.	Boston College	7-4-1	236
24.	Mississippi State	8-4-0	160
25.	Texas	8-4-0	90

The University of Nebraska

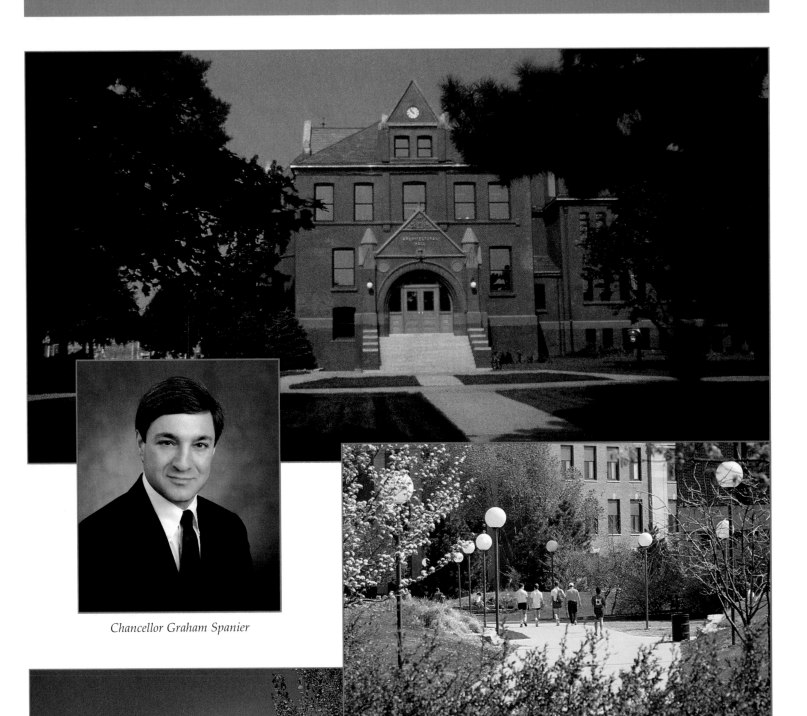

Chancellor Graham Spanier

Athletic Department

Glen Abbott
Equipment
Manager

Dr. Lonnie Albers
Director of Athletic
Medicine

Chris Anderson
Sports Information
Director

Mike Arthur
Assistant Director of
Athletic
Performance

Bryan Bailey
Coordinator of
Reconditioning

Cindy Bell
Ticket Manager

Kevin Best
Assistant Sports
Information
Director

Jon Bostick
Development
Officer

John Bousek
Video Assistant

Don Bryant
Associate A.D.,
Public Relations

Craig Busboom
Accounting
Manager

Bryan Carpenter
Computer Video
Technician

Dr. Pat Clare
Chief of Staff,
Orthopedic
Surgeon

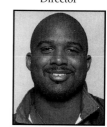
Kevin Coleman
West Stadium
Strength Coach

Dave Crum
Assistant Ticket
Manager

Heidi Cuca
Marketing Director

Bob Devaney
Athletic Director
Emeritus

Joni Duff
Football Secretary

Dr. Robert Dugas
Team Orthopedist

Dave Ellis
Director of Performance
Nutrition

Boyd Epley
Assistant A.D.,
Director of Athletic
Performance

Dave Finn
Director of Video
Operations

Gary Fouraker
Assistant A.D.,
Business & Finance

Sam Gdowski
Assistant
Marketing Director

Randy Gobel
Coordinator of
Strength &
Conditioning

Dr. Tom Heiser
Team Orthopedist

Dr. Barbara Hibner
Associate A.D.,
Senior Women's
Administrator

Butch Hug
Events Manager

John Ingram
Facilities
Operations
Manager

Nick Joos
Associate Sports
Information
Director

Monica Kelly
Assistant to the
Director of Athletic
Development

Norma Knobel
Administrative
Services Manager

Paul Koch
Devaney Center
Strength Coach

Trina Kudlacek
Academic
Counselor

Roland "Duke" LaRue
Assistant Athletic
Trainer

Athletic Department

Dennis Leblanc
Assistant A.D.,
Academic
Programs/Services

Pat Logsdon
Assistant to the
Director of Football
Operations

Mike Mason
Assistant
Equipment
Manager

George Mauzy
Assistant Sports
Information Director

Paul Meyers
Development
Officer

Brian Mohnsen
Computer Video
Technician

Marc Munford
Development
Officer

Jack Nickolite
Associate Director
of Athletic
Medicine

Dr. James O'Hanlon
Institutional
Representative

Doak Ostergard
Associate Head
Athletic Trainer

Al Papik
Senior Associate
A.D., Compliance
Coordinator

Chris Peterson
Associate A.D.,
External Operations

Jack Pierce
Director of Athletic
Development

Dr. Matt Reckmeyer
Team Orthopedist

Jeff Schmahl
Video Production
Specialist

Joe Selig
Assistant A.D.,
Facilities & Events

Bill Shepard
Grounds Manager

Jack Stark
Performance
Psychologist

George Sullivan
Head Football
Trainer, Assistant
Chief of Staff

Curt Thompson
Coordinator of
Performance Ed.
Services

Vince Ullman
Video Electronic
Technician

Sonya Varnell
Coordinator of
Multicultural
Affairs

Jerry Weber
Head Athletic
Trainer

Mary Lyn Wininger
Coach Osborne's
Secretary

Kathi Woody
Football Recruiting
Secretary

Keith Zimmer
Asst. Director of
Academic & Student
Services

Managers and Trainers

EQUIPMENT MANAGERS
(left to right): Head Equipment Manager Glen Abbott, Orlando Maldanado, Matt Geiser, Shawn Davis, Assistant Equipment Manager Mike Mason.

UNDERGRADUATE ASSISTANTS
Back Row (left to right): Kyle Emsick, Jon Pedersen, Jim Ryan. Front Row: Chad Young, Damon Schmadeke, Jason Simdorn. Not Pictured: Merritt Nelson.

STUDENT MANAGERS
Back Row (left to right): Jason McNeely, John McNeely, Jason Koch, Mike Shukei, John Meier, Head Student Manager Brandon Hamer. Front Row: Kevin Ridley, Jeff Knox, Ryan Ricenbaw, Adam Kucera, Lowell Miller. Not Pictured: Travis Hopkins, Todd Liberty.

ATHLETIC TRAINERS
Back Row (left to right): Cindy Barker, Associate Head Athletic Trainer Doak Ostergard, Asst. Chief of Staff and Head Football Trainer George Sullivan, Head Athletic Trainer Jerry Weber, Roland "Duke" LaRue, Associate Director of Athletic Medicine Jack Nickolite, Sara Weinberg. Front Row: Graduate Assistant Trainers Glenda Quarles, Doug Edwards, Chris Froiland, Scott Gardner and Ruth Cook.

Cheerleaders and Marching Band

JANUARY 9, 1995 • $2.95 (CAN. $3.95)

Sports Illustrated

How Sweet It Is!

Tom Osborne celebrates Nebraska's national championship

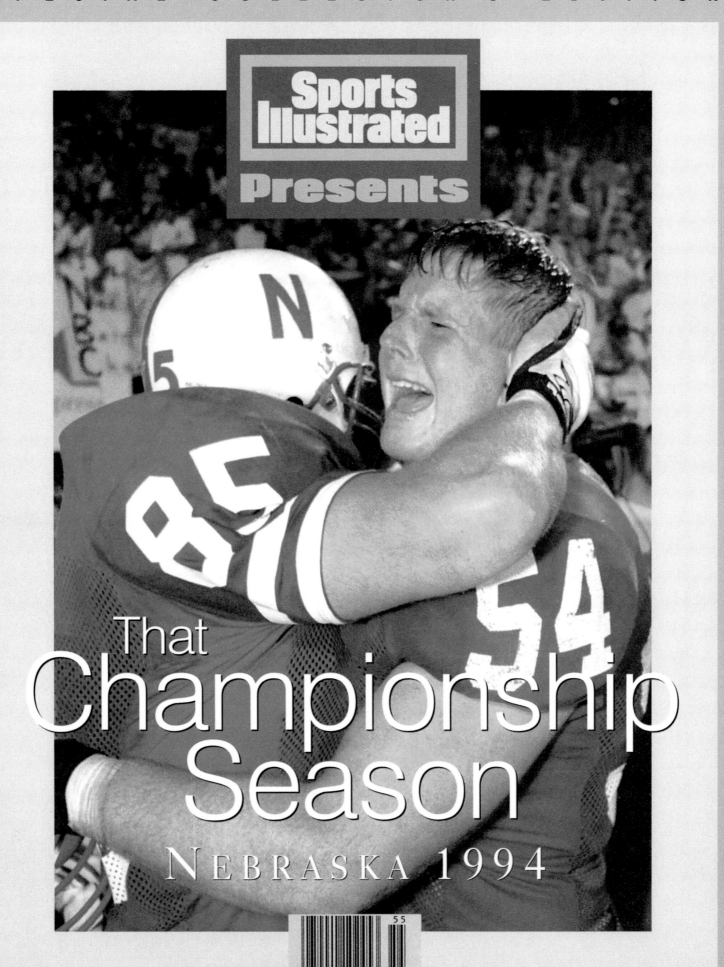

Sports Illustrated
Presents

That
Championship
Season

NEBRASKA 1994

Huskers Win Miami Thriller
AT LAST!

VICTORY RIDE: Nebraska kick holder Jon Vedral, No. 25, and another Husker player carry Coach Tom Osborne after the victory over Miami that is expected to give the coach his first national title.

WHAT A RIDE!

Daily
Nebraskan

1994 NATIONAL CHAMPIONSHIP
SOUVENIR EDITION
$3.00

THE QUEST   1994 · 1995